Modern Families

Modern Families brings together research on parenting and child development in new family forms including lesbian mother families, gay father families, families headed by single mothers by choice, and families created by assisted reproductive technologies such as in vitro fertilization (IVF), egg donation, sperm donation, embryo donation, and surrogacy. This research is examined in the context of the issues and concerns that have been raised regarding these families. The findings not only contest popular myths and assumptions about the social and psychological consequences for children of being raised in new family forms, but also challenge well-established theories of child development that are founded upon the supremacy of the traditional family. It is argued that the quality of family relationships and the wider social environment are more influential in children's psychological development than are the number, gender, sexual orientation, or biological relatedness of their parents, or the method of their conception.

SUSAN GOLOMBOK is Professor of Family Research and Director of the Centre for Family Research at the University of Cambridge and Professorial Fellow at Newnham College, Cambridge.

Criticism of the wide variety of newly emerging family arrangements has often been justified by claims that they fail to provide adequate support for the cognitive, social and emotional development of children. In her comprehensive and extremely well-written summary of research evidence, Susan Golombok provides solid, welcome reassurance to parents, policy-makers and family service providers that children growing up in a variety of non-traditional family environments fare equally well and sometimes even better than children growing up in traditional families.

Philip A. Cowan and Carolyn Pape Cowan
University of California, Berkeley

In this fascinating and very readable book, Susan Golombok has brought together her own research spanning several decades with that of other scholars who have studied lesbian mother families, gay father families and families built through donor conception, surrogacy and other forms of assisted reproductive technology. *Modern Families* takes us inside and across these diverse family structures to focus on what really matters for children – family processes and dynamics much more than visible features such as the number of parents, their sexual orientation, or the method by which the children were conceived. This book underscores the adaptive capacity of families while highlighting the basic ingredients that families need to provide for their children. It should be required reading for family scholars, policy-makers and anyone who cares about child well-being.

Harold D. Grotevant
Rudd Family Foundation Chair in Psychology,
University of Massachusetts Amherst

An absolutely splendid book that provides an understanding of family relationships as a whole, and not just those in new family forms. The book reflects, with appropriate caveats on its limitations, a large research base but it is written using engaging, non-technical language that is easy to follow.

Michael Rutter
Professor of Developmental Psychopathology,
King's College London

Since the 1970s, when human family forms began to mushroom in variety, Susan Golombok has been at the forefront of every research endeavor concerning the effects upon children of being raised by lesbian or gay parents, or children who have been conceived by the new reproductive technologies. Her and others' work largely confirms that "the kids are alright." In this book, Susan masterfully summarizes the state of scientific knowledge concerning diverse family forms and child outcomes. It is essential to the training of undergraduate and advanced graduate students in developmental and clinical psychology, as well as the allied professions of nursing, pediatrics, family medicine, social work, psychotherapy and public policy as concerns child and family health. This highly accessible book will be a vital core reference for many years to come.

Howard Steele
Professor and Director of Graduate Studies,
New School for Social Research

Modern Families

Parents and Children in New Family Forms

SUSAN GOLOMBOK

CAMBRIDGE
UNIVERSITY PRESS

CAMBRIDGE
UNIVERSITY PRESS

University Printing House, Cambridge CB2 8BS, United Kingdom

Cambridge University Press is part of the University of Cambridge.

It furthers the University's mission by disseminating knowledge in the pursuit
of education, learning and research at the highest international levels of excellence.

www.cambridge.org
Information on this title: www.cambridge.org/9781107650251

First published 2015

Printed in the United Kingdom by Clays, St Ives plc

A catalog record for this publication is available from the British Library

Library of Congress Cataloging in Publication data
Golombok, Susan.
Modern families : parents and children in new family forms / Susan Golombok.
   pages   cm
Includes bibliographical references and index.
ISBN 978-1-107-05558-2 (hardback) – ISBN 978-1-107-65025-1 (paperback)
1. Parenting.   2. Child development.   3. Families.   4. Mother and
child.   I. Title.
HQ755.8.G654 2015
306.874–dc23
2014043722

ISBN 978-1-107-05558-2 Hardback
ISBN 978-1-107-65025-1 Paperback

To my father

" 'He's just my *real* dad,' Sophie Mol said. 'Joe's my dad. He never hits. Hardly ever.' "

Arundhati Roy, The God of Small Things

Contents

Preface

In 1976, the feminist magazine *Spare Rib* published an article
on the plight of lesbian women who fought for custody of their
children when they divorced. Without exception, these women lost.
Custody was awarded to their ex-husbands on the grounds that it
was not in children's best interests to be raised by lesbian mothers.
It was argued that children who grew up with lesbian mothers
would develop psychiatric disorders, would be ostracized by their
peers and, most troubling of all to the courts, would grow up to
be lesbian or gay themselves. The decision to award custody to
heterosexual fathers in preference to lesbian mothers is particularly
striking, as the custody of children following their parents' divorce,
at that time, was always granted to mothers unless their physical
or mental health rendered them unfit as parents. These judgments,
both in the UK and the USA, were made in the absence of research
on what actually happens to children in lesbian mother families.

The *Spare Rib* article called for someone to conduct an
objective study of the development of children in lesbian mother
families. I volunteered. At that time, I was a young student of
developmental psychology with an interest in women's issues
and thought that this would be a novel and worthwhile topic for
my Master's dissertation. Little did I know that I would still be
researching this topic today! As attention turned from custody
disputes to adoption by lesbian women, to access to assisted
reproduction by lesbian women, to same-sex marriage, the same
questions about the well-being of children arose, over and over
again. These very same questions are now being asked about the
children of gay fathers. In the intervening period, as a result of
scientific advances in assisted reproductive technologies, other new

family forms have emerged, including heterosexual parent families created through in vitro fertilization (IVF), donor insemination, egg donation, embryo donation and surrogacy. Yet again, questions have been raised about the development and well-being of children in these families. The aim of this book is to bring together the findings of research on parents and children in all of these new family forms.

The present book follows an earlier volume on this topic, *Parenting: What Really Counts?*, (2000). In that book, I examined the aspects of parenting that matter most for children's psychological well-being, as well as the available research on new family forms. Since that time, there has been an explosion of research on new family forms, which is the primary focus of this book. In spite of conceptual and methodological advances in family research over the past 15 years, the characteristics that are generally considered to represent good and bad parenting remain largely the same, and the summary in Chapter 1 closely resembles that of the earlier volume. My thanks to Taylor & Francis for permission to draw from this material. The quotations from family members (both published and unpublished) come from participants of studies carried out by the Centre for Family Research at the University of Cambridge.

Unlike other areas of academic study, most people have views on modern families, not least because they have a family of their own. These views are often based on speculation and assumption, rather than empirical research. It is hoped that this book will enhance the debate by shedding light on modern family life.

Acknowledgments

Much of the research on modern families described in this book would not have happened without the insight, expertise and enthusiasm of the outstanding researchers with whom I have had the privilege and pleasure to work at the University of Cambridge Centre for Family Research – John Appleby, Shirlene Badger, Lucy Blake, Polly Casey, Irenee Daly, Sarah Evans, Tabitha Freeman, Susanna Graham, Zeynep Gurtin, Elena Ilioi, Susan Imrie, Humera Iqbal, Vasanti Jadva, Sarah Jennings, Pamela Jimenez-Etcheverria, Nishtha Lamba, Laura Mellish, Sherina Persaud, Elizabeth Raffanello, Jennifer Readings, Jenna Slutsky and Sophie Zadeh – and at the former Family and Child Psychology Research Centre at City University, London, in particular, Rachel Cook, Emma Goodman, Emma Lycett, Fiona MacCallum, Claire Murray, Lucy Owen and Fiona Tasker. This research depends on innovative funders as well as innovative people and also would not have been possible without a series of project and program grants from the Wellcome Trust dating back to the 1980s and most recently in the form of a Senior Investigator Award which has provided the freedom and flexibility to study new family forms as they emerge. I am also indebted to Sir Michael Rutter for supporting this fledgling area of research from the very early days, at a time when few other academics saw it as interesting or worthwhile, and to the late Sir Robert Edwards who encouraged research on the psychological wellbeing of IVF children right from the start.

My heartfelt thanks go to my colleagues at the Centre for Family Research: Helen Statham for enabling me to take time off to complete the book, Claire Hughes for knowing just the right reference at just the right time, Martin Richards for always being willing to talk, and Abby Scott for keeping everything calm and under control. Special thanks are due to Kathy Oswald for carrying out the lengthy and painstaking task of compiling the reference list with her insatiable good humor. I am also very fortunate to have Melissa Hines and Michael Lamb as close colleagues and appreciate our conversations about aspects of modern family life that are covered in this book. Thanks are also due to Michael Attwell and Douglas Chirnside for the title and for showing me that interest in research on modern families extends beyond the world of academia, and to my Editor, Hetty Marx, for encouraging me to write this book in the first place.

Our studies would not have been possible without the collaboration of fertility clinics of which the London Women's Clinic, CARE Fertility and Bourn Hall deserve special mention, as well as the British Association for Adoption and Fostering. I am especially grateful to all of the parents and children who have spoken to us over the years about their families and trust that their experiences have enhanced the lives of others. Last but not least, I would like to thank John and Jamie for giving me a family of my own.

1 Introduction

The popular American sitcom *Modern Family*, featuring the trials, tribulations and, in many ways, very ordinary lives of three related contemporary families, including Jay, a middle-aged father who is remarried to a much younger Columbian woman who has a son from a previous marriage, Jay's daughter and her traditional family with a hands-on father and their three children, and Jay's gay son, his male partner and their adopted Vietnamese daughter, highlights the diverse ways in which families are formed today. Although *Modern Family* is a parody of present-day family life, the reality is even more extraordinary. The traditional nuclear family of a heterosexual married couple with biologically related children is now in the minority. Instead, a growing number of children are raised by cohabiting, rather than married, parents, by single parents, by stepparents and by same-sex parents, with many children moving in and out of these different family structures as they grow up. More remarkably, it is now possible for a child to have up to five "parents" instead of the usual two. These may include an egg donor, a sperm donor, a surrogate mother (who hosts the pregnancy) and the two social parents who are known to the child as mum and dad. Recent years have also seen the emergence of co-parenting arrangements, whereby a man and a woman who are not in a relationship together – who may live in different households or who may have met over the Internet with the sole purpose of becoming parents – raise children jointly. These real modern families are the subject of this book.

THE RISE OF NEW FAMILY FORMS

Changes to the structure of the family have been taking place since the 1970s. Whereas less than 10 percent of families were headed by single parents at the beginning of the 1970s, this figure has now risen to around 30 percent in both the USA (US Census Bureau, 2012a) and the UK (Lloyd and Lacey, 2012a, b). The increase in single-parent families has been paralleled by a decline in marriage rates and a rise in divorce rates in both the USA and in Europe (Amato, 2014; US Census Bureau, 2012b). Although divorce rates are now decreasing, divorce statistics do not give the whole picture, as there are no official statistics on separation rates among cohabiting couples. Across the USA and Europe, cohabitation has become commonplace. Around half of the children born to unmarried mothers in the USA are born to mothers who are cohabiting with their children's father (McLanahan and Beck, 2010), and rates of cohabitation are also high in Western Europe (Wik, Keizer, and Lappegard, 2012). In an examination of the marital status of first-time mothers, only 59% in the USA and 53% in the UK were married, whereas 24% and 31%, respectively, were cohabiting and 17% and 16% were single (Amato, 2014). There has also been a striking increase in the number of stepfamilies in many Western societies. Forty percent of all marriages in the UK are remarriages for one or both partners (Lloyd and Lacey, 2012a, b), and approximately 10 percent of children in the USA live with a stepparent (Kreider and Ellis, 2011).

Families headed by single parents, cohabiting parents or stepparents are often referred to collectively as "non-traditional families," and result largely from parental separation or divorce and the formation of new cohabiting or marital relationships. The impact on children of being raised in such families has been widely studied (for a review, see Golombok and Tasker, 2015). However, the focus of the present book is on "new families," rather than "non-traditional families." The term "new families" is used to refer to family forms that either did not exist or were hidden from society until the latter part of the twentieth century, and that represent a more fundamental shift away from traditional family structures than do non-traditional families formed by relationship breakdown and reformation. These include lesbian mother families, gay father families, families headed by single mothers by choice and families created by assisted reproductive technologies involving in vitro fertilization (IVF), egg donation, donor insemination, embryo donation and surrogacy. Some of these families became visible following the growth of the women's liberation and gay rights movements in the 1970s, and others only became possible following the introduction of in vitro fertilization (IVF) in 1978. Although new families are distinct from non-traditional families, they are not mutually exclusive. It is not unusual for new families also to be non-traditional – for example, when parents of children born through egg or sperm donation divorce and remarry to form stepfamilies.

In spite of the rise in new family forms, the traditional nuclear family is still generally considered the best environment in which to raise children, and remains the gold standard against which all other family types are assessed. It is commonly assumed that the more a family deviates from the norm of the traditional two-parent heterosexual family, the greater the risks to the psychological well-being of the children. But is this really the case? Are children less likely to thrive in families headed by same-sex parents, single mothers by choice or parents who conceived them using assisted reproductive technologies? And will children born to gay fathers through egg donation and surrogacy be less likely to flourish than children conceived by IVF to genetically related parents? The answer to these questions depends on the extent to which these new families differ from traditional families in the aspects of family life that matter most for children's healthy psychological development and, particularly, the extent to which they provide a less supportive family environment for children. Before exploring parenting and child development in new family forms, it is therefore important to examine factors associated with the optimal development of children in traditional families. Family influences on child development are often conceptualized in terms of three interrelated components: the psychological well-being of the parents; the quality of parent–child relationships; and the psychological characteristics of the child. Each of these must be viewed in the context of the social environment in which the family is based.

TRADITIONAL FAMILIES

Psychological well-being of parents

Quality of marriage. What are the consequences of an unhappy marriage for children, and just how bad does it have to be before they are affected? It is surprising to note that studies of the association between bad marriages and negative outcomes for children have found the link between the two to be weaker than expected. A closer look shows that much of the research has examined whether or not parents are satisfied with their relationship with their partner, and findings have shown that marital dissatisfaction appears to have little effect on children. What does make a difference is marital conflict (Cummings and Davies, 1994, 2010; Grych and Fincham, 1990, 2001; Reynolds, Houlston, Coleman, et al., 2014). Children whose parents are in conflict have been found to be more aggressive, disobedient and difficult to control, more likely to become involved in delinquent behavior and to perform poorly at school, more likely to be anxious and depressed, and more likely to have difficulty in getting on with peers relative to children whose parents are happily married (Cummings and Davies, 1994, 2010; Emery, 1988; Grych and Fincham, 2001; Reynolds, Houlston, Coleman, et al., 2014).

But just because parents are in conflict does not mean that their children will suffer psychological problems. Almost all children see their parents argue and most are not affected by this. Indeed, it is thought that it can be good for children to be exposed to arguments, because they will learn how to resolve disagreements and make up. Thus, what seems to matter for children is not whether their parents fight, but *how* they fight. Aspects that are harmful to children include the following: frequent fighting; a belief that the fighting is heralding their parents' separation; severe hostility (especially physical violence); being the subject of their parents' rows; and parents' inability to make up (Cummings and Davies, 1994, 2010; Davies and Cummings, 1994; Grych and Fincham, 1993, 2001; Reynolds, Houlston, Coleman, et al., 2014).

The process through which marital conflict affects children has been the subject of much debate (Cummings and Davies, 2010; Grych and Fincham, 2001; Reynolds, Houlston, Coleman, et al., 2014). Some believe that marital conflict is bad for children because of its indirect effects on parenting. Parents who are wrapped up in their own disputes may show hostility toward their children or may not properly monitor or discipline their children or give sufficient attention to them. Marital conflict may also interfere with parents' emotional relationships with their children. As discussed below, parents who are emotionally available to their children, sensitive to their needs and appropriately responsive to them are most likely to have securely attached children. Conflict between parents may undermine children's sense of emotional security, and may jeopardize the security of children's attachment to their parents (Cummings and Davies, 2010). Exposure to parents' fighting also has a direct effect on children's psychological well-being, in that seeing parents argue is, in itself, distressing (Cummings and Davies, 1994; Emery, 1988). Confirmation that parental conflict has a direct effect on children comes from a series of experiments by Mark Cummings and his colleagues, in which children were exposed to arguments between adults and their reactions were monitored. It was consistently found that being exposed to adults' arguments, even if the arguments did not involve the children, was distressing for children (Cummings and Davies, 1994). It is now generally agreed that marital conflict may have both indirect and direct effects on the psychological well-being of children (Reynolds, Houlston, Coleman, et al., 2014). As well as interfering with the relationships between the parents and the child, hostility between parents appears to be upsetting in its own right. Evidence that both processes are at work comes from a study of young adolescents who were followed up over a period of 2 years (Harold and Conger, 1997). An indirect effect of marital conflict on the relationship between parents and children was found, in that parents who were more hostile to each other were also more hostile to their children. There was also a direct relationship between the frequency of marital conflict and the degree of child distress.

Investigations of the impact of the quality of the parents' marriage on the development of their children have focused on the adverse effects of hostile marriages, rather than the beneficial effects of harmonious marriages. However, there is growing evidence that the more favorable outcomes for children of happily married parents do not simply result from the absence of serious conflict, but, instead, are more directly associated with positive aspects of the relationship, such as the way in which parents communicate with each other and show each other affection (Goldberg and Carlson, 2014; Ratcliffe, Norton, and Durtschi, 2014). This emerging area of research has the potential to increase our understanding of the types of marriage that are good for children and not just those that are bad.

Parents' psychological state. Parents' psychological adjustment can also affect the psychological well-being of children (Goodman and Brand, 2008; Papp, Cummings, and Goeke-Morey, 2005; Zahn-Waxler, Duggal, and Gruber, 2002). Among the many studies of the consequences for children of parents' psychiatric disorder, the impacts of parental depression have received the greatest attention. Children of depressed parents have consistently been found to show elevated rates of behavioral, social and emotional problems. Studies that have diagnosed the presence or absence of psychiatric disorder in both children and their parents have shown that children whose parents are depressed are not only more likely to show a wide range of psychological problems, but are also more likely themselves to become depressed (Orvaschel, Walsh-Altis, and Ye, 1988; Weissman, Gammon, Merikangas, et al., 1987; Weissman, Warner, Wickramaratne, et al., 1997).

It is perhaps not surprising that depression in parents is associated with psychological problems in children. Of particular interest to psychologists are the mechanisms involved in this association. One explanation is that depression reduces a parent's ability to parent effectively (Cummings and Davies, 1994; Cummings and Davies, 2010). Just as with marital conflict, depression is thought to interfere with parents' control and discipline of their children, and also with their emotional availability and sensitivity to them, thus jeopardizing children's security of attachment. Studies have shown that depressed parents tend to be either very lenient or very authoritarian (in terms of monitoring and disciplining their children's behavior), and often switch between the two (Kochanska, Kuczynski, Radke-Yarrow, et al., 1987). Detailed analyses of video-recordings of mothers interacting with their babies have also shown that, compared with other mothers, depressed mothers are less warm and less responsive (Tronick, 1989). Furthermore, when depressed and non-depressed mothers were observed playing with their 1- and 2-year-old children, depressed mothers were less likely to adjust their behavior to that of their children (Jameson, Gelfand, Kulcsar, et al., 1997).

When mothers are depressed, their unstimulating and unresponsive behavior is reflected in their babies, who also seem depressed. These babies are more withdrawn, less active, more irritable and less smiley than are other babies. It is interesting to note that when mothers who are not depressed are asked to "act depressed," their babies immediately become distressed and look away, which shows that a mother's behavior toward her infant has a marked effect on the infant's emotional state. It is not just with their depressed mother that babies seem withdrawn; they also appear less happy and less active when interacting with other adults, and can even cause non-depressed adults to act in a less animated and enthusiastic way toward them (Field, 1995). Studies have shown that children of depressed mothers are more likely than children of non-depressed mothers to be insecurely attached (Murray, 1992; Radke-Yarrow, Cummings, Kuczynski, et al., 1985).

Another explanation is that the greater marital conflict in couples in which one partner is depressed – rather than the depression itself – is responsible for the behavioral and emotional problems of the children of depressed parents. But whether marital conflict, on its own, can account for the psychological difficulties experienced by children of depressed parents remains an open question. In a review of relevant studies, Downey and Coyne (1990) found that, although marital discord was linked to conduct problems such as aggression and disruptive behavior in the children of depressed parents, it could not explain the high rates of childhood depression. It was concluded that marital conflict in families with a depressed parent increases children's risk for conduct problems, and the parent's depression – rather than the associated marital discord – increases children's own risk for depression. To complicate the issue further, depression and marital conflict may each be caused by external factors, and these external factors may, in themselves, be implicated in children's development of psychological problems. Depressed parents and their children often experience a range of difficulties, including financial hardship, poor housing and a lack of social support. These stressors not only increase the risk of both depression and marital conflict in parents, but also pose a direct threat to the psychological adjustment of children, as discussed below.

Children whose parents are dependent on alcohol or drugs are also at a disadvantage (Mayes and Truman, 2002). Compared with other children, they are more likely to show conduct problems, including antisocial behavior and delinquency. An obvious explanation is that parents who are often drunk or drugged, or whose attention is focused on obtaining their next supply, cannot properly care for their children. But this is not the only reason why these children are at risk. Parents who become dependent on alcohol, or on addictive drugs such as heroin or cocaine, often live in conditions of extreme poverty. They may also suffer from a psychiatric disorder such as depression, which, as already discussed, is associated with the development of psychological problems in children. A high rate of neglect and abuse has been found among the children of alcoholic and drug-addicted parents. It is not unusual for these children to grow up in an atmosphere of threat and violence, and many end up living apart from their parents – either with other family members or, as discussed in Chapter 7, with foster or adoptive parents. A study that followed up babies born to mothers on heroin found that half were living elsewhere by the time they were 1 year old (Wilson, 1989). In addition to the life experiences that place these children at risk for psychological problems, they may also inherit a vulnerability toward alcohol or drug dependence themselves (Schuckit and Smith, 1996).

For children whose mothers consume large amounts of alcohol or drugs during pregnancy, there are additional risks (Mayes and Truman, 2002). In addition to reduced birth weight, many babies of alcoholic mothers show delayed development in infancy, as well as intellectual impairment, hyperactivity and difficulty in concentrating throughout their childhood and adolescent years. Infants whose mothers are dependent on heroin are born addicted to this drug. Not only do these newborns experience unpleasant withdrawal symptoms beginning in their first days of life, but they may also suffer from long-lasting effects such as poor physical coordination, poor attention and hyperactivity as they grow up. The effects of prenatal exposure to cocaine are less clear-cut, although there is evidence that babies whose mothers took cocaine during pregnancy are slower to develop (Singer, Arendt, Farkas, et al., 1997). It is not certain whether the problems experienced by school age children whose mothers were addicted to alcohol or drugs during pregnancy result from their exposure to these substances in the womb or from being raised by an addicted parent. Once again, it seems most likely that several factors contribute to the difficulties of these children. Prenatal exposure to alcohol or drugs makes infants difficult to handle, which, in turn, results in less sensitive and responsive parenting by drug- or alcohol-dependent parents, who may have difficulty coping with even the easiest of babies. Investigations of the ways in which addicted mothers interact with their infants have shown them to be less involved and more hostile than other mothers, and their infants more likely to be insecurely attached (Mayes and Truman, 2002).

Quality of parent–child relationships

The question of what it is to be a good parent has been a major focus of psychological enquiry since the days of Sigmund Freud. Whereas much of the research on parenting has stemmed from attachment theory (Bowlby, 1969) other researchers have examined the influence of parenting on children's psychological adjustment more generally (for reviews see Bornstein, 2002, 2006; Collins, Maccoby, Steinberg, et al., 2000; Lamb, 2012; Lamb and Lewis, 2011; Maccoby, 2000).

Attachment theory. Much of the knowledge we have today about the aspects of parenting that matter most for children's psychological adjustment comes from the ground-breaking work of the psychiatrist John Bowlby and the psychologist Mary Ainsworth, who highlighted the importance for children of feeling secure in their relationships with their parents. According to Bowlby, infants have an innate tendency to use their parents as a secure base from which to explore the world and as a source of comfort when they are distressed.

Bowlby argued that the quality of a child's relationship with his or her mother in the first years of life determines the child's future well-being (Bowlby, 1969). His views were encapsulated in a report written for the World Health Organization on children who had lost their parents in World War II (Bowlby, 1951), in which he stated: "An infant and young child should experience a warm, intimate, and continuous relationship with his mother (or permanent mother substitute – one person who steadily 'mothers' him) in which both find satisfaction and enjoyment." A certain number of Bowlby's beliefs have now been questioned. It is no longer thought that the mother must be the child's primary attachment figure; instead, it is understood that the person most involved in looking after the child – generally the mother – will become the primary attachment figure. Also, it is now accepted that children can become attached to more than one person, usually in a clear order of preference. Indeed, Bowlby himself changed his views on these issues in his later years (Bowlby, 1988). For the sake of simplicity, the term "mother" will be used below to refer to the primary attachment figure.

Unless children experience extreme deprivation early in life – as was the case with the children in Romanian orphanages discussed in Chapter 7 – they will form attachments to their primary caregivers. However, not all children become securely attached to these caregivers. Mary Ainsworth was particularly interested in the ways in which securely and insecurely attached children differ from each other, and devised the Strange Situation Test to explore these differences (Ainsworth and Wittig, 1969). In the Strange Situation Test, the mother and infant are observed in an unfamiliar playroom during a series of increasingly distressing events designed to elicit attachment behavior in the infant, such as the mother leaving the child alone in the room and the infant being left alone with a stranger. The infant's attachment behavior is classified as either "secure," "insecure-resistant," or "insecure-avoidant," according to the infant's exploration of the playroom when the mother is present, the infant's response to the stranger, the infant's reaction to the mother leaving the room and, in particular, the infant's behavior toward the mother on her return. The way in which an infant reunites with his or her mother following separation is viewed as an indicator of the extent to which the infant expects to receive comfort from her when distressed. Infants who are considered "securely attached" are confident about exploring the room and playing with toys in their mother's presence, and are not distressed by the arrival of the stranger when their mother is there; they greet their mother warmly on her return from leaving the room and, if they have been upset by her absence, are easily comforted by her and soon return to play.

Infants classified as "insecurely attached" behave in one of two ways. Those classified as "insecure-resistant" often seem wary of exploring the playroom, even when their mother is present; they become extremely distressed when their mother leaves the room and, on her return, clearly want to turn to her but resist contact and are difficult to comfort. In contrast, "insecure-avoidant" infants tend to explore the playroom immediately and show little distress when the mother leaves the room and little interest in her return. Instead, they often carry on with whatever they are doing and appear to ignore her presence. More recently, a fourth category, "insecure-disorganized," was identified (Main and Solomon, 1990). Unlike insecure-resistant children (who are distressed by the Strange Situation Test) and insecure-avoidant children (who show a lack of concern), these children do not seem to have a consistent way of responding to stress. Instead, they appear disorientated by the experience; they sometimes become completely motionless, as if frozen to the spot, or move in odd ways in their mother's presence. This pattern of behavior is most often seen among children who have been neglected or abused.

Mary Ainsworth was also interested in the question of why some children become securely attached, whereas others form insecure attachments. From observations of a large number of mothers and their babies, both in Africa and the USA, she found a link between mothers' behavior toward their infants and the type of attachment infants had to their mothers (Ainsworth, 1985; Ainsworth, Blehar, Waters, et al., 1978). Her observations show that mothers of securely attached infants tend to be responsive to their infants and sensitive to their needs. They also smile, talk to and touch their infants often, and engage in synchronized interactions with them. Mothers of insecure-resistant infants appear to be unpredictable in their behavior. Sometimes they are responsive to their infants but, at other times, they are unavailable or unresponsive to them; they sometimes misinterpret their infants' signals, respond inappropriately and have difficulty establishing synchronized routines. The ambivalent nature of the insecure-resistant infant's response to the mother on reunion with her in the Strange Situation Test (seeking contact but resisting it) is thought to reflect the infant's uncertainty about whether or not she will be comforting. In contrast, mothers of insecure-avoidant infants appear to be actively rejecting. They are often unresponsive to their infants' signals, and unaffectionate and impatient with them. In the Strange Situation Test, it seems that these infants have learned to defend themselves against rejection by showing little emotion and avoiding their mother on her return. Mothers of insecure-resistant infants and insecure-avoidant infants have been respectively described as unpredictably responsive and predictably unresponsive, in comparison with the predictably responsive behavior of mothers of securely attached infants (Steele and Steele, 1994).

Over the years, there has been some controversy over the origins of secure and insecure attachment relationships – not only in regard to the importance of mothers responding sensitively to their infants, but also in relation to the aspects of maternal sensitivity that make a difference. Whether maternal sensitivity (in its narrow sense, of recognizing and responding promptly and appropriately to an infant's signals) is the key to secure attachment, rather than other maternal behaviors (such as affection and close physical contact) are questions that have intrigued researchers for some time. These questions culminated in a review in 1997 of all studies that have investigated whether a mother's sensitivity is associated with the attachment security of her baby (De Wolff and van IJzendoorn, 1997). From a statistical analysis of all of the studies, combined, it was concluded that maternal sensitivity is an important factor in whether or not infants become securely attached; infants whose mothers respond appropriately and promptly to their signals are almost twice as likely to become securely attached. However, this does not mean that all infants with sensitive mothers become securely attached or that all infants whose mothers do not respond sensitively develop an insecure attachment relationship. Other aspects of parenting, it seems, are also at play in the formation of early attachment relationships, including the mother's expression of affection and the amount of stimulation she gives to her baby. Maternal sensitivity goes some way toward explaining why some infants develop secure, and others insecure, attachments to their mothers, but it is not the whole answer.

Central to Bowlby's theory is the concept of "internal working models" of attachment relationships – the idea that, through early experiences with their mothers or other attachment figures, children build up representations of these relationships in their minds (Bowlby, 1969). According to Bowlby, these internal working models influence not only children's expectations of, and behavior toward, their attachment figures, but also how they come to see themselves. Thus, securely attached children have internal working models of their mothers as available and responsive, and internal working models of themselves as lovable. Insecure-resistant children have internal working models of their mothers as persons they cannot *depend* on to be available when needed, whereas insecure-avoidant children have internal working models of their mothers as persons they cannot *expect* to be available when needed. Both types of insecure children, argued Bowlby, are likely to have internal working models of themselves as persons who are unworthy of being loved. Internal representations of attachment figures, and of the self, are believed to influence children's relationships with others as they grow up.

Much of the early research on attachment has focused on the first two years of life using the Strange Situation Test. Although observation of actual behavior has proved fruitful in studying attachment in infancy, this approach has been less appropriate for examining the attachment relationships of older children. The older that children become, the more difficult it is to assess what is going on in their unconscious minds by simply observing their behavior. The growing interest in internal working models has resulted in new techniques that focus on thought and language as ways of tapping into internal representations of attachment relationships (Main, Kaplan, and Cassidy, 1985). For example, children might be shown pictures of a child being separated from his or her parents and be asked to talk about how they think the child in the picture would feel, or they might be asked to give the ending to a story involving a child in distress. These procedures have been shown to be good indicators of how children view their relationships with their attachment figures.

A central question for attachment theorists is the extent to which the type of attachment infants form with their mother or primary attachment figure remains stable over time. Studies that have assessed children in the Strange Situation Test on more than one occasion have shown that secure infants can become insecure, and that insecure infants can become secure, depending on whether the circumstances of their lives change for better or for worse (Thompson, 2006). Previously secure children, for example, can become insecure if their family is placed under stress – perhaps if a parent becomes unemployed or falls seriously ill.

Interest in the assessment of attachment in later childhood has given researchers the opportunity to examine whether attachment classifications in infancy remain the same in the early school years. Studies in the USA (Main and Cassidy, 1988) and in Europe (Grossman and Grossman, 1991) have assessed children's attachment security at the age of 1 year using the Strange Situation Test, and again at the age of 6 years using a modification of the Strange Situation Test that focuses on the child's behavior toward the mother on reunion following a 1-hour separation. How a child greets his or her mother on her return, and whether the child talks to her freely about what happened in her absence, are considered good indicators of attachment security. In these studies, the large majority of children were found to have the same type of attachment on both occasions. This suggests that, although attachment relationships can change, in most cases, the type of attachment formed with the mother during infancy remains stable throughout the preschool years.

A related question that has been of interest to attachment theorists is whether insecure attachment leads to the development of psychological problems in children. A number of studies have addressed this question by using the Strange Situation Test to classify children as securely or insecurely attached, then following them up to determine whether insecurely attached children show higher levels of emotional and behavioral problems than do their securely attached peers. Many of these studies have identified a link between attachment security in infancy and various aspects of behavior in later childhood (Belsky and Cassidy, 1994; Erikson, Sroufe, and Egeland, 1985; Sroufe, 1986; Suess, Grossman, and Sroufe, 1992; Youngblade and Belsky, 1992). Insecurely attached children are, for example, less likely to play enthusiastically and cooperatively, have high self-esteem, be popular with other children, interact positively with visitors to their home, show independence at school, show competence in carrying out problem-solving tasks and ask for help when appropriate. It seems, therefore, that insecure attachment relationships in infancy are associated with less positive outcomes for children in the preschool and early school years. An association has also been identified between disorganized attachment and later behavioral problems (van IJzendoorn, Schuengel, and Bakermans-Kranenburg, 1999). However, just as children's attachment classifications may change over time according to changes in their experiences, it is not inevitable that children who have insecure attachments in the first years of their life will experience psychological difficulties as they grow up, or that all securely attached infants will grow into well-adjusted children (Thompson, 2008). Children's psychological adjustment is influenced not only by the security of their attachment relationships, but also by the wider social context in which these relationships are formed. It appears that early security is more likely to be associated with positive psychological outcomes when children continue to experience sensitive parental care (Thompson, 2008).

A major breakthrough in attachment research was the development of the Adult Attachment Interview by Mary Main (Booth-LaForce and Roisman, 2014; George, Kaplan, and Main, 1985; Main, Goldwyn, and Hesse, 2003). This interview, designed to assess adults' internal working models of their attachment relationships, provided a means of not only studying attachment in adulthood but also of examining links between parents' attachment relationships and those of their children. During the interview, information is obtained about the person's childhood experiences with attachment figures and how these experiences are currently viewed. The material of interest is not so much the actual content of the accounts, but how individuals talk about their experiences. In discussing issues such as feelings of rejection in childhood, the coherence of their accounts, the ease with which they remember and can talk about past events and the way in which they understand the past – referred to as "reflexive functioning" – have proven to be more informative to researchers than their actual experiences.

On the basis of a person's response to the interview, he or she is classified according to one of four patterns of attachment. Those classified as "autonomous secure" can talk easily about their relationships with their parents. They give coherent and consistent accounts of their childhood experiences with them and are open about both positive and negative aspects of these relationships. A secure childhood is not necessary for people to be given this classification, but if their childhood was difficult, they must have since come to an understanding of how that difficulty came about.

The "dismissing-detached" classification includes people who dismiss attachment relationships as having little importance in their lives. They often describe their parents positively, but can provide little supportive evidence and may even describe events that contradict their statements about a happy family life. They tend not to remember much about their relationships with their parents, although they can remember other aspects of their childhood and express little concern over unhappy experiences in the past. Those given the classification "preoccupied-entangled" still appear to be involved in unresolved struggles with their parents and trying to please them, and often appear confused or angry with them. It seems difficult for them to break free, and they often describe conflicts with parents that are still ongoing. The fourth classification, "unresolved-disorganized," applies to people who have experienced the traumatic loss of (or separation from) an attachment figure, or neglect or abuse, and are still focussed on unresolved issues from the past.

One of the most interesting findings to emerge from research using the Adult Attachment Interview is that the quality of a woman's childhood relationship with her mother appears to be related to the quality of that woman's relationship with her own child. This suggests that the type of attachment a daughter has with her mother can be passed on from one generation to the next. Evidence for this phenomenon comes from studies that have assessed both mothers' attachment classifications and those of their children (van IJzendoorn, 1995). These studies have consistently shown that autonomous-secure mothers most often have securely attached children and that mothers with insecure Adult Attachment Interview classifications are most likely to have insecurely attached children. Of particular interest is a study that found a link between mothers' attachment classification and that of their infants when the mothers' interviews were conducted before the children were born and thus could not have been influenced by their actual relationships with their babies (Fonagy, Steele, and Steele, 1991). In this study, it was possible to successfully predict in 75 percent of all cases whether the infant would be securely or insecurely attached on the basis of the mother's attachment classification made dur- ing pregnancy. By chance, alone, this would have been true of only 50 percent.

The suggestion that patterns of attachment may be transmitted from one generation to the next has led to speculation about the ways in which this might happen (Fox, 1995; Steele and Steele, 1994; van IJzendoorn, 1995). One idea is that parents' internal working mod- els of their attachment relationships may influence their behavior toward their children – in particular their ability to respond sensi- tively to their children, which, in turn, influences children's security of attachment (Steele and Steele, 2013). Thus, it has been suggested that autonomous parents who have a positive view of their child- hood attachment relationships, or who have come to terms with their unhappy experiences, may be better able to respond to their infants' needs than dismissing or preoccupied parents; dismissing parents might rebuff children's attachment behavior in stressful situations because behaviors such as crying may trigger unwanted attachment-related memories in themselves, and preoccupied par- ents may still be focused on their own attachment experiences and therefore unable to attend fully to their children. But the mechanism linking mothers' classification on the Adult Attachment Interview to their infants' classification on the Strange Situation Test is far from understood. The mother's attachment status does not have a one-to-one relationship with her responsiveness to her baby, and, as we have already seen, maternal responsiveness does not explain fully the type of attachment the baby has to her.

Not everyone in the field is convinced that security of attach- ment in adulthood is directly related to childhood attachment secur- ity. Instead, the Adult Attachment Interview may simply measure a person's current view of attachment relationships and may be unre- lated to his or her security of attachment in infancy (Cassidy and Shaver, 1999). In order to address this question it would be necessary to follow up individuals over many years, obtaining their Strange Situation Test classification in infancy and their Adult Attachment Interview classification in adulthood. The few long-term longitudinal studies conducted so far have failed to find a direct link between a person's security of attachment as a baby and their security of attachment as an adult. However, when positive and negative experiences in the person's family life are taken into account, it seems that changes in attachment can be explained in a meaningful way (Grossman, Grossman, and Waters, 2005). In the largest study to date, there was some evidence for stability in attachment between infancy and early adulthood, and changes in attachment were meaningfully associated with changes in life experience (Booth-LaForce and Roisman, 2014).

In general, it seems that securely attached children fare better than do their insecurely attached counterparts. However, not all insecurely attached children will do badly; neither is it guaranteed that all securely attached children will do well. What this research shows us is that secure attachment is more likely to result in positive outcomes for children, but other factors are also involved.

Parenting styles and practices. While attachment theory has made a considerable contribution to our understanding of the processes through which parents influence their children, other aspects of parenting, such as warmth and affection, and the ability to discipline and control children appropriately, are also of importance (Bornstein, 2002; Collins, Maccoby, Steinberg, et al., 2000; Lamb, 2012; Maccoby and Martin, 1983). A distinction has been made between parenting styles, which refer to the overall emotional climate of the parent–child relationship, and specific parenting practices, such as checking children's whereabouts (Darling and Steinberg, 1993). This distinction is important as the same parenting practice may have very different outcomes when implemented with one parenting style (relaxed and cheerful) than when implemented with another (intrusive and hostile) (Darling and Steinberg, 1993; Steinberg and Silk, 2002).

Diane Baumrind, who was at the forefront of research on parenting styles, identified four styles of parenting, each of which is associated with particular outcomes for children (Baumrind, 1971; 1989, 1991). According to Baumrind, authoritarian parents are very controlling, expect their children to do as they say and rarely negotiate with them. Their children are more likely than other children to be defiant, socially incompetent and dependent. Permissive parents are loving parents but exert little control over their children's behavior and make few demands of them. As a result, their children tend to be lacking in self-assertiveness and uninterested in achievement. Indifferent parents either reject or neglect their children. They are not supportive and do not monitor what their children are doing. The children of these parents tend to be the most likely to develop emotional and behavioral problems and to perform poorly at school. The most positive style of parenting is an authoritative style, combining warmth and affection with firm control. Authoritative parents control their children's behavior through negotiation, rather than punishment and exertion of power. Children of these parents are more likely to be self-controlled, responsible, cooperative and self-reliant than are children of the other types of parents.

Another method of studying parenting styles has been to examine links between parenting and child adjustment according to specific dimensions of parenting rather than typologies. This dimensional approach has been applied to relationships between adolescents and their parents.Three overarching dimensions have been identified (Steinberg and Silk, 2002). These include autonomy (the extent to which the adolescent is under the control of the parents), harmony (the extent to which the parent–child relationship is warm, involved and emotionally close) and conflict (the extent to which the parent–adolescent relationship is contentious and hostile).

There is now a large body of research on parenting styles showing that adolescents who have been reared by authoritative parents are more psychosocially competent than their peers from authoritarian, permissive or indifferent homes (Steinberg, 2001; Steinberg and Morris, 2001). There is also substantial empirical evidence in support of associations between the parenting dimensions of autonomy, harmony and conflict, and adolescent adjustment (Steinberg and Silk, 2002). From their review of the field, it was concluded by Steinberg and Silk (2002) that adolescents benefit from having parents who are warm, firm and accepting of their need for autonomy.

The work of Gerald Patterson has also increased our understanding of parenting by focusing on the mechanisms through which parental discipline practices influence children's behavior. Patterson and his colleagues have examined effective and ineffective ways of controlling children's behavior, concentrating on bidirectional influences between parents and their children (Patterson, 1982; Patterson, DeBaryshe, and Ramsey, 1989; Patterson and Fisher, 2002; Patterson, Reid, and Dishion, 1992). This research shows that, when parents react to their children's antisocial behavior in an accepting or positive fashion, the children are more likely to behave badly in the future in order to achieve what they want. Parents who give in to their child's demands in order to prevent a tantrum, for example, will find that their child will repeat or escalate the tantrum the next time around. This pattern of coercive behavior is particularly associated with childhood conduct disorder.

Children's wider social world and individual characteristics

The social environment in which children grow up has a major impact on their lives. Children raised in poverty, in comparison with children from affluent backgrounds, are more likely to perform poorly at school, drop out of school early, become involved in delinquent and criminal behavior, have unwanted pregnancies and develop emotional problems in their teenage years (Bradley and Corwyn, 2002; Brooks-Gunn, Britto, and Brady, 1999; Evans and Kim, 2013; McLoyd, 1998). Poverty interferes with children's psychological development in many ways. Even before birth, children are at a disadvantage; they are more likely to be exposed to drugs, alcohol and malnutrition in the womb, and to be born prematurely. As they grow up, they are less likely to have access to toys and books at home and to attend high quality schools, both factors mitigating against high academic achievement. Moreover, poverty has a pervasive and damaging effect on the quality of parenting that children receive. Parents who are faced with the pressures of economic hardship often become depressed, their marriages deteriorate and the demands of their children become a further source of stress.

This finding was clearly demonstrated in a study conducted in the rural Midwest of the USA, following a serious economic crisis in the 1980s that had a devastating effect on family life. The increase in antisocial and aggressive behavior among children was found to be a direct consequence of the deterioration of their relationships with their parents, which stemmed from their parents' increased marital conflict and psychological distress (Conger, Conger, Elder, et al., 1992; Conger and Donnellan, 2007; Conger, Ge, Elder, et al., 1994). Similar findings were obtained from a comparison of delinquent city children in a study designed to answer the question of why some boys raised in poor neighborhoods become delinquent, whereas others do not (Sampson and Laub, 1994). The link between poverty and delinquency was found to be mediated, to a large extent, by parents' inability to discipline their children effectively. Parents who were unable to control their children and who punished them in a harsh and rejecting manner were most likely to have delinquent adolescents, whereas parents who monitored their children's activities and disciplined them in such a way that their children still felt loved and accepted were less likely to have delinquent children, even when they lived in conditions of extreme economic disadvantage. It seems that the link between poverty and delinquency results, at least in part, from the insidious effects of poverty on family relationships.

However, not all children raised under even the most extreme conditions of social disadvantage develop psychological difficulties. We sometimes hear of highly successful people coming from violent, abusive or impoverished family backgrounds from which they have managed to escape. Why is it that some children are able to overcome early adversity, whereas others become so badly affected that their early experiences continue to have a destructive influence on their psychological well-being throughout their lives? One answer to this question is that some children are more resilient than others (Garmezy, 1991; Luthar, Crossman, and Small, 2015; Masten and Coatsworth, 1998; Rutter, 1987, 2012; Zimmerman, Stoddard, Eisman, et al., 2013). These children seem to be much less affected by the kinds of stressors that, for other children, would lead to psychological problems. They may be raised in conditions of extreme poverty or they may be victims of abuse, but, however bad their experiences, they seem to bounce back. What is different about these children?

One of the first studies to address this question was carried out on a Hawaiian island, where many children were being raised under extreme hardship (Werner and Smith, 1982, 1992). The resilient children were found to be different right from the start. As babies, they were more affectionate, more active and had fewer eating and sleeping problems. At school, they were higher achievers and more independent, and had more interests, better relationships with their peers, higher self-esteem and a greater perceived control of their lives. They were also more likely to be girls than boys. But these children were set apart by more than just their characteristics. The resilient children were also more likely to have a close and affectionate relationship with at least one parent or parent-figure, and received emotional support from outside the family – from a teacher or other interested adult. A warm and supportive relationship with at least one person was found to be an important factor in protecting vulnerable children from the adverse effects of the stressors in their lives. So, it seems that children are protected both by their own characteristics and by close relationships with others. Whatever the type of adversity studied in more recent investigations – be it poverty, divorce, abuse or a parent's psychiatric disorder – the factors associated with resilience have been found to be strikingly similar to those originally identified in Hawaii, with relationships with caring adults found to be particularly important (Luthar, 2006; Masten, Cutuli, Herbers, et al., 2007; Zimmerman, Stoddard, Eisman, et al., 2013). These factors have been shown to operate in different ways: they may counteract exposure to risk, they may reduce the negative effects of risk or they may inoculate against further exposure (Zimmerman, Stoddard, Eisman, et al., 2013).

Right from birth, infants show different characteristics from each other. Some cry more than others, some are more active than others and some like being cuddled, whereas others do not. In the 1960s, Alexander Thomas, Stella Chess and colleagues were the first to study differences in the behavior of newborn babies (Thomas, Chess, Birch, et al., 1963). They showed that, early in infancy, babies could be classified as "easy," "difficult" or "slow to warm up." "Easy" babies were in a good mood most of the time, adapted well to new experiences and showed regular patterns of eating and sleeping. In contrast, "difficult" babies were irritable, reacted badly to new situations and showed irregular eating and sleeping habits. Those classified as "slow to warm up" took time to adapt to changes in their routine.

Since that time, researchers have come up with a variety of ways in which infants are thought to differ from each other. Though there is lack of agreement over which of these factors is most important, there is general consensus that infants do differ in temperament, even as newborns (Goldsmith, Buss, Plomin, et al., 1987; Shiner, Buss, McClowry, et al., 2012; Zentner and Shiner, 2012). Key differences include how active the baby is, how easily the baby becomes distressed or frightened, how irritable the baby is, the ease with which the baby responds to new situations and the extent to which the baby likes being with people and expresses enjoyment by smiling or appearing content. Although not included in the review by Goldsmith, Buss, Plomin, et al. (1987), attention and self-regulation are now considered important aspects of temperament (Shiner, Buss,

McClowry, et al., 2012; Zentner and Shiner, 2012). Infants' temperaments can have a profound effect on the behavior of their caregivers.
For example, a mother may be more likely to pick up a crying baby
who is easily soothed than a baby who continues to cry no matter
what the mother does to help.

For the reason that babies show differences in temperament from birth, it was believed that they may inherit a predis-
position to behave in certain ways, and that their experiences in
the environment in which they live might minimize or maximize
these behavioral tendencies (Goldsmith, Buss, Plomin, et al., 1987;
Kohnstamm, Bates, and Rothbart, 1989). Thus, a child with a genetic disposition toward behavioral problems was thought to be
more likely to develop such problems when faced with a hostile
family environment, relative to a child in a similar family environment with no genetic risk. However, in contrast to the view that
biologically based temperamental differences are influenced by
environmental experiences, more recent conceptualizations view
temperament as the result of biological and environmental factors
working together, from the prenatal period, onwards (Shiner, Buss,
McClowry, et al., 2012).

A question of enduring interest to researchers is how genes
and the environment interact to produce behavioral characteristics
(Rutter, 2006). Early research compared identical twins (who share
all their genes) and non-identical twins (who share half their genes)
to establish whether identical twins were more similar to each other
on a particular psychological characteristic than were non-identical
twins. Positive findings signified that a characteristic was inherited
and, if this were found to be the case, researchers sought to determine the extent to which the characteristic was genetically transmitted. Another method for establishing the relative contribution
of genes and the environment to the development of behavioral
characteristics has been to examine children adopted at birth or in
early infancy to compare the effects of the biological parents (who
provided the genes but did not raise the children) and the adoptive

parents (who raised the children but were genetically unrelated to them). These studies have shown that behavioral characteristics result from a complex interplay between genes and the environment. For example, children born to antisocial mothers were more likely to show disruptive behavior and, consequently, to experience negative parenting from their adoptive parents which contributed further to their conduct problems (O'Connor, Deater-Deckard, Fulker, et al., 1998).

A different type of adoption study has examined the similarities of siblings who have been adopted into different families, in comparison with the similarities of siblings who have been raised by their biological parents. These studies have provided an insight into whether resemblance between siblings is a result of shared genes or shared family environment. If siblings reared together are more similar than are siblings reared apart, this tells us that the characteristics they have in common are more influenced by their shared family environment than by their shared genes. (If shared genes were to be responsible, then siblings would be just as likely to show the same characteristics whether or not they were raised in the same family environment.) What these studies have shown, once again, is that most psychological characteristics are influenced by both genes and the environment.

Studies have also been carried out of children of different biological parents who have been adopted into the same family. In spite of growing up in the same home, these children have not been found to resemble each other with respect to their psychological characteristics. Behavioral geneticists have examined the extent to which the differences in their behavior result from differences in their environment as opposed to differences in their genes and have come up with a surprising result: the environmental influences that shape children's development are different for children in the same family (Plomin, 1990, 1994; Plomin and Daniels, 1987).

This finding changed our understanding of how families influence children. It used to be believed that children in the same family were exposed to the same environment. Whether parents had a happy marriage or were in conflict, and whether parents were psychologically stable or disturbed, were circumstances that were assumed to affect all children in the family, equally. Differences between siblings were thought to result from differences in their genetic makeup, not differences in their family environment. After Plomin's findings, however, it seemed that this assumption was wrong. Although children may be exposed to an identical family environment, the impact of that environment may differ for each child. Plomin argued that the environmental influences specific to an individual child, rather than those that are common to all children in the family, are more important in shaping the child's development. Although there is disagreement about the relative importance of these two processes (Maccoby, 2000; Rutter, 2006), the unique environmental influences help explain why children in the same family can be so different. For example, a mother may be more affectionate toward one sibling than another, often because of temperamental differences between them. Evidence that children in the same family have different experiences comes from studies of siblings' perceptions of their relationships with parents (Dunn and Plomin, 1990). Siblings commonly report differential treatment by their parents, such that one child is perceived to be "the favorite."

What can be concluded from this research? One thing is clear: in considering how families affect children, we can no longer assume that children growing up in the same family have identical experiences. A much loved child may share a home with a less valued brother or sister. Changes in family life may also impact differently on one sibling than on another. For instance, parents' divorce may be devastating to one child, whereas another may be relatively unharmed. But this does not mean that experiences that are common to all children in the family do not matter. Shared family experiences can also have an important influence on children (Maccoby, 2000; Rutter, 2006; Rutter, Silberg, O'Connor, et al., 1999a, b).

NEW FAMILY FORMS

From the discussion above, it seems that whether children's experiences of growing up in their particular families promote either psychological adjustment or psychological problems depends not simply on the psychological well-being of their parents, the quality of parenting they experience, their individual characteristics or the social world in which they live, but also on the complex interactions between these factors. It is clear, however, that parents have an important influence on the psychological well-being of their children, whether through the direct effects of parenting or the indirect effects of the environment in which their children are raised. The specific questions addressed in the following chapters are as follows: how does the parenting experienced by children in new family forms differ from that of children in traditional families? And what are the psychological consequences for the child?

Studies of the psychological development of children in new family forms are not simply of interest in their own right, but also provide "natural experiments," whereby factors that usually go together can be examined independently (Rutter, 2007; Rutter, Pickles, Murray, et al., 2001). Thus, studies of new family forms can shed light on the influence of structural aspects of the family on child development. These include the number of parents in the family, the gender of the parents, their sexual orientation, their genetic relatedness to their children, their gestational relatedness to their children and whether or not their family was created by assisted reproductive technologies such as in vitro fertilization (IVF).

The most common ways in which the new family forms discussed in this book differ from the traditional family are as follows: (a) families headed by lesbian couples differ with respect to the gender of the parents (two female parents and no male parent in the family home), the sexual orientation of the parents (lesbian, rather than heterosexual), the use of assisted reproduction in some cases (donor insemination) and genetic relatedness to the child (absence of a genetic link between the non-biological mother and the child, or between both mothers and the child in the case of adoption); (b) "test-tube baby" families differ in terms of the use of assisted reproduction (IVF or intra-cytoplasmic sperm injection [ICSI]); (c) donor conception families differ in the use of assisted reproduction (sperm, egg or embryo donation) and genetic relatedness (the absence of a genetic link between one or both parents and the child); (d) surrogacy families differ with respect to the use of assisted reproduction (IVF in gestational surrogacy), gestational relatedness (a surrogate mother hosts the pregnancy) and, sometimes, genetic relatedness (the absence of a genetic link between the mother and the child in genetic surrogacy); (e) single mothers by choice differ in the number of parents (one, rather than two), the gender of parents (female) and the use of assisted reproduction in some cases (donor insemination); and (f) gay father families differ with respect to the gender of the parents (two male parents and no female parent in the family home), the sexual orientation of the parents (gay, rather than heterosexual), the use of assisted reproduction in some cases (surrogacy and egg donation), genetic relatedness (the absence of a genetic link between the non-genetic father and the child, or between both fathers and the child in the case of adoption) and gestational relatedness (a surrogate mother hosts the pregnancy or the child is given up for adoption by the birth mother). By comparing these various family types with the traditional family and with each other, the role of family structure in child development may be explored.

In addition to theoretical questions about the role of structural aspects of the family in child development, research on new family forms addresses everyday questions that are of universal interest: how does it feel to be a "test-tube baby"? Should children conceived by egg or sperm donation be told that their mother or father is not their genetic parent? How do children born through surrogacy feel about their surrogate mother as they grow up? Will children with lesbian mothers or gay fathers become lesbian or gay themselves? Do children of single mothers by choice wish to know their biological father? These are just some of the questions that will be examined in this book. The focus will primarily be on children's psychological adjustment, but, where relevant, other aspects of child development such as gender development and cognitive development will also be explored.

2　Lesbian mother families

"Ban These Babies!" This was the headline to an article in a London newspaper in 1978 following the revelation that lesbian women were having children through donor insemination with the help of a doctor whom the journalist dubbed "Dr Strangelove." At that time, the fact that lesbian women were raising children was not generally known, and the discovery that a medical doctor was helping lesbian women to become pregnant produced widespread outrage. The matter even reached Parliament, with Rhodes Boyson, MP, a prominent member of the British government, stating in the House of Commons: "This evil must stop for the sake of the potential children and society, which both have enough problems without the extension of this horrific practice. Children have a right to be born into a natural family with a father and a mother. Anything less will cause lifelong deprivation of the most acute kind for the child."

Similar views were expressed in the House of Lords, the upper house of the British Parliament. According to Lord Kilbrandon, the children of lesbian parents were deemed to be at risk of "severance from normal society, to psychological stresses and unhappiness and possibly even to physical experiences which may scar them for life."

At the same time, lesbian motherhood was being condemned in the USA. In Texas in the mid 1970s, a former Baptist Sunday school teacher and nurse, who lived with her female partner following her divorce, lost custody of her son despite her being described as an exceptional parent by psychologists and her ex-husband's dubious fitness as a father. One of the most extreme cases took place in Florida in the 1990s. A divorced lesbian woman lost custody of her 11-year-old daughter to her ex-husband, who had murdered his first wife during a custody dispute and was later accused of trying to sexually abuse the daughter from his first marriage. A 2012 documentary about this case, *UNFIT: Ward vs. Ward*, included a clip of a television interview with the father, who said: "I shot her three times in the upper left shoulder. She told me not to kill her, she would give me the baby and a divorce. I fired three times point blank into the heart ... I reloaded and shot her six more times."

In fact, very few lesbian women were having children through donor insemination in the 1970s. The majority of lesbian mothers at that time had given birth to their children while they had been married or cohabiting with a male partner and had later left that relationship to set up home with a female partner or as a single lesbian mother. Thus, their children were generally of preschool or school age when they entered a lesbian mother family, having spent their early years living with their father. Custody battles involving lesbian mothers were particularly fierce. In the 1970s, sole custody was almost always awarded to the mother in heterosexual families, unless she was mentally or physically incapable of caring for her children. As mothers were viewed as children's primary attachment figures, it was believed that a child's continuous relationship with the mother promoted secure attachment and positive psychological adjustment (Goldstein, Freud, and Solnit, 1973). In stark contrast, custody was almost always awarded to the father in cases involving a lesbian mother, on the grounds that it was not in a child's best interests to be raised in a lesbian mother household (Rivers, 2010). Custody disputes were played out in courts of law by expert witnesses, with the expert on the father's side (often a psychoanalyst) arguing that growing up in a lesbian family would have a damaging effect on children's psychological well-being; the expert on the mother's side (usually a child psychiatrist) would argue that what mattered most for children's psychological well-being was the quality of family relationships. In the absence of empirical data on the actual outcomes for children of growing up in lesbian mother families, judges awarded custody to the heterosexual father, who often had a new female partner by the time the case came to court, and thus offered children a traditional family – a situation that was preferred to a lesbian mother family.

There were three main arguments for denying lesbian mothers custody of their children. First of all, it was claimed that lesbian women would be inadequate parents because they were less nurturing than heterosexual women and their children would develop psychological problems as a result. Secondly, it was expected that the children would be teased and rejected by their peers, which would again result in psychological disorder. Thirdly, it was believed that the children would show atypical gender development such that boys would be less masculine in their identity and behavior, and girls less feminine, relative to boys and girls from heterosexual homes. Arising from this belief was the concern that the children would grow up to be lesbian or gay themselves, an outcome that was viewed as highly undesirable by courts of law.

How much justification was there for these assertions? From the perspective of psychological theory, no clear predictions could be made about the likely consequences for children of growing up in lesbian mother families. As discussed in Chapter 1, theories that focused on the influence of parenting on child adjustment stressed the importance of factors such as parental warmth, sensitivity, involvement and appropriate control for children's psychological well-being. However, in spite of the commonly voiced assumption that lesbian women were not suited to parenting, it was not known whether lesbian mothers exhibited a poorer quality of parenting than did heterosexual mothers and, thus, whether the children of lesbian mothers were more at risk for psychological problems than were their counterparts from heterosexual homes. In terms of peer relationships, it was recognized that hostility and rejection by peers was associated with psychological difficulties in children (Coie, Coie, Lochman, et al., 1992; DeRosier, Kupersmidt, and Patterson, 1994; Ladd, 1990; Parker and Asher, 1987, 1992). What was not known was the extent to which children with lesbian mothers experienced victimization by their peers.

Furthermore, the prominent psychological theories of the day could shed little light on the likely impact of lesbian motherhood on children's sex-typed behavior, as each theory led to a different prediction about the consequences of growing up in a lesbian mother family for children's gender development. A range of theories were put forward to explain the processes involved in gender development, and the most influential of these were psychoanalytic (Freud, 1905/1953, 1920/1955, 1933), social learning (Bandura, 1977; Mischel, 1966, 1970), cognitive developmental (Kohlberg, 1966; Martin, 1993) and biological (Money and Ehrhardt, 1972) theories. Opinion varied among these theorists over the extent to which parents could influence the gender development of their children, and thus the extent to which children's sex-typed behavior could be influenced by the sexual orientation of their mothers. It was generally believed, however, that failure to conform to traditional gender role behaviors was a negative developmental outcome.

Psychoanalytic theorists stressed the importance of two heterosexual parents for the successful resolution of the Oedipal conflict, which was viewed as central to boys' identification with their fathers and girls' identification with their mothers, and the acquisition of male or female identity and behavior. It was predicted that children raised by lesbian mothers would show atypical gender development because they lacked a father figure and their mother had adopted a non-traditional female role. Specifically, it was argued that boys would fail to identify with a male role and would thus be less masculine in terms of their identity and behavior, and girls would identify with a non-traditional female role and would thus be less feminine. From a psychoanalytic perspective, the acquisition of non-traditional gender role behavior was viewed as a negative outcome of the unsuccessful resolution of the Oedipal conflict.

Social learning theorists also viewed parents as influential in the gender development of their children. The two processes that were believed to be important were children's modeling of the parent of the same sex as themselves and parents' differential reinforcement of the sex-typed behavior of their daughters and sons. It was thought that boys with lesbian mothers might be less masculine, owing to the lack of a father as a same-sex role model and possible differences in lesbian mothers' reinforcement of male behavior. Similarly, it was thought that girls might be less feminine due to the presence of non-traditional female role models, as well as possible differences in the reinforcement of female behavior. In particular, it was felt that children with lesbian mothers might be less likely to be discouraged from engaging in non-conventional gender role behavior and also, because of their mothers' atypical parental roles, might hold less rigid stereotypes about what constitutes acceptable male and female behavior and thus engage in less conventional gender role behavior themselves. Nevertheless, social learning theorists believed that adults other than parents were important role models and reinforcers of sex-typed behavior in children; thus, these theorists viewed parents as less influential in their children's gender development than did psychoanalytic theorists.

Cognitive developmental theorists placed even less importance on the role of parents in the gender development of their children, arguing that children integrate information about sex-typed behavior from their wider social environment. Cognitive developmental explanations of gender development emphasized that children actively construct what it means to be male or female from the gendered world around them and adopt behaviors and characteristics that they perceive to be consistent with their own sex. Gender stereotypes, rather than parents, were viewed as the primary source of gender-related information. From this perspective, children with lesbian mothers were not expected to differ in gender role behavior from children in heterosexual families.

Similarly, from a biological perspective whereby sex-typed behavior was considered to be determined prenatally, parental behavior was thought to make little difference to children's gender development. Instead, differences in prenatal hormones, particularly prenatal androgens, in the developing embryo were viewed as fundamental to the subsequent sex-typed behavior of boys and girls.

As no systematic information existed about the psychological consequences for children of growing up in a lesbian family – and little could be determined from psychological theories – the first empirical studies were initiated in the 1970s.

POST-DIVORCE LESBIAN MOTHER FAMILIES

The early studies focused on families formed following the mother's separation or divorce from the father of her children and addressed the questions raised in child custody cases regarding lesbian mothers' quality of parenting and the psychological development of their children. Two studies were carried out in the USA, one on the east coast (Green, Mandel, Hotvedt, et al., 1986) and the other on the west coast (Kirkpatrick, Smith, and Roy, 1981), and a study was also conducted in the UK (Golombok, Spencer, and Rutter, 1983). These investigations adopted a similar design, comparing children in lesbian mother families to children in families headed by single heterosexual mothers. The rationale for the comparison group was that both groups of children were being raised by women without a father in the family home, with their mothers' sexual orientation the main difference between them. Thus, any differences identified between children in the two family types were not confounded by the presence or absence of a father, but, instead, could be attributed to differences in maternal sexual orientation. As the lesbian mothers had experienced divorce or separation – which has been shown to contribute to the development of psychological problems in children – it was important that the comparison group had also been through a divorce to control for the potentially negative effects of marital discord and family disruption on children. Otherwise, any differences identified between family types may have arisen from divorce, rather than maternal sexual orientation. A further study focused specifically on children's development of sex-typed behavior (Hoeffer, 1981).

Green and colleagues compared 50 lesbian mothers and their 56 children with a demographically matched group of 40 single heterosexual mothers and their 48 children. Around half of the lesbian mothers were cohabiting with their female partner. The children ranged from 3 to 11 years in age, and all had lived without adult males in the household for a minimum of 2 years (Green, Mandel, Hotvedt, et al., 1986). The mothers were interviewed and they also completed questionnaire assessments of attitudes toward family life, personality and their children's gender development, and the children were interviewed and administered tests of IQ, gender development, peer group popularity and family relationships. Although feelings for other women had contributed to the divorce of almost half of the lesbian mothers, other reasons for divorce were similar for the two groups of mothers and included sexual dissatisfaction, infidelity and the husband's alcoholism, compulsive gambling or physical abuse. The lesbian and heterosexual mothers held similar attitudes toward divorce, sex roles, the sex education of children and child discipline. However, the lesbian mothers were more self-confident than were the heterosexual mothers. The children in the two family types did not differ in IQ scores or in popularity with their peers.

Gender development is generally examined in terms of three components: gender identity, which is a person's sense of being male or female; gender role behavior, which refers to behavior that is typical for males and females in a particular culture; and sexual orientation, which is a person's identity as lesbian, gay, bisexual or heterosexual. There were no differences between children from the two family types on projective tests of gender identity or in their wish to be the other sex, and none of the children showed evidence of gender identity disorder. Moreover, the boys and girls showed typical patterns of gender role behavior. Although the daughters of lesbian mothers were less traditionally feminine in some ways, their behavior did not stand out from that of other girls of their age. The children were too young for an assessment of sexual orientation.

The study by Kirkpatrick, Smith and Roy (1981) compared 20 lesbian mother families with 20 single heterosexual mother families, matched for demographic background. The children were aged between 5 to 12 years, with 10 girls and 10 boys in each family type. Mothers were interviewed about their developmental history, and children took part in a playroom interview about their early memories, dreams, future plans and gender-related interests, such as their favorite toys and the sex of their preferred playmates. Their response to toys in the playroom was also assessed. In addition, the children were administered projective tests of psychological disorder and gender identity, as well as an IQ test. Almost all of the lesbian mothers cited the absence of psychological intimacy as the reason for their divorce, and half of these mothers had been involved in a lesbian relationship at the time of separation that was described as having provided the intimacy their marriages had lacked. In contrast, the large majority of heterosexual mothers reported their husbands' drug or alcohol abuse, infidelity or physical abuse as the cause of divorce, as opposed to a lack of intimacy. The regularity of fathers' visits or involvement with the children following the divorce was reported to be no more reliable in one group than the other. The children did not differ in IQ test scores; neither did they differ in the presence or severity of psychological disorders, with two children of lesbian mothers and three children of heterosexual mothers rated as severely disturbed, by a child psychiatrist and a psychologist who were unaware of the children's family type. Using a range of indices of gender identity and gender role behavior, no differences in gender development were found between children brought up by lesbian and single heterosexual mothers.

In the UK, 27 lesbian mother families and their 37 children were compared with 27 single heterosexual mother families and their 38 children (Golombok, Spencer, and Rutter, 1983). The children were aged from 5 to 17 years with an average age of 9 to 10 years. Around half of the lesbian mothers' marriages had ended for reasons associated with their sexual orientation, and, at the time of the study, half of the lesbian mothers were cohabiting with their female partner. Their relationships were generally harmonious, as judged by a well-validated assessment, with only two couples showing relationship difficulties. Mothers were administered a standardized interview designed to assess family relationships and the social, emotional and gender development of their children. A section of the interview obtained detailed information on the children's psychological problems, if any, and was rated for the presence of psychiatric disorder by a child psychiatrist, who was unaware of the children's family type. In addition, the children were interviewed about family and peer relationships and gender role behavior. Mothers and teachers also completed a questionnaire measure of children's psychological adjustment. Only a small minority of the children showed serious psychological problems, with no differences identified between the children in lesbian families and those raised by single heterosexual mothers, as measured by mothers' and teachers' questionnaires and the standardized ratings of the interview transcripts by a child psychiatrist. Indeed, where differences were identified between children in the two family types, psychological problems appeared to be more common among the children of single heterosexual mothers. With respect to gender identity, all of the boys were happy to be male and all of the girls were happy to be female, and none wished to be the other gender. Neither was there a difference in gender role behavior between family types, as assessed by mothers and the children themselves. The sons of lesbian mothers were no less masculine in their interests and behavior, and the daughters no less feminine, than were the sons and daughters of heterosexual mothers. The majority of the children were too young to make a meaningful assessment of sexual orientation.

In an investigation of children's gender role behavior, Hoeffer (1981) compared the play and activity interests of 20 6- to 9-year-old children of lesbian mothers and a demographically matched group of 20 children of the same age who were being raised by single heterosexual mothers. Each family type had 10 boys and 10 girls. The majority of mothers were separated or divorced from their child's father (83 percent), and the remainder had never been married. Using a measure of children's preferences for typically masculine (e.g. train, truck, tool kit), feminine (e.g. doll, tea set, beads) and neutral (e.g. marbles, seashells, colored pens) toys, gender role behavior was assessed according to the extent to which children preferred the toys associated with their own gender. In addition, mothers' encouragement of gender role behavior was measured by asking them to rate the toys according to those that they most, somewhat, and least preferred for their children. Mothers were also interviewed about the ways in which they encouraged play with their children's eight favorite toys and activities; for example, by suggesting play with the toys, showing approval or disapproval of the toys and modeling play with the toys. There was no difference in toy preferences between the boys and girls with lesbian mothers and their counterparts with heterosexual mothers. However, mothers' sexual orientation did make a difference to the toys the mothers preferred for their children. The lesbian mothers preferred a more equal mixture of masculine and feminine toys than did the heterosexual mothers, and appeared more willing to encourage – or at least less likely to discourage – their children's play with toys that were stereotypically associated with the other gender. Nevertheless, their children were highly sex-typed in their toy and activity preferences, suggesting that lesbian mothers' greater preference for an equal mixture of masculine and feminine toys for their children had little impact on the toys and activities chosen by their daughters and sons.

Less is known about adolescents than about younger children in post-divorce lesbian mother families. However, Huggins (1989) studied self-esteem in 18 adolescents aged from 13 to 19 years from lesbian mother families and 18 adolescents in the same age range from heterosexual mother families. Ten of the 16 lesbian mothers were living with a female partner and four of the 16 heterosexual mothers had remarried or were living with a male partner. No differences in self-esteem were found between the adolescents with divorced lesbian mothers and the adolescents with divorced heterosexual mothers. Although the sample size was too small for statistical analysis, the findings produced tentative suggestions of factors that may be associated with low self-esteem in the daughters of lesbian mothers. These included feeling negatively about their mothers' lesbian identity, learning about their mother's sexual orientation at an older age, having a father who was unaccepting of their mother's sexual orientation and having a mother who was single.

The children in the UK study were followed up when they reached early adulthood, in order to address the criticism voiced in courts of law that "sleeper effects" may be operating in lesbian mother families such that the negative effects of lesbian motherhood would not become apparent until the children had grown up. It was argued that children who had been raised by lesbian mothers would experience psychological problems and difficulties in forming intimate relationships in adulthood. In addition, as discussed above, it was believed that they would be lesbian or gay themselves, which was often the basis for custody to be awarded to heterosexual fathers, rather than lesbian mothers. The children in the study were re-contacted when they were around 23 to 24 years old, and assessments of the young adults' family relationships, peer relationships, psychological adjustment and sexual orientation were carried out by standardized interviews and questionnaires (Tasker and Golombok, 1995, 1997). It was possible to trace 25 young adults from the lesbian families and 21 young adults who had been raised by single heterosexual mothers, who, together, represented around 60 percent of the initial sample who had participated 14 years earlier. Although the sample size was small, an advantage of the study was that the children had been recruited before their sexual orientation was known; thus the potential for selection bias associated with their sexual identity was reduced.

During the children's adolescence, all but one of the original single heterosexual mothers had had at least one new male partner, and all but one of the original lesbian mothers had had at least one female partner, with almost all these new partners residing with the family. There was no difference between young adults from the two family types in the quality of their relationship with their mother or their father when they were in their mid twenties. However, the young adults from lesbian families were more positive about their relationship with their mother's female partner than were those from heterosexual families regarding their mother's male partner. The reason for this seems to lie in the pattern of family relationships, more generally. Young adults from lesbian mother families usually maintained a relationship with their mother, their father and their mother's partner, who was viewed as an additional parent; contrastingly, in heterosexual families, it was more likely that contact with the father would be lost and the mother's partner would be viewed as a less favored replacement parent. Although the young adults with lesbian mothers were no more likely to report having been teased or bullied in adolescence, the focus of the victimization differed according to family type. Those from lesbian families were more likely to have been teased or bullied about their own or their mother's sexual orientation than were their counterparts from heterosexual homes. Whether this was actually the case or whether young people with lesbian mothers were simply more likely to recollect such bullying in adolescence because they were more sensitive to it cannot be determined from retrospective reports. However, it seems likely that the answer lies somewhere between these two possibilities. No differences were identified between the two groups of young people in their experience of anxiety or depression, with scores on standardized measures falling within the normal range.

Sexual orientation was assessed in terms of same-gender sexual attraction since adolescence, same-gender relationships since adolescence and current sexual orientation (Golombok and Tasker, 1996). Although there were no differences between young adults in the two family types in ratings of same-gender attraction, those from lesbian families were more likely to have experienced same-gender relationships. With respect to sexual orientation, the large majority of young people identified themselves as being heterosexual in adulthood, with only two women from lesbian mother families identifying themselves as lesbian. Other studies of sexual orientation have produced similar findings. In the study of adolescent children of lesbian and heterosexual mothers by Huggins (1989), reported above, only one child – that of a heterosexual mother – identified herself as lesbian. Gottman (1990) focused on the adult daughters of lesbian and heterosexual mothers and found that around 16 percent of the young women reported same-gender sexual fantasies and 8 percent reported a female sexual object choice, with no differences according to family type. However, actual sexual behavior was not assessed.

PLANNED LESBIAN MOTHER FAMILIES

The growth of assisted reproductive technologies in the 1980s and 1990s resulted in donor insemination becoming a more accessible route to parenthood for lesbian women. For the first time, rather than fighting for custody of their children following an acrimonious divorce, lesbian couples began to plan their family together after coming out. Planned lesbian mother families were also created by adoption, by sexual intercourse with a man who would not be a father to the child and by co-parenting, whereby the mother had a child with a man who was not her partner but played a role in raising the child. The rapid increase in openly lesbian women having children at that time became known as "the lesbian baby boom" (Patterson, 1995).

From a psychological perspective, planned lesbian mother families were of particular interest, as they enabled researchers to address theoretical questions about the role of fathers in children's development. If the children of planned lesbian mother families were not found to differ from the children in traditional families, then this would suggest that fathers are not essential. A further reason for studying these families was that the research on divorced and separated lesbian mothers had been criticized on the grounds that the children had grown up with their father in their early years. Thus, to the extent that early experience influences later development, it was not possible to generalize from these children to children raised in father-absent lesbian mother families from birth.

A number of studies of planned lesbian mother families with young children were carried out. In the USA, Chan, Raboy and Patterson (1998) investigated 55 lesbian mother families and 25 heterosexual parent families, some headed by couples and others headed by single parents. All had conceived their children through donor insemination and the average age of the children was 7 years. No differences were found between the lesbian and heterosexual families in terms of parental well-being, as assessed by standardized measures of stress associated with parenting, depression, self-esteem and, for two-parent families, the couple's relationship quality. Neither were differences found between the psychological adjustment of children in the two family types, as rated by parents and teachers, and the children were found to be well-adjusted in relation to population norms.

Also in the USA, Flaks, Ficher, Masterpasqua and Joseph (1995) compared 15 lesbian couples with children aged from 3 to 9 years who had been conceived by donor insemination with a demographically matched group of 15 heterosexual couples with children of the same age. Parents were administered an interview assessment of parenting awareness skills and a questionnaire measure of their relationship quality. The children were administered an IQ test and their psychological adjustment was assessed using a standardized questionnaire completed by their biological mothers and their teachers. The lesbian and heterosexual couples were not found to differ from each other with respect to relationship quality. Moreover, the lesbian couples' scores did not differ from norms for married heterosexual couples on this measure. Although the lesbian mothers showed greater parenting awareness skills than did the heterosexual parents, this appears to have been related to the parents' gender, rather than their sexual orientation, as both the lesbian and heterosexual mothers showed greater awareness of parenting skills than did the heterosexual fathers. No differences in either cognitive functioning or psychological adjustment were found between children in the two family types, with the scores of both groups of children comparing favorably with population norms.

In Belgium and the Netherlands, 30 lesbian mother families with a child conceived by donor insemination were compared with 38 heterosexual families with a child conceived by donor insemination and 30 heterosexual families with a naturally conceived child. The children were aged between 4 and 8 years (Brewaeys, Ponjaert, Van Hall, et al., 1997). The inclusion of these two groups of heterosexual families allowed the impact of sexual orientation to be examined independently of conception by donor insemination. All lesbian couples who had given birth to a child through donor insemination in a major fertility center during a 6-year period took part in the study; thus the sample was representative of lesbian mothers who had conceived their children by donor insemination at a clinic. In both the lesbian and heterosexual families, an anonymous sperm donor had been used. The quality of the couple's relationship was assessed by questionnaire, and the quality of the parent–child relationship was evaluated through a standardized interview with the parents. In addition, parents completed questionnaire measures of children's adjustment and gender development. The quality of the couples' relationships and the quality of interaction between the biological mother and the child did not differ between the lesbian mother families and either of the heterosexual parent groups. However, co-mothers in lesbian families were found to interact more with their children than were fathers. The children in lesbian mother families did not differ in psychological adjustment from the children in the heterosexual parent comparison groups, and were found to be well-adjusted in relation to population norms. In terms of gender development, neither the boys nor the girls raised by lesbian mothers differed in sex-typed behavior from the boys and girls from heterosexual homes.

As occurred in response to research on post-divorce lesbian mother families, questions were raised about the psychological consequences for children in planned lesbian families upon reaching adolescence. Longitudinal studies in Europe and the USA addressed this issue. In the UK, 30 lesbian mother families were first compared with 42 families headed by single heterosexual mothers and 41 two-parent heterosexual families when the children were 6 years old (Golombok, Tasker, and Murray, 1997). The inclusion of a comparison group of single heterosexual mothers in addition to the two-parent heterosexual comparison group allowed the effects of the absence of a father in the home to be teased apart from the effects of maternal sexual orientation. It was found that mothers in female-headed families, irrespective of their sexual orientation, showed greater warmth toward their children, interacted more with them and also had more serious disputes with them, than did mothers in father-present families. No differences were identified between the lesbian mother and single heterosexual mother families. This suggests that, regardless of sexual orientation and the number of parents in the family, mothers in female-headed families have warmer but more conflicted relationships with their children. The children in female-headed families did not show raised levels of emotional and behavioral problems. However, they perceived themselves as less physically and cognitively competent. When followed up in early adolescence at 12 years of age, the children in female-headed families continued to engage in greater interaction with their mothers and had more serious disputes with them than did their peers from father-present homes (MacCallum and Golombok, 2004). They also perceived their mothers as more available and dependable, but did not experience greater maternal warmth. The early adolescent children of lesbian mothers did not differ in terms of social and emotional development from those with single heterosexual mothers or those with two heterosexual parents. Regarding gender development, boys in father-absent families showed more feminine – but no less masculine – characteristics of gender role behavior in that they were more sensitive and caring. When the adolescents reached the age of 18, the female-headed families were similar to the heterosexual two-parent families on a range of measures of parenting quality and young adults' psychological adjustment, with scores on these measures reflecting positive family relationships and high levels of psychological well-being (Golombok and Badger, 2010). Where differences were identified, these pointed to more positive family relationships and greater psychological well-being among those raised in female-headed homes. Although the lesbian and single heterosexual mothers continued to show very similar patterns of parenting, the lesbian mothers experienced greater conflict with their young adult children and were similar to the heterosexual two-parent families in that respect.

A qualitative longitudinal study, the US National Longitudinal Lesbian Family Study, was initiated in 1986 to provide in-depth data on lesbian families with children conceived by donor insemination (see Gartrell, Peyser, and Bos, 2012 for a review). This study has maintained a remarkably low level of sample attrition. Eighty-four families were recruited to the study during insemination or pregnancy, of which 73 were headed by a couple and 11 were headed by a single mother at the time of the child's birth. Subsequent data collection took place when the children were 2, 5, 10 and 17 years old, by which time 93 percent of the families were still participating in the study. Thus, the sample has not been biased by the attrition of those who have not functioned well. Although the study does not include a comparison group, the children's scores on a standardized measure of adjustment have been compared with US norms. At the age of 10 years (Gartrell, Deck, Rodas, et al., 2005) and at the age of 17 (Gartrell and Bos, 2010), the study children showed fewer emotional and behavioral problems than did the general population of children of the same age, and the 17-year-olds showed higher social, academic and general competence, and lower social and behavioral problems. In order to assess positive functioning – as opposed to psychological problems – the quality of life of the 17-year-olds from lesbian families was compared with that of a matched group of adolescents with heterosexual parents who had been recruited from a representative sample (van Gelderen, Bos, Gartrell, et al., 2012). The two groups of adolescents showed positive psychological adjustment and did not differ in ratings of their quality of life.

In terms of sexual orientation, the 17-year-olds completed an online questionnaire that included questions about their sexual behavior, and were also asked to specify their sexual identity on a seven-point scale ranging from exclusively heterosexual to exclusively homosexual (Gartrell, Bos, and Goldberg, 2011). For boys, 2.7 percent rated themselves as bisexual and 5.4 percent rated themselves as predominantly to exclusively homosexual. No girls rated themselves as predominantly to exclusively homosexual. However, 18.9 percent of girls rated themselves as bisexual. When compared with boys of the same age in the National Survey of Family Growth, the sons of lesbian mothers were found to be no more likely to have engaged in same-sex sexual behavior. However, the daughters of lesbian mothers were more likely to have had same-sex sexual contact than were girls of the same age.

In the Netherlands, 100 two-parent lesbian mother families were compared with a demographically matched sample of 100 two-parent heterosexual families, all with children aged from 4 to 8 years (Bos, van Balen, and van den Boom, 2004, 2007). The lesbian biological mothers reported higher levels of emotional involvement with, and concern about, their children than did the heterosexual mothers. The same was true of co-mothers, compared to fathers in heterosexual families. The co-mothers also showed less power assertion than did the fathers; however, this finding is more likely to be associated with the gender of the parent rather than the parent's sexual orientation. No differences in child adjustment were identified between children in the two family types at the child's age of 4 to 8 years (Bos, van Balen, van den Boom, et al., 2007) or 8 to 12 years (Bos and van Balen, 2008). When the children from the Dutch study were aged 11 years, on average, they were compared with children in the US National Longitudinal Lesbian Family Study at the age of 10 years in order for cultural influences on the functioning of planned lesbian families to be examined (Bos, Gartrell, van Balen, et al., 2008). These two countries differ markedly in social attitudes toward same-sex parenting, with more accepting attitudes prevailing in the Netherlands, which, in 2001, was the first country in the world to institute same-sex marriage. The American children were found to be less open to their peers about their lesbian family and experienced more homophobia. They also showed higher levels of emotional and behavioral problems than did the Dutch children. This difference in the psychological adjustment of children in the two countries was shown to be related, at least in part, to the greater homophobia experienced by the American children. The Dutch study also examined children's gender development at around 11 years old (Bos and Sandfort, 2010). There were no differences in gender identity between children from lesbian and heterosexual families as assessed by the extent to which children felt they were typical of, and happy with, their gender. However, children in lesbian families felt less parental pressure to conform to gender stereotypes and were more uncertain about future heterosexual romantic involvement – an indirect measure of developing sexual orientation.

Studies of children raised by lesbian mothers have focused almost exclusively on families in which children have been born to the mothers. Few studies have considered families that have been created by adoption. Indeed, the studies that exist have focused on adoptive gay father families, with adoptive lesbian mother families included as a comparison group. For this reason, research on adoptive lesbian mother families will be discussed in Chapter 7.

POPULATION SAMPLES

A problem in carrying out research on lesbian mother families is the difficulty in obtaining representative samples. The early research relied on volunteers, who were generally recruited through lesbian social groups and the lesbian press. Owing to the prejudice and discrimination faced by lesbian women raising children, it is likely that sampling biases occurred, although the nature and extent of these biases are not known. It is possible that mothers who were in danger of losing custody of their children would have been disinclined to take part in research, in case it could be used against them. Alternatively, mothers in this situation may have been more likely to perceive a need for such research and thus may have been more inclined to volunteer. It is also conceivable that mothers whose children were experiencing problems would have been less likely to participate in research, which would have resulted in artificially positive findings on the psychological well-being of children raised in lesbian mother homes. Samples of lesbian mother families with children who had been conceived through a sperm bank or fertility clinic were generally representative of planned lesbian mother families with donor-conceived children, as it was possible to invite all women who attended a specific sperm bank or clinic to participate in the research and to calculate participation rates, which were generally very high (e.g. Brewaeys, Ponjaert, van Hall, et al., 1997; Chan, Raboy, and Patterson, 1998). Nevertheless, these families represented only a subsample of planned lesbian mother families; they did not include lesbian mother families that had been created through sexual intercourse, through privately arranged donor insemination or through adoption. Owing to the use of potentially biased volunteer and convenience samples, it was argued that the findings of research on lesbian mother families could not be generalized to lesbian mother families as a whole.

In the 1990s, the first opportunities arose for studying representative samples of lesbian mother families recruited from the general population. One such investigation was conducted in the UK and the other in the USA. In the UK, a study of lesbian mother families with 7-year-old children (Golombok, Perry, Burston, et al., 2003), was carried out in collaboration with the Avon Longitudinal Study of Pregnancy and Childhood, a large geographic population study of 14,000 mothers and their children, beginning at the time of the mother's pregnancy. In the USA, a study of lesbian mother families with 14-year-old children (Wainright, Russell, and Patterson, 2004) was conducted in collaboration with the National Longitudinal Study of Adolescent Health (Add Health), involving a large, national sample of adolescents who were recruited through schools.

The Avon Longitudinal Study of Pregnancy and Childhood enrolled any woman expecting a baby over a period of 21 months in the early 1990s. Women were selected from a clearly defined area of England with a population of 1 million people that included a large city, moderately sized towns and rural areas. The demographic characteristics of the families were closely comparable to those of families in the UK as a whole. The lesbian mothers in the study were first identified, then snowballing procedures were used to enrol lesbian mother families who had moved into the area after the birth of their children, as these families would not have been identified through the initial recruitment process. This process produced 39 lesbian mother families, who were compared with carefully matched groups of 74 two-parent heterosexual families and 60 families headed by single heterosexual mothers, to allow the effects of the number and gender of parents in the family to be examined alongside the effects of parental sexual orientation. The quality of parent–child relationships and the socio-emotional and gender development of the children were assessed through in-depth interviews and questionnaires administered to parents, children and teachers. The findings reflected positive parent–child relationships in lesbian mother families and well-adjusted children with typically developing gender role behavior

(Golombok, Perry, Burston, et al., 2003). The only robust difference found between family types was that fathers showed greater smacking of their children than did co-mothers. A novel feature of this investigation was the use of a measure of children's play narratives to assess parent–child relationships from the child's point of view. The children from lesbian mother and heterosexual families evaluated their mothers as equally positive, equally negative, and similar in their levels of discipline (Perry, Burston, Stevens, et al., 2004).

In the USA, Add Health recruited two schools in each of 80 communities, stratified to ensure that they were representative in terms of region, urbanicity, school type, ethnicity and school size. The 90,000 adolescents attending these schools were asked to complete a questionnaire designed to assess different aspects of psychosocial functioning. In addition, a subsample of 12,000 adolescents was interviewed at home. Forty-four adolescents living in two-parent lesbian families were identified, and a carefully matched comparison group of 44 adolescents living in two-parent heterosexual families was also obtained. No differences in psychosocial adjustment, including anxiety, depression and self-esteem, were identified between adolescents from the two family types (Wainright, Russell, Patterson, et al., 2004). Neither was there a difference in adolescents' feelings of warmth from their parents, perceived care from adults and friends, integration into their neighborhood, perceived autonomy or experiences of sexual and romantic relationships. Although adolescents with lesbian mothers did not differ from those with heterosexual parents in measures of school adjustment – such as academic achievement and getting into trouble – they were found to be more connected at school; they felt closer to other students, safer at school and happier at school than did those with heterosexual parents. In terms of peer relationships, the adolescents with lesbian mothers did not differ from those with heterosexual parents in the quality of their relationships with peers, their number of friends, the presence of a best friend and support from male and female friends (Wainright and Patterson, 2008). In addition, reports by peers showed no differences in the popularity or centrality within their friendship networks of children in lesbian and heterosexual families. The adolescents from both family types showed low levels of alcohol, tobacco and marijuana use, and no differences were identified between them (Wainright and Patterson, 2006).

A further investigation conducted in the UK identified 18 adolescents living in two-parent lesbian mother families from a large, school-based survey of around 2,000 12- to 16-year-olds (Rivers, Poteat, and Noret, 2008). These adolescents were pair-matched with 18 adolescents living with two heterosexual parents based on their school, school year, age, sex, race, socio-economic status and sexual orientation. The 14 participating schools were representative of the 47 schools in the region with respect to the students' socio-economic status, gender, ethnicity and urban versus rural mix. The children raised in lesbian mother families did not differ from those in heterosexual parent families in their reports of victimization or in their psychosocial functioning, which included symptoms of psychological distress such as anxiety and depression, and concerns relating to family, friends, school work, bullying, appearance and drug or alcohol use. Although the children of lesbian mothers reported various forms of victimization by peers, the children of heterosexual parents reported similar experiences.

Some studies have focused on school achievement. The impact of the timing and number of family transitions (e.g. from a two-parent family to a single-parent family or a single-parent family to a stepfamily) on children's mathematics scores was the focus of a study by Potter (2012), based on the Early Childhood Longitudinal Study – Kindergarten Cohort, an investigation of 20,000 children from kindergarten to eighth grade in the USA. Although data on parental sexual orientation was not obtained directly, 158 same-sex parent families were identified through the information children provided about the gender and relationship status of adults residing in the household. These families were all two-parent families, with more than 90 percent headed by lesbian mothers. Although the mathematics scores of children with same-sex parents appeared to be lower than those of children with married heterosexual parents, this gap disappeared after the number of family transitions that the children had experienced was controlled for. Children who entered same-sex parent families following the divorce or separation of their parents would necessarily have experienced a family transition, whereas children in two-parent heterosexual families were much less likely to have experienced such a transition between kindergarten and eighth grade.

The first investigation of the academic performance of a large, nationally representative sample of children raised by same-sex couples in the USA was conducted by Rosenfeld (2010), using US census data. In an examination of progress through school – that is, normal progress versus being held back a grade – children of same-sex couples were compared with children from other family types. The sample included 3,502 children of same-sex couples, of whom 2,030 lived with lesbian mothers and 1,472 lived with gay fathers, and more than 700,000 children from other family types. Although the children of heterosexual married couples had lower rates of grade retention (6.8%) than did the children of lesbian mothers (9.5%) and gay fathers (9.7%), this difference was mostly owing to the higher socio-economic status of the heterosexual married couples and disappeared when socio-economic status was controlled for in the statistical analyses. Indeed, the grade retention rates for children of lesbian and gay parents were lower than those found for children of cohabiting heterosexual parents (11.7%) and children of single parents, which ranged from 11.1% to 12.6%. Thus, it was concluded that children with same-sex parents make normal progress through school.

More negative findings were reported from Canadian census data on high school graduation rates (Allen, 2013). An advantage of the Canadian data was that same-sex couples and their children could be directly identified. Although the children of lesbian mothers were only 60 percent as likely to complete high school as were children from families headed by married heterosexual parents, the study did not control for either socio-economic status or the number of family transitions, which are both associated with school performance. It is particularly important to control for socio-economic status in comparisons of lesbian mother and heterosexual parent families, as same-sex parent families have lower incomes and are twice as likely to have household incomes near the poverty threshold as their heterosexual counterparts (Gates, 2013).

CHILDREN'S EXPERIENCES

Although much can be learned from the controlled, quantitative studies of parenting and child development in lesbian mother families described above, these studies do not tell us about the day-to-day experiences of children raised in lesbian mother homes or what these children themselves think. How do young children respond to having two mothers? How do older children react to stigmatization? And how do young adults who have been raised in lesbian mother families reflect upon their upbringing? These are just some of the questions that have been raised in relation to the lived experiences of children of lesbian mothers.

One question that has often been asked is whether young children favor their biological mother over their non-biological mother. In order to examine this issue, lesbian couples were interviewed about the parental preferences of their 3.5-year-old children (Goldberg, Downing, and Sauck, 2008). Although, as infants, they were reported to prefer their biological mother – which was attributed to factors such as breastfeeding and the mother's greater time spent with the child – by the time the children were aged 3.5, most mothers felt that their children had an equal preference for both mothers. In the study by Brewaeys, Ponjaert, van Hall, et al. (1997), a projective test of children's perceptions of their relationship with each parent, the Bene Anthony Family Relations test, was conducted with 4- to 8-year-old children. No difference was found in the degree to which children attributed positive feelings to the biological mother in lesbian families and to the biological mother in the comparison group of heterosexual families. However, within lesbian families, children appeared to attribute more positive feelings to the biological mother than to the non-biological mother. Since this test is projective, whereby feelings toward parents are inferred from a doll play task, firm conclusions should not be drawn from these findings. When followed up at age 10, the quality of children's relationships with non-biological mothers was similar to that with biological mothers according to both children and mothers (Vanfraussen, Ponjaert-Kristoffersen, and Brewaeys, 2003).

A key issue for children once they start school is the nature and extent of victimization that they experience in response to their lesbian mother family. A qualitative study of 82 children and young people with lesbian and gay parents between the ages of 4 and 27 in the UK identified aspects of the school environment that can cause distress (Guasp, Statham, and Jennings, 2010). Although experiences of bullying were found to be low, the children felt that, when instances did occur, teachers often did not respond as severely as they would to racist bullying. The difficulties faced by children were generally more subtle than overt teasing or bullying. The children were distressed by the way in which the word "gay" was used as an insult. As one girl said:

> When I'm in school it's a bit hard, especially when children go … as an insult they go oh that's so gay about something they don't like. Say they might have done a drawing they didn't like and they go oh, that's so gay, and they've done a bad piece of work, oh that's so gay.

Also, they often had to answer questions about their family from their classmates, which made them feel unusual and uncomfortable. Although the questions stopped once their peers understood their family situation, questioning began again when the children moved to a different class or school. As one 8-year-old described it:

> In most people's families you don't have to explain to everybody about your whole family, but I do in the playground. People will be like oh, how come you've got two mummies, you can only have one, and then I have to explain it all, but other people don't really have to do that.

This 7-year-old had a similar experience:

> Well, people ask me ... it's impossible to have two mums and
> dads ... it's not possible, it's above human abilities ... stuff like
> that and I say it's obviously possible ... I just go yes it's possible
> and then they say ... no it's not ... and I say yes it is ... and then
> they say no it's not and then I say oh yes, just be quiet, yes it is.

Another major issue for these children was that lesbian or gay people
or families were never mentioned in schools, which made them feel
invisible:

> The videos that they used to show you in school, all about life
> and everything, it would be the conventional family with a mum,
> dad, kids and dog. And it wasn't two mums and two dads. It was
> always a mum and dad.

The experience of this 12-year-old was not unusual:

> I can still remember when I was younger we had to draw a medal
> that said No. 1 dad. I said I didn't want to do it. And they just
> said ... well, my teacher, it was like a supply teacher, and if I'd
> had my normal teacher I think she would have said well you
> could draw one for your mum, but she just sort of said ... well
> just do one, don't moan. And I found that really hard.

In schools that were unsupportive, some children came to the conclusion that it was safer to keep their family a secret:

> I wish I could talk openly about it to people. I'm too scared to, too
> scared of what would happen, of what they would say, what about
> if they told someone ... I said not to tell anyone and they told
> somebody, and although it might not seem a big thing to anybody
> else, it does to me.

When asked to suggest ways in which schools could become more
friendly toward children of same-sex parents, the young people

recommended that teachers talk about different kinds of families, not assume that everyone has a mum and dad, include examples of lesbian and gay people in their lessons, and stop homophobic bullying, as this would enable them to be themselves at school.

Stigmatization associated with growing up in a lesbian mother family was also studied in Henny Bos and colleagues' study of planned lesbian mother families in the Netherlands. At around 11 years of age, the children were asked about their experiences of stigmatization. Although they reported low levels, overall, boys, more than girls, felt excluded by peers because of their lesbian family, whereas girls more often reported that other children gossiped about their family (Bos and van Balen, 2008).

Children in the US National Longitudinal Lesbian Family Study were interviewed at age 10 about their family and their experiences of homophobia (Gartrell, Deck, Rodas, et al., 2005). By this age, 57% were completely out to their peers about coming from a lesbian family, 39% were out to some and 4% concealed information about their family from their classmates. Although unanimously positive about their family, 43 percent had experienced homophobia outside the family home, and the majority of these children had been distressed by these incidents. At the age of 17, the adolescents were asked about their everyday life experiences (Gartrell, Bos, Peyser, et al., 2012).These young people were found to be academically successful with active social networks and close friendships that had lasted for many years. Most felt comfortable bringing friends home, informing their friends of their mothers' sexual orientation and confiding in their mothers about their lives. Almost all described their mothers in highly positive terms. However, half had experienced negative reactions to their lesbian family at school, through teasing, rejection, exclusion or the derogatory use of the words "lesbian" or "gay" (van Gelderen, Gartrell, Bos, and van Rooij, 2012).

Studies have also been conducted on the perspective of young adults who have grown up in lesbian mother families. In the longitudinal study of post-divorce lesbian mother families conducted in the

UK, Tasker and Golombok (1995) explored factors associated with young people's positive and negative attitudes toward their families in adolescence and early adulthood. The young adults were generally affirmative about their lesbian family. However, adolescence was remembered as a more difficult time for some. Feelings of hostility or embarrassment about their lesbian family in adolescence were expressed by young people who recollected peer group stigma – especially if they remembered being teased about their own sexual identity – and by those who felt that their mother had been too open about her lesbian identity, preventing them from being in control of who was told about their family, and when. Other factors that appeared to be at play for adolescents who had negative feelings about their family included their friends not being welcomed at home, their mothers' disapproval of their boyfriends or girlfriends and their mothers' negative attitude toward men. Acceptance of their family during adolescence was associated with close and stable family relationships, the absence of peer stigma and the mother and her partner providing constructive help in bridging the gap between school and home. The geographical location of the family also appears to have made a difference, with those living in rural environments and small cities experiencing greater stigmatization than those from London and the south of England. After growing up and leaving home, these experiences became less important and many young adults began to take pride in their lesbian family background.

The experiences of 46 adults with lesbian, gay or bisexual parents in the USA, 80 percent of whom had lesbian mothers, were examined by Goldberg (2007), with an emphasis on their perceptions of how their upbringing had influenced them. Many thought that they were more tolerant of other minority groups as a result of having grown up in a society that judged and marginalized their families and themselves. They also thought that they were more sensitive to, and distressed by, homophobia, and felt protective of their parents and the gay community, with some making great efforts to defend their parents to peers, family members and society. Related to this was a feeling of pressure to present themselves as upstanding, well-adjusted adults in order to protect their families against negative opinion.

A crucial issue for many lesbian mother families is whether the couple have the right to marry. Goldberg and Kuvalanka (2012) interviewed young adults with lesbian, gay and bisexual parents to examine their perspectives on marriage equality. Three-quarters gave their unconditional support for marriage equality, with the remaining quarter in favor but critical of the institution of marriage, in general. In addition to the practical benefits of marriage, including equality with respect to financial matters and obviation of the need for second-parent adoption by a non-legal parent, symbolic benefits were emphasized, including greater recognition of parents' relationships and the potential decrease in stigma to which children of same-sex parents are commonly exposed.

INDIVIDUAL DIFFERENCES

Although few differences have been identified *between* lesbian mother and heterosexual parent families when groups of children from each family type have been compared, variation has been found *within* each family type in the psychological well-being of the children. Several studies have examined factors associated with positive and negative psychological outcomes for children in lesbian mother families and a number of key factors have emerged, the most important of which appear to be the psychological well-being of parents including the quality of the couple's relationship, the quality of parenting experienced by children and the degree of stigma to which children are exposed.

The role of family processes in the psychological adjustment of children in lesbian mother families has been the focus of much of the work of Charlotte Patterson and her colleagues. In their study of lesbian mother families with donor-conceived children, stress associated with parenting was found to be associated with children's behavior problems. In addition, for the two-parent families, children were rated as better adjusted when their parents reported greater relationship satisfaction, higher levels of love and lower levels of conflict, irrespective of parents' sexual orientation. Parents who experienced higher levels of parenting stress and lower levels of relationship quality had children with greater behavioral problems (Chan, Raboy, and Patterson, 1998). Similarly, in their Add Health study, adolescents who had positive relationships with their parents were more likely to be functioning well at school (Wainright and Patterson, 2008; Wainright, Russell, and Patterson, 2004). With respect to gender development, a study of lesbian and heterosexual parents with preschool children showed that, regardless of parental sexual orientation, the children of couples who engaged in a more equal division of childcare and paid labour had less traditional occupational aspirations (Fulcher, Sutfin, and Patterson, 2008).

Stigmatization associated with lesbian mother families has also been shown to have a negative impact on the psychological adjustment of children in these families. In an investigation of post-divorce lesbian mother families, Gershon, Tschann and Jemerin (1999) found lower self-esteem among adolescents who had been exposed to greater homophobia. As discussed above, the study by Henny Bos and colleagues of planned lesbian mother families in the Netherlands found that the mothers generally reported low levels of stigmatization. However, those who experienced ridicule, marginalization or exclusion in relation to their family were more likely to report emotional and behavioral problems in their 4- to 8-year-old children (Bos, van Balen, and van den Boom, 2004). When children were around 10 to 12 years old, higher levels of stigmatization – as reported by the children themselves – were associated with greater behavioral problems among boys and lower self-esteem among girls (Bos and van Balen, 2008). Similarly, 10-year-olds in the National Longitudinal Lesbian Family Study who had been stigmatized because of their lesbian mother family showed raised levels of problem behavior (Bos, Gartrell, Peyser, et al., 2008). At the age of 17, those who had experienced stigmatization reported greater mood, anxiety and conduct problems (Bos and Gartrell, 2010; Bos, Gartrell, and van Gelderen, 2013).

Although the stigma experienced by those who grow up with lesbian mothers can take its toll on the psychological well-being of some children, the absence of overall differences in psychological problems between children with lesbian and heterosexual parents suggests that other children are resilient to the effects of stigmatization. This raises the following question: what factors protect children against the negative effects of stigmatization? In their Dutch study, Bos and van Balen (2008) found that 8- to 12-year-old children benefited from contact with other children with same-sex parents. In addition, findings from the National Longitudinal Lesbian Family Study show that positive relationships with mothers and fitting in well with a peer group helped to protect adolescents of lesbian mothers from the negative effects of homophobic stigmatization (Bos and Gartrell, 2010; van Gelderen, Gartrell, Bos, et al., 2012). Attending a school that teaches students about lesbian and gay lifestyles and mothers' involvement in the lesbian community were also found to be associated with positive adjustment in these children (Bos, Gartrell, Peyser, et al., 2008; Bos, Gartrell, van Balen, et al. 2008). The beneficial effects of lesbian- and gay-friendly school environments found in these studies add weight to the pleas of the children described above for schools to exhibit more inclusivity to families with same-sex parents. Interestingly, the protective effects of mothers' involvement in the lesbian community are in stark contrast to the outcomes of early child custody cases, in which mothers were allowed custody or visitation rights to see their children only if they had *no* involvement in the lesbian community.

LIMITATIONS

Much criticism has been directed at the body of research on lesbian mothers and their children. Indeed, this area of research has probably attracted more scrutiny than any other within the field of developmental psychology, with detailed examinations of the methodological veracity of the research carried out at the level of the US Supreme Court and equivalent bodies in other countries, in relation to issues such as adoption by same-sex parents and marriage equality. Whereas some of the criticisms are valid and should be borne in mind in any consideration of the studies described above, there has been a concerted attempt by anti-gay organizations to undermine these research findings as a deliberate strategy to reinforce heterosexual marriage.

So, what can be concluded about the methodological status of existing research on lesbian mother families? An important limitation concerns the generally small samples studied. As a result, comparisons between lesbian mother and heterosexual parent families may lack sufficient statistical power to detect differences between them, in the direction of either more negative or more positive outcomes for the children of lesbian mothers. One approach that has been used to compensate for small sample sizes in other areas of psychological research is meta-analysis, a statistical procedure that combines the findings of comparable investigations on a specific topic to increase statistical power and thus enable the identification of significant effects, should they exist. A meta-analysis of 18 studies of the parenting practices, emotional well-being and sexual orientation of young people raised in lesbian mother families was conducted by Allen and Burrell (1996). No differences were revealed between lesbian mother and heterosexual parent families for any of these constructs, as assessed by parents, teachers or the children themselves. The authors concluded that the meta-analysis had sufficient statistical power to detect large and medium effects and that the probability of the existence of undetected small effects was low.

A meta-analysis of 19 studies involving 564 same-sex parent families and 641 heterosexual parent families by Crowl, Ahn and Baker (2008) examined children's gender identity, gender role behavior, sexual orientation, cognitive functioning, psychological adjustment and quality of relationships with parents. The proportion of families headed by lesbian mothers and gay fathers was not reported, although the large majority were likely to have been lesbian mother families, given the far greater number of studies of lesbian mother families that have been carried out. Although no differences were found between the children according to family type, the quality of parents' relationships with their children was found to be better in families headed by same-sex parents. This finding was based on data obtained from parents, but not from children. Fedewa, Black and Ahn (2014) also included both lesbian mother and gay father families in their meta-analysis of 33 studies but again the majority of families were headed by lesbian mothers. The quality of parent–child relationships was found to be higher, and the children were found to show higher levels of psychological adjustment and more traditional gender role behavior, in families with same-sex rather than heterosexual parents. However, the effect sizes were very small, which suggested that there were no meaningful differences between the two family types. No differences were identified for children's cognitive development, gender identity or sexual orientation. From these meta-analyses, it appears that the failure to find greater psychological problems among the children of lesbian mothers in individual studies has not simply resulted from a lack of statistical power.

Other criticisms of this research literature include a failure to detect differences between lesbian mother and heterosexual parent families as a result of the following: lesbian mothers tending to present their families in the best possible light in order to counteract criticism about the quality of their parenting and the well-being of their children; use of measures that lack satisfactory reliability and validity; and sample bias, such that families with problems may be less likely to participate in research than well-functioning families, and thus artificially positive findings may be produced. Related to this latter criticism is the reliance on predominantly white, middle-class samples. Nevertheless, a large number of studies of children with lesbian mothers have been carried out using the following: (a) different types of measures with sound psychometric properties, including standardized interviews, questionnaires, observational assessments and children's psychological tests; (b) multiple informants, including mothers, fathers and children, as well as teachers, to provide an independent assessment; and (c) different types of samples, including volunteer samples, consecutive samples of specific kinds of lesbian mother families (such as those with donor-conceived children) and samples that are representative of the general population. Clearly, some studies stand up to methodological scrutiny more than do others, as is true for all areas of psychological research. However, what is striking about these investigations, conducted in different geographic locations over a period of 40 years, is the consistency of the findings, given the diversity of methods used.

CONCLUSIONS

In the years that have passed since lesbian mothers first hit the headlines and judges were required to base child custody decisions on speculation over the consequences of growing up in a lesbian mother family in the absence of empirical research, a large number of investigations of what really happens to children with lesbian mothers have been carried out. Is it the case that these children experience psychological disorder, problems with their peers and atypical gender development, as suggested by the major psychological theories and predicted so fervently by the media, mental health professionals and the public at large?

With respect to psychological adjustment, not a single study has shown that children raised by lesbian mothers are more at risk for emotional or behavioral problems than are their peers from heterosexual homes. Not only have no differences been identified when lesbian mother and heterosexual parent families have been directly compared, but also children in lesbian mother families have been shown to function within the normal range; that is, they are no more likely than children in the general population to experience psychological disorder. This is the conclusion of studies of post-divorce lesbian mother families, of planned lesbian mother families and of general population samples. On the whole, it seems that lesbian mothers have well-adjusted children.

At school, children with lesbian mothers generally appear to perform no differently from children with heterosexual parents. Some show high levels of academic achievement, whereas others do not; but the children's academic performance does not appear to be associated with maternal sexual orientation. The findings on peer relationships are not so clear cut. Although outright victimization in the form of teasing, bullying and rejection by peers seems less prevalent than previously assumed and is determined, to some extent, by societal factors such as geographical location, low level stigmatization based on homophobic attitudes remains a fact of life for children of lesbian mothers. This stigmatization may take the form of the use of the word "gay" as a pejorative term or the invisibility of same-sex parent families in the school environment. Moreover, children's reports of victimization represent an underestimation, as some children avoid distress by choosing not to disclose details of their family to peers.

Although comparisons between lesbian mother and heterosexual parent families have not identified overall differences in parenting quality or child adjustment, there is variation among the children of lesbian mothers in the presence and severity of emotional and behavioral problems (as is also true for heterosexual families). Why is it that some children in lesbian mother families experience psychological difficulties, whereas others do not? The answer to this question is, to some extent, the same as for children in any family type. The studies show that children whose mothers are experiencing personal or relationship difficulties are themselves more likely to have psychological problems. However, children with lesbian mothers face specific challenges that place them at risk for psychological difficulties – particularly the stigmatization of their lesbian mother family in the wider social world. The adverse effect of stigmatization on children's well-being does not mean that lesbian mothers fail to provide a positive family environment for their children. The stigmatization that children experience results from their lesbian mother family, but is not a necessary consequence of it. Although it is not possible for parents to isolate their children from homophobic attitudes and behavior, they can protect them, to some extent, by giving constructive help in dealing with stigmatization and by providing a supportive home environment.

Investigations of gender development have focused on the separate components of gender identity, gender role behavior and sexual orientation. Although it might seem strange today, when lesbian mothers first caught the attention of the public, it was thought that their children would be confused about their gender identity; that is, it was assumed that they would be unsure of whether they were male or female. However, in all the studies conducted so far, not one child with gender identity disorder has been identified. The girls have been found to be secure in their identity as female, and the boys have been found to see themselves as male. Although the predominant theories of the day encouraged an open mind about gender role behavior, research on this aspect of gender development has shown girls to be no less feminine, and boys to be no less masculine, than girls and boys from heterosexual homes. This finding is in spite of lesbian mothers' greater preference for less sex-typed toys and activities for their daughters and sons. Moreover, non-traditional gender role behavior is no longer seen as a negative attribute.

In terms of sexual orientation, the large majority of children raised in lesbian mother families identify as heterosexual in adulthood. Thus, the commonly held assumption that children brought up by lesbian mothers will themselves grow up to be lesbian or gay is not supported by the evidence. Nevertheless, more young people from lesbian families, especially young women, engage in same-sex relationships. This is probably because growing up in an accepting environment enables those who are attracted to same-sex partners to pursue these relationships; young people in lesbian mother families generally do not face the same disapproval as experienced by their peers from heterosexual homes.

The research conducted in the latter part of the twentieth century that sought to establish whether or not children of lesbian mothers differed from other children was based on the premise that any differences identified would point to more negative outcomes for children in lesbian families. However, a landmark paper by Stacey and Biblarz (2001) argued that the focus on negative outcomes meant that positive differences and differences that were neither positive nor negative – simply differences – had been overlooked. This paper served an important function by highlighting that difference does not necessarily imply deficit, and proved to be a turning point in the field.

In the relatively short period of time between the 1970s – when lesbian mothers first became visible – and the present, the population of lesbian mother families has grown exponentially. The early research, conducted in a climate of homophobia, set out to shed light on previously unexplored assumptions about the harmful psychological consequences for children. Today, lesbian mothers can marry each other, adopt children jointly and be the joint legal parents of children born through donor insemination, depending on where in the world they live. Although these changes have come about through more accepting social attitudes toward lesbian mother families and less discriminatory policies and legislation, the psychological research described above has also played a part by challenging the widely held belief that growing up in a lesbian family is psychologically damaging to children.

3   "Test-tube" baby families

Just at the time when lesbian mother families were beginning to enter public awareness, a new and even more controversial family was created through in vitro fertilization (IVF). In 1978, the first "test-tube" baby, Louise Brown, was born in the UK (Steptoe and Edwards, 1978). As reported in the *Guardian* newspaper (in an article entitled "Test tube mother has a girl," on July 26, 1978): "Mrs Lesley Brown, the world's first test-tube mother, gave birth to a baby girl at Oldham General Hospital, Lancashire, last night after a caesarean section delivery. The historic birth took place shortly before midnight. The baby weighed in at 5lb 12ozs. Medical staff said later that the condition of both mother and daughter were 'excellent.'" The

Daily Express newspaper reported on July 11, 1978, "The baby of the century is born. The first ever to be conceived in the laboratory. And it's a girl."

For the first time, a human life had been created in the laboratory. The mother's egg was fertilized by the father's sperm in a Petri dish and the embryo that was to become Louise was transferred to her mother's womb. Louise entered the world on July 25, 1978 to a fanfare from the world's media. As reported by *The Economist* magazine (in an article entitled "No IVF please, we're British," on July 17, 2008): "The world's press was camped outside; the front doors locked and staff forced to sneak in and out via a side entrance. Patrick Steptoe and Robert Edwards, the obstetrician and physiologist who had, nine months before, taken an egg from one of Mrs Brown's ovaries under anaesthetic and fertilized it in vitro with her husband's sperm, were in hiding." It was, said *Time* magazine (in an article entitled "The first test-tube baby," on July 31, 1978), "The most awaited birth in perhaps 2,000 years."

But the route to this historic birth was not straightforward. In a lecture in honor of Robert Edwards's Nobel Prize in 2010, Martin Johnson, a reproductive biologist who had been a Ph.D. student of Robert Edwards in the early days of IVF, described the hostile opposition that Edwards and Steptoe had faced (Johnson, 2010, 2011). As Johnson described it, on publication of the first scientific paper on IVF in humans on February 14, 1969, "all hell was let loose." Edwards and Steptoe were attacked by the media, the Roman Catholic Church and their professional colleagues, and, on April 1, 1971, their application for funding to pursue their research on in vitro fertilization was eventually rejected: "It was not until 1989 ... that the UK Parliament finally gave its stamp of approval to his visionary work, and then only after a fierce battle lasting some 11 years" (Johnson, 2010, p. 251, 2011). And it was not until 32 years after the birth of Louise Brown that Robert Edwards won the Nobel Prize. As Patrick Steptoe had died in 1988, he was not eligible to be a joint recipient of this award.

In the years since Louise Brown's birth, IVF has made the transition from the realms of science fiction to become a commonly accepted treatment for infertility, with more than 5 million IVF babies born worldwide (Adamson, 2012). In 1978, however, Louise's birth was met by the general public with opposition and fear. Some of the original mothers who had had children in this way were shunned or shouted at in the street, and even close relatives were suspicious of the new addition to their family. As one of the first IVF mothers said: "I think my mother-in-law thought he was going to come out with two heads ... She does love him, I'm sure she does, but there's always been that little something ... even when she came to the hospital after he was born, she didn't pick him up."

In spite of the hullabaloo surrounding Louise's birth, Louise was the genetic child of her mother and father. Apart from the circumstances of her conception, she was no different from any other child, as she was raised by the parents who had conceived and given birth to her. Just as the introduction of the contraceptive pill was criticized for the separation of sex from reproduction, much was made of the separation of reproduction from sex that followed the introduction of IVF. Nevertheless, Louise was, in every sense, the child of her parents – she was the genetic child of her mother and father, her mother had been pregnant and given birth to her, and she grew up both socially and legally as the daughter of Mr. and Mrs. Brown.

The establishment of IVF paved the way for increasingly "high-tech" reproductive procedures. In the early 1990s, a new technique was introduced – intra-cytoplasmic sperm injection (ICSI) – whereby a single sperm is injected directly into an egg in order to fertilize it (Palermo, Joris, Devroey, et al., 1992). This was the first treatment for male infertility, and it has since enabled men with abnormal sperm or a low sperm count to become fathers. As in IVF, when the mother's egg and father's sperm are used in ICSI and the mother undergoes the pregnancy, the parents have both a genetic and a gestational connection to their child in the same way as do parents of naturally conceived children.

For many infertile couples, IVF or ICSI is their treatment of choice as they wish to have biologically related children. As an IVF father said:

I think it's the most, the closest thing to natural really. I mean everything else is a step further away, isn't it? At least it's my sperm and [partner's] eggs, you know, it's just a bit of help if you like rather than anything else. If we'd adopted I'm sure we would have loved the children just as much but ideally you want to have your own children, don't you?

An IVF mother put it like this:

We always said that the reason we wanted children was to create something between us two. So we didn't really want to think about egg or sperm donation or adopting until we'd given IVF a try, using our own egg and sperm first. And we were very, very lucky that it worked.

Considerable concern has been expressed about the possible risks of "high-tech" reproductive procedures such as IVF and ICSI. Whereas much of this anxiety has focused on the health and physical development of children born through these techniques because of the handling of eggs and sperm and the early development of the embryo in a culture medium outside the mother's body (see Fauser, Devroey, Diedrich, et al., 2014 for a review), there have also been concerns about the potentially adverse effects of these techniques on parenting and the psychological development of the children they help to conceive. Owing to the stressful nature of infertility and its treatment, which often lasts for many years, it was thought that parenting difficulties might arise following the eventual birth of a long-awaited baby. Specifically, it was argued that parents who had had difficulty in conceiving might become emotionally over-invested in their much wanted children (Burns, 1990; Covington and Burns, 2006), and that those who had become parents after a period of infertility may be overprotective of their children, or have unrealistic expectations of them or of themselves as parents (Colpin, Demyttenaere, and Vandemeulebroecke, 1995; Hahn and DiPietro, 2001; McMahon, Ungerer, Beaurepaire, et al., 1995; Mushin, Spensley, and Barreda-Hanson, 1985; van Balen, 1998). Moreover, it was suggested that the stress of infertility and its treatment may lead to psychological disorders and marital problems for parents that may, in turn, have negative psychological consequences for their children (McMahon, Ungerer, Beaurepaire, et al., 1995).

A concern relating to ICSI over and above those of IVF was the potential risk for children of the use of abnormal sperm, the bypass of the usual natural selection process of sperm and the potential for physical damage to the egg or embryo which may produce changes in genetic material (Pinborg, Henningsen, and Malchau, 2013; Ponjaert-Kristoffersen, Bonduelle, Barnes, et al., 2005; te Velde, van Baar, and van Kooij, 1998) and may thus have implications for children's psychological development.

MULTIPLE BIRTHS

One important reason why having a child by IVF or ICSI may result in a rather different experience for families is the high incidence of twin and triplet births that arise from these procedures – a consequence of the use of multiple embryos in an IVF or ICSI cycle. More than one-quarter of births resulting from IVF and ICSI in Europe in the 1990s (Nygren and Andersen, 2002), and more than 40 percent of IVF and ICSI births at a similar time in the USA (Wright, Schieve, Reynolds, et al., 2001), produced twins or triplets. This contrasts sharply with the same period's multiple-birth rate for naturally conceived pregnancies of around 1 percent (Bergh, Ericson, Hillensjö, et al., 1999). The problem of multiple births has been greatest in developing and newly industrialized regions such as Latin America, where the multiple-birth rate for assisted reproduction pregnancies in 2000 was 50 percent, and over 13.5 percent of IVF and ICSI births involved triplets or quadruplets (Zegers-Hochschild, 2002). The most extreme example occurred in California in 2009, when Nadya Suleman, a 33-year-old single woman nicknamed by the media as "Octomom," gave birth to IVF octuplets, all of whom survived.

Owing to the physical risks associated with multiple births, including perinatal mortality, preterm deliveries, low birth weight and neonatal problems and disability, some countries have introduced regulations to limit the number of embryos used in an IVF or ICSI cycle. As a consequence, by 2009, the multiple-birth rate resulting from IVF and ICSI in Europe had declined to 20 percent (Ferraretti, Goossens, Kupka, et al., 2013). However, in the USA, the incidence of multiple births following IVF and ICSI remains above 30 percent (Society for Assisted Reproductive Technology, 2012; Zegers-Hochschild, Mansour, Ishihara, et al., 2013).

Parents who have multiple births have to cope not only with two or more infants born at once, but also with infants who may have greater needs as a result of prematurity and low birth weight. Studies of naturally conceived twins and triplets have shown that parents are faced with many stressors that can negatively affect family relationships (Bryan, 1992; Lytton and Gallagher, 2002). Raising two or three children of the same age places enormous demands on parents' time, often resulting in exhaustion, lack of personal time, depression and financial difficulties. As a consequence, twins and triplets have less one-to-one interaction with their parents than do singleton children. As they grow older, children from multiple births often show delayed language development and obtain lower scores on cognitive and reading tests (Hay, Prior, Collett, et al., 1987; Lytton and Gallagher, 2002; Rutter and Redshaw, 1991). A study of a general population sample found that the language development of twins at 3 years of age lagged 3 months behind that of singleton children, after the most premature twins and those with neurological damage were excluded and the gestational age of the twins at birth was adjusted for (Rutter, Thorpe, Greenwood, et al., 2003). As the language delay was found in children without disabilities and the study took account of the twins' shorter gestation, it was concluded that this was not a result of brain damage or biological immaturity but, instead, reflected a real difference between twins and singleton children. Rather than biological factors, the delayed language development in twins was found to be associated with a lower quantity and quality of mother–child interaction (Rutter, Thorpe, Greenwood, et al., 2003).

Although studies of families with naturally conceived multiples are informative, families with twins or triplets who have been conceived through IVF or ICSI may differ in ways that impact on parenting and child development. Parents may find coping with twins or triplets to be particularly stressful following their experience of infertility and its treatment. On the other hand, these parents may be more accepting of a multiple birth. Those undergoing assisted reproduction will almost certainly have considered this outcome and will have made the decision to proceed. Indeed, for a high proportion of those who embark on assisted reproduction, the idea of a multiple birth seems preferable to childlessness, and the prospect of twins is viewed positively as a way of completing the family without the need for further stressful, risky and expensive medical treatment (Gleicher, Campbell, Chan, et al., 1995; Goldfarb, Kinzer, Boyle, et al., 1996; Murdoch, 1997). As one mother put it: "We always say it was buy one, get one free because it literally was! We buy one, we get one free!"

Studies of families with assisted reproduction twins (Colpin, De Munter, Nys, et al., 1999; Cook, Bradley, and Golombok, 1998; Glazebrook, Sheard, Cox, et al., 2004; Olivennes, Golombok, Ramogida, et al., 2005) and triplets (Garel, Salobir, and Blondel, 1997; Golombok, Olivennes, Ramogida, et al., 2007) have revealed higher levels of anxiety and depression among these parents than among parents of singleton children, in spite of the fact that parents of twins and triplets have generally shown greater openness to multiple births. Some investigations have focused on the development of assisted reproduction children who have been born as part of a multiple birth. In a comparison between 2-year-old twins and singletons born through IVF/ICSI (Bonduelle, Ponjaert, Van Steirteghem, et al., 2003), the twins obtained lower scores on the Bayley Scales of Infant Development. Similarly, in a comparison between 2- to 5-year-old IVF/ICSI twins and singletons, the twins showed lower levels of cognitive functioning as assessed by the parent completion version of the Denver Developmental Screening Test, particularly with respect to language development and fine motor skills (Olivennes, Golombok, Ramogida, et al., 2005). No differences were identified for emotional or behavioral problems. Triplets have also been found to show cognitive impairment in comparison with both twins and singletons (Feldman, Eidelman, and Rotenberg, 2004; Feldman and Eidelman, 2005; Garel, Salobir, Lelong, et al., 2001; Golombok, Olivennes, Ramogida, et al., 2007). Findings relating to the psychological adjustment of triplets have been inconclusive, with one investigation of 2-year-olds reporting raised levels of emotional problems (Feldman and Eidelman, 2005) and another investigation of 2- to 5-year-olds reporting no such finding (Golombok Olivennes, Ramogida, et al., 2007).

Few studies have compared IVF/ICSI twins with naturally conceived twins. In an investigation of cognitive and motor development in a large representative sample of 3- to 4-year-olds, no differences in language or motor development were identified (Pinborg, Loft, Schmidt, et al., 2004). Tully, Moffitt and Caspi (2003) focused on behavioral problems in 5-year-olds. Again, no differences were found.

The delayed cognitive development shown by twins and triplets born by IVF and ICSI, when compared with IVF/ICSI singletons, indicates that the greater desire for twins among couples who embark upon assisted reproduction does not ameliorate the cognitive impairment shown in children who are twins. The same is true regarding the greater emotional problems shown by parents of IVF/ICSI triplets and twins. The impact of multiple births on parenting and child development must be considered separately from the impact of IVF and ICSI per se. The investigations described below focus on families with singleton children born as a result of IVF or ICSI, to avoid the potentially confounding effects of multiple births.

PARENTING IN IVF FAMILIES

Do mothers and fathers who become parents through IVF behave differently toward their children than do mothers and fathers of naturally conceived children? A number of studies have been carried out to address this question, focusing on children of different ages. Research on infants has been conducted in Greece and Australia. Although the samples in the Greek study were small, the findings are of interest, as detailed micro-analytic assessments of mother–infant interaction were conducted on four occasions when the infants were between 4 and 21 weeks of age (Papaligoura and Trevarthen, 2001). Few differences were identified between IVF and natural conception families. However, at 21 weeks, mothers whose children had been born through fertility treatment showed greater attention to their infants' physical state and spent longer trying to calm their infants when their infants were distressed.

In the Australian study, 70 IVF families and a comparison group of 63 natural conception families, each with a singleton child, were recruited during pregnancy and followed up when the infants were 4 months old and 1 year old (McMahon and Gibson, 2002). At the 4 month and 1 year assessments, mothers and fathers completed questionnaires designed to assess their feelings of competence as parents and their satisfaction with parenting. An observational measure of mother–child interaction was also administered when the babies were 4 months old, in order to assess maternal sensitivity. At 4 months, the IVF mothers felt less able than the natural conception mothers to understand their infants' signals and to soothe them (McMahon, Ungerer, Tennant, et al., 1997) and, at 1 year, the IVF mothers saw their children as more vulnerable and "special" (Gibson, Ungerer, Tennant, et al., 2000). Nevertheless, the IVF mothers did not differ from the natural conception mothers in sensitivity toward their infants at either 4 months or 1 year (Gibson, Ungerer, McMahon, et al., 2000). For fathers, no differences were identified between those with IVF and naturally conceived children in perceptions of parenting competency at 4 months (McMahon, Ungerer, Tennant, et al., 1997) or 1 year (Gibson, Ungerer, Tennant, et al., 2000).

Families with 2-year-old children were investigated in Belgium (Colpin, Demyttenaere, Vandemeulebroecke, et al., 1995), where 31 IVF families were compared with 31 natural conception families through observational assessments of mother–child interaction and questionnaire assessments of attitudes and feelings toward their children completed by mothers and fathers. No differences were found between family types with respect to the children's behavior toward their mothers or the mothers' behavior toward their children in the interaction task, or for mothers' and fathers' thoughts and emotions regarding their children. In a follow-up study when the children were 8 to 9 years old, the IVF families did not differ from the natural conception families in mothers' or fathers' reports of parenting behavior or parenting stress (Colpin and Soenen, 2002).

IVF families with 4- to 8-year-old children were the focus of the first phase of the European Study of Assisted Reproduction Families conducted in the UK, the Netherlands, Spain and Italy (Golombok, Brewaeys, Cook, et al., 1996; Golombok, Cook, Bish, et al., 1995). The study recruited 116 families with children conceived by IVF, and comparison groups of 115 families with children adopted in infancy and 120 families with naturally conceived children. A group of 111 families with children conceived by donor insemination was also recruited (see Chapter 4). An in-depth semi-structured interview designed to assess quality of parenting and the Parenting Stress Index, a questionnaire measure of stress associated with parenting, were separately administered to mothers and fathers. Information obtained from the interview was coded according to a standardized coding scheme. The IVF mothers were found to show greater warmth toward their children, to be more emotionally involved with them, to interact more with them and to report less stress associated with parenting than were the natural conception mothers. IVF fathers were reported by mothers to interact with their children more than were natural conception fathers, and the fathers themselves reported less parenting stress. The adoptive parents fell between the IVF and natural conception parents on these measures. In the first study to be conducted in a non-western culture, Hahn and DiPietro (2001) examined IVF families with preschool and early school-age children in Taiwan. The quality of parenting was generally found to be good, although IVF mothers showed greater protectiveness over their children. The children's teachers, who were unaware of the nature of the children's conception, rated the IVF mothers as more affectionate toward their children, but not more protective or intrusive, than the natural conception parents.

In order to examine the functioning of IVF families when the children were approaching adolescence, the parents and children in the European Study of Assisted Reproduction Families were reassessed using standardized interview and questionnaire assessments of parent–child relationships when the children reached the age of 12 years. The IVF mothers and fathers were generally found to have positive relationships with their adolescent children, involving a combination of affection and age-appropriate control (Golombok, Brewaeys, Giavazzi, et al., 2002; Golombok, MacCallum, and Goodman, 2001). The few differences that were identified reflected more positive functioning among the IVF than among the adopted and natural conception families, with the exception of the over-involvement with their children of a small proportion of IVF parents. The UK families were followed up once again when the children were aged 18 years (Owen and Golombok, 2009). The IVF mothers and fathers did not differ from the other mothers and fathers on any of the variables relating to warmth or conflict, apart from disciplinary indulgence, which was shown more by IVF mothers. The 18-year-olds were, themselves, administered a standardized interview and questionnaires to assess the quality of their relationship with their parents (Golombok, Owen, Blake, et al., 2009). The IVF young adults were found to have good relationships with their parents. Similar findings to those found in the UK were reported in a follow-up of the Belgian study when the children were aged 15 to

16 years (Colpin and Bossaert, 2008). A standardized questionnaire assessment of the parenting style constructs of responsiveness, behavioral control, psychological control and autonomy support was completed by mothers, fathers and adolescents, separately for each parent. There were no differences in parenting style between IVF and natural conception families as rated by mothers, fathers or adolescents.

So, is it the case that the mothers and fathers of children born through IVF experience difficulties in parenting their long-awaited children? It seems that IVF mothers may be less confident in the children's early months of infancy than are mothers who have not undergone fertility treatment. However, this difference seems short lived. In children's preschool and early school years, IVF mothers and fathers appear to show more positive parenting than do natural conception parents, although there may be a tendency toward over-involvement and overprotection among a minority of mothers. By the time children reach adolescence, IVF mothers and fathers seem very similar to those who have conceived their children naturally in both their approach to parenting and in the quality of their relationships with their children. In general, mothers and fathers whose children have been conceived through IVF appear to be highly committed and involved parents – a finding that is perhaps not surprising given the obstacles they faced in their quest for a child.

CHILDREN IN IVF FAMILIES

So, what about the children? Do IVF children experience psychological difficulties associated with the method of their conception? The Australian study found some evidence of elevated levels of behavioral difficulties in IVF infants, compared with naturally conceived infants. IVF mothers rated their infants as more temperamentally difficult at 4 months than did natural conception mothers (McMahon, Ungerer, Tennant, et al., 1997), and as showing more behavioral problems and more difficult temperaments at age 1 (Gibson, Ungerer, Leslie, et al., 1998). However, there was no difference at age 1 in the proportion of IVF and natural conception infants classified (according to the Strange Situation test) as securely attached (Gibson, Ungerer, McMahon, et al., 2000). In a Swedish study, a comparison of 121 IVF infants and a matched group of 110 naturally conceived infants found the IVF infants to be more manageable, attentive and habitual, but also more sensitive to strong stimuli, as assessed by the Toddler Behavior Questionnaire when the children were 1 year old (Sydsjö, Wadsby, Kjellberg, et al., 2002).

The European Study of Assisted Reproduction Families assessed the psychological adjustment of 4- to 8-year-old IVF children using the Strengths and Difficulties Questionnaire, a widely used measure of behavioral and emotional problems, completed by mothers and teachers (Goodman, 1994, 1997, 2001). In addition, the children were administered tests of self-esteem and of feelings toward their parents. The IVF children did not differ from the naturally conceived children on these measures (Golombok, Brewaeys, Cook, et al., 1996; Golombok, Cook, Bish, et al., 1995). In the UK, only, an assessment was made of the children's security of attachment to their parents using the Separation Anxiety Test, and interview transcripts relating to children's psychological functioning were rated by a child psychiatrist who was unaware of the children's family types. No differences between IVF and naturally conceived children were found for either security of attachment or the incidence of psychological disorder (Golombok, Cook, Bish, et al., 1995). In the Belgian study, mothers, fathers and teachers completed the Child Behavior Checklist (Achenbach and Rescorla, 2000) when the children were 8 to 9 years old (Colpin and Soenen, 2002). There were no differences in child adjustment between the IVF and naturally conceived children, as rated by parents or teachers. Only one study, conducted in Israel, reported raised levels of emotional problems among IVF children of middle school age (Levy-Shiff, Vakil, Dimitrovsky, et al., 1998). In comparison with naturally conceived children, IVF children showed poorer adjustment to school, as rated by teachers, and reported themselves to be more aggressive, anxious and depressed. Although the reason for the discrepancy between the findings of this study and those of the other studies is not known, it might be associated with the older age of the IVF, than the natural conception, parents in the Israeli sample.

In the European Study of Assisted Reproduction Families, parents and teachers again completed the Strengths and Difficulties Questionnaire when the children were aged 12 years (Golombok, Brewaeys, Giavazzi, et al., 2002; Golombok, MacCallum, and Goodman, 2001). No differences were found between family types for either mothers' or teachers' ratings. At the age of 18, no differences between the IVF adolescents and the comparison groups of early adopted and natural conception adolescents were found on a self-report measure of anxiety, depression, hostility and interpersonal sensitivity (Golombok, Owen, Blake, et al., 2009). This study provided the first opportunity for researchers to ask young people how they felt about the unusual nature of their conception. Although a small minority reported a negative reaction on finding out, by the age of 18, not one was distressed about having been conceived by IVF.

Wagenaar and colleagues (Wagenaar, van Weissenbruch, Knol, et al., 2009a) compared the behavior and socio-emotional functioning of 139 IVF children with that of 143 children born spontaneously to parents who had previously experienced fertility problems. The mean age of the children was 13.5 years. Parents completed the Child Behavior Checklist (Achenbach and Rescorla, 2000) and teachers completed the companion Teacher Report Form. The adolescents were found to be functioning within the normal range, as assessed by the scores of both parents and teachers. Where differences were identified, these reflected higher levels of adjustment among the IVF children, particularly in relation to behavioral problems. A non-significant trend in the same direction was also found for teachers' ratings of behavioral problems. When the adolescents themselves reported their behavioral and socio-emotional functioning by completing the Youth Self-Report, no differences were identified according to family type (Wagenaar, van Weissenbruch, et al., 2011). Colpin and Bossaert

(2008) administered the Child Behavior Checklist (Achenbach and Rescorla, 2000) to mothers and fathers, and the Youth Self-Report to 15- to 16-year-old adolescents, in their longitudinal study in Belgium. No differences in adjustment between adolescents who had been conceived by IVF and those who had been conceived naturally were found in either parents' or adolescents' ratings. Similarly, two other studies that used the Child Behavior Checklist (Achenbach and Rescorla, 2000) found no indication of raised levels of psychological problems in children who had been conceived by IVF, compared to general population norms (Cederblad, Friberg, Ploman, et al., 1996; Montgomery, Aiello, and Adelman, 1999).

Wagenaar and colleagues also studied children's cognitive development. In a comparison between the school functioning of 233 IVF children aged 8–18 years, and a matched group of 233 children born spontaneously to parents with fertility problems, no differences were found on measures of educational level, general cognitive ability or school performance, including the need for extra help, special education or repeating a grade (Wagenaar, Celeen, van Weissenbruch, et al., 2008). Those children who had reached puberty, comprising 139 adolescents conceived by IVF and 143 adolescents from the comparison group, were administered assessments of information processing, attention and visual-motor functioning. No differences between the two groups of adolescents were found with the exception of lower motor speed in the IVF children which was within the normal range (Wagenaar, van Weissenbruch, Knol, et al., 2009b).

Contrary to the fears voiced in the early days of IVF, children conceived in this way appear to show low levels of emotional and behavioral problems and no evidence of cognitive impairment. Although there is some evidence of temperamental problems in infancy, this may reflect the perceptions of anxious mothers, rather than the difficulties of their infants. IVF children are just as likely as their naturally conceived counterparts to be securely attached to their mothers. No studies that used either the Strengths and Difficulties Questionnaire (Goodman, 1994, 1997, 2001) or the

Child Behavior Checklist (Achenbach and Rescorla, 2000), the two most reliable and valid measures of child adjustment, found raised levels of psychological problems in IVF children. As some studies also administered these questionnaires to teachers in order to obtain independent reports, greater confidence can be placed in the findings than would otherwise be possible had the questionnaires been completed by parents alone. It seems, therefore, that the tendency toward overprotection by IVF mothers does not result in psychological problems for children. Neither does the greater quality of parenting shown by IVF parents result in even more positive child adjustment.

PARENTING IN ICSI FAMILIES

Although concerns about ICSI families have centered on the effects on children (rather than on parents), the same concerns that have been expressed in relation to IVF parents, such as the possibility of their overprotecting their children, also apply to ICSI parents. For this reason, researchers have examined parenting in ICSI families. A large-scale, multisite study of 540 ICSI, 439 IVF and 542 natural conception families with 5-year-old children was conducted in Belgium, Denmark, Greece, Sweden and the UK. Mothers and fathers completed the Parent–Child Dysfunctional Interaction subscale of the Parenting Stress Index and the Parental Acceptance–Rejection Questionnaire. Few differences in parenting were identified between family types, although ICSI mothers reported fewer hostile or aggressive feelings toward their children and higher levels of commitment to parenting than did the mothers of naturally conceived children (Barnes, Sutcliffe, Kristoffersen, et al., 2004). The children were administered the Bene-Anthony Family Relations Test to provide an assessment of parent–child relationships from the perspective of the children. This involved the children attributing feelings and behaviors to their fathers and mothers through a play task, whereby they posted positive and negative statements to them. No differences were identified according to family type for children's positive or negative feelings toward their mothers or fathers, or their involvement with their mothers or their fathers. Similar findings were reported from a study in the Netherlands of 87 ICSI families, 92 IVF families and 85 natural conception families with 5- to 8-year-old children (Knoester, Helmerhorst, van der Westerlaken, et al., 2007). There were no differences between family types on the Dutch version of the Parenting Stress Index, apart from higher scores for the ICSI and IVF parents relating to children's hyperactivity. In a study of 8-year-olds in Belgium (Leunens, Celestin-Westreich, Bonduelle, et al., 2006), there were no differences in parenting stress reported by mothers and fathers on the Dutch version of the Parenting Stress Index. It appears, therefore, that parents of ICSI children are similar to parents of IVF children, in that they are highly committed to parenting and have positive relationships with their children.

CHILDREN IN ICSI FAMILIES

Whereas initial anxieties about IVF families arose largely from speculation and fear of the unknown, ICSI raised more tangible concerns owing to the direct manipulation of eggs and sperm in the fertilization process. As a result, a number of studies have examined the psychological development of ICSI children. Investigations of ICSI families have generally included larger samples than have studies of IVF families, and have thus provided greater statistical power to detect the adverse effects of ICSI, should these exist.

With respect to psychological adjustment, Barnes, Sutcliffe, Kristoffersen, et al. (2004) found no differences between ICSI children and comparison groups of IVF and natural conception children for behavioral or emotional problems, as rated by mothers and fathers on the Child Behavior Checklist (Achenbach and Rescorla, 2000). The Child Behavior Checklist was also administered to mothers by Knoester, Helmerhorst, van der Westerlaken, et al. (2007). Although no differences were identified between ICSI, IVF and naturally conceived boys, a difference was found between ICSI and IVF girls. Rather than indicating raised levels of adjustment difficulties in ICSI girls, this finding resulted from the particularly low scores of the IVF girls.

Owing to the specific concerns regarding ICSI noted above, attention has focused on the cognitive development of ICSI children. In Belgium, the Bayley Scales of Infant Development were administered to 201 ICSI children at 2 years of age, and no evidence was found of delayed development in relation to norms for this age group (Bonduelle, Joris, Hofmans, et al., 1998). A comparison of 439 ICSI children and 207 IVF children aged 2 years by the same research team found no differences in Bayley Scale scores (Bonduelle, 2003). Similar findings were reported in the UK following the administration of the Griffiths Mental Development Scales to a representative sample of 208 ICSI children and a comparison group of 221 naturally conceived children aged 1 to 2 years (Sutcliffe, Taylor, Saunders, et al., 2001). In contrast, significantly poorer Bayley Scale scores, particularly for boys, were found when 89 1-year-old ICSI children were compared with 84 IVF and 80 naturally conceived children in Australia (Bowen, Gibson, Leslie et al., 1998). Seventeen percent of the ICSI children showed mildly or significantly delayed development, compared with 2 percent of the IVF and 1 percent of the natural conception children.

In order to address the controversial question of whether or not the ICSI children showed developmental delay, the Australian children were followed up at age 5 years and the sample size was increased to 97 ICSI, 80 IVF and 110 naturally conceived children (Leslie, Gibson, McMahon, et al., 2003). No differences were identified between the ICSI children and the comparison groups of IVF and natural conception children for IQ scores or the proportion of children who showed delayed development. In line with this finding, a study of 5-year-olds conducted in Belgium, Denmark, Greece, Sweden and the UK (Ponjaert-Kristoffersen, Bonduelle, Barnes, et al., 2005), in which 511 ICSI children were compared with 424 IVF children and 488 naturally conceived children on the Revised Wechsler Preschool and Primary Scale of Intelligence (WPPSI-R) and the Motor Scale of the McCarthy Scales of Children's

Abilities, identified no differences between the ICSI, IVF and natural conception children. In a parallel study that included the Belgian and Swedish children, as well as children from the USA (Ponjaert-Kristoffersen, Tjus, Nekkebroek, et al., 2004), no differences in IQ were identified between the 300 ICSI children and the comparison group of 260 naturally conceived children, as assessed using the WPPSI-R, although the ICSI children obtained lower scores on some of the visual-spatial subscales.

In a different Belgian sample, the cognitive development of ICSI children and a comparison group of naturally conceived children was examined at age 8 years (Leunens, Celestin-Westreich, Bonduelle, et al., 2006) and age 10 years (Leunens, Celestin-Westreich, Bonduelle, et al., 2008), using the Wechsler Intelligence Scale for Children – Revised (WISC-R). Although the ICSI children obtained higher scores at age 8, there were no differences between the ICSI and the natural conception children at age 10. In the Netherlands, 5–8-year-old ICSI children obtained significantly lower IQ scores than a comparison group of naturally conceived children, but did not differ from IVF children, on the Revised Amsterdam Child Intelligence Test. The lower IQ scores of the ICSI children are likely to have resulted from the lower socio-economic status of the ICSI fathers. Moreover, the IQ scores of the ICSI children were above average for the general population (Knoester, Helmerhorst, Vandenbroucke, et al., 2008). Thus, in spite of earlier concerns, there is little evidence to suggest that ICSI results in cognitive impairment in children.

PARENTS' EXPERIENCES

For those who undergo IVF or ICSI, the experience can be extremely difficult. As one father described it:

> I think for anyone going through it it's hard, the ups and downs, you know the little victories when the injections start reacting and working and then you're counting the embryos and then you see the little picture of the two cell or four cell embryos; and they're

highs. And then the lows when it doesn't work. And knowing you've got to wait and go through it all again. It's really hard.

Another father said:

I've always wanted a family and it was hard – it was a long hard slog to get the family. I'd quite happily give everything up and spend all my time with them.

Some mothers commented on the lack of understanding of others, which they found difficult:

I don't think my mother-in-law realizes quite how much we went through to have children. It's all very well saying "Oh yeah we underwent IVF" – if only it was that simple.

I want to increase awareness of it and for people to realize that it's normal. That's one of the things I found really hard when we were having treatment. People have this perception that "Oh it's alright, you can just have IVF and then you'll have a baby," and I feel like I've got to educate people that it's not easy. And sometimes I felt that some people might have a prejudice about it as well that "Oh it's not natural" to conceive in that way and I just want to say "Look I have perfectly normal, healthy, happy children."

However, those whose treatment was successful generally felt that it was all worthwhile:

They're miracles. They are absolute miracles. She came out of the freezer and he was fresh.

I tell her that she's very special but then, you know, all children are, but personally I think IVF babies are a little bit, little bit more.

I'm actually really proud that we've had IVF and that it's actually worked. I think it's an absolute miracle and if it wasn't for IVF then I wouldn't be a mum. So I'm happy to broadcast it, promote it, talk about it, because I just think it's a magical, stressful experience. But well worth it.

CONCLUSIONS

Although highly contentious when first introduced, IVF and associated assisted reproductive technologies (such as ICSI) have now become commonplace treatments for infertility. It seems that families created with these technologies function well, and the fears expressed about the potentially negative impact these technologies may have on parenting and child development are unfounded. The most problematic aspect of "high-tech" procedures such as IVF and ICSI is the high proportion of twins and triplets that ensue. However, this is not a direct result of the procedures themselves; instead, it is a product of the number of embryos used. Countries that have instituted regulation to limit the number of embryos transferred in IVF or ICSI treatment have shown a decline in multiple births.

4   Donor conception families

Before Robert Edwards embarked on the scientific work that was eventually to lead to IVF as a treatment for infertility, and long before Robert Edwards and Patrick Steptoe joined forces, doctors had begun to help childless couples through a procedure known as artificial insemination by donor (AID), now known as donor insemination (DI), to avoid the negative connotations of the term "artificial." This procedure involves the insemination of a woman with the semen of a man who is not her husband or partner. The first reported case of donor insemination was in 1884, when a French doctor inseminated a woman without her knowledge, with the doctor and her husband agreeing that it was best for her not to know. Although donor insemination has caused less of a public outcry than has IVF, it has had a more fundamental impact on the family. Whereas children conceived by IVF are genetically related to both of their parents, children conceived by donor insemination lack a genetic link to one parent – the person they know as their father.

Although donor insemination has been practiced for many years, it was not until 1984, 100 years after the first reported case of donor insemination, that advances in IVF led to the birth of a child conceived using a donated egg (Lutjen, Trounson, Leeton, et al., 1984). Egg donation is like donor insemination, in that the child is genetically related to only one parent; however, in the case of egg donation, it is the mother, not the father, to whom the child lacks a genetic link. Egg donation is a much more complex and intrusive procedure than is donor insemination. The egg donor must take hormonal medication and then undergo a surgical procedure for her eggs to be extracted. The father's sperm is then used to fertilize the donated eggs by IVF and the resulting embryo(s) are transferred to the womb of the woman who will be the mother of the child. Egg donation has, for the first time, enabled women to become pregnant and give birth to children who are not genetically their own.

With embryo donation, both the egg and sperm are donated and neither parent is genetically related to the child. This situation is similar to adoption, except the parents experience pregnancy and the child's birth. For this reason, embryo donation is sometimes referred to as "prenatal adoption." Embryo donation most commonly takes place when couples have produced more embryos than they need for their own IVF treatment and donate their additional embryos to another couple. When donated eggs and sperm from separate donors are used this is often referred to as "double donation."

Many questions have been raised about the psychological consequences of sperm, egg and embryo donation: what is the psychological impact of growing up with genetically unrelated parents? Does this affect children's relationships with their parents, or make a difference to how they see themselves? How do donor-conceived children feel about their donor and his or her family – the genetic relatives they do not, and may never, know? This chapter will examine these questions through the findings of research on families created in this way. For the sake of simplicity, the terms "donor conception" and "gamete donation" will be used interchangeably to refer collectively to sperm, egg and embryo donation.

It has often been suggested that the creation of families using donated sperm, eggs or embryos may have negative consequences for parenting and children's psychological adjustment (Baran and Pannor, 1993; Blyth, 2004; Daniels, Gillett, and Grace, 2009; Daniels and Taylor, 1993; McGee, Brakman, and Gurmankin, 2001). Two key mechanisms have been proposed: secrecy about the child's genetic origins and the absence of a genetic relationship between one or both parents and the child.

SECRECY

The use of donated eggs and sperm (gametes) to conceive a child has, until recently, been surrounded by secrecy. Those who have become parents in this way have tended not to tell their children about their donor conception; thus, the majority of these children have grown up unaware that their fathers (in cases of sperm donation), mothers (in cases of egg donation) or both parents (in cases of embryo donation) are not their genetic parents. The issue of whether or not parents should disclose donor conception to their children is highly contentious. Until relatively recently, fertility doctors advised parents not to tell their children about the nature of their conception, with some doctors suggesting that the couple have sexual intercourse at the time of the insemination to create the possibility that the child would be genetically their own. However, attention has been drawn to the potentially negative effects of secrecy (Daniels and Taylor, 1993; Baran and Pannor, 1993). As a result, parents have been encouraged to be open with their children about the nature of their conception (Blyth, 2002; Daniels and Thorn, 2001; Nuffield Council on Bioethics, 2013). The view that donor-conceived people should be entitled to know the identity of their donor led to the enactment of legislation in some countries to remove donor anonymity and to bring the law on donor conception more in line with that of adoption (adopted children have the right to obtain the identity of their birth parents in adulthood). In a number of countries including Sweden, Norway, the Netherlands, Switzerland, New Zealand, Australia and the UK, people conceived using donated gametes now have the right to obtain the identity of their donor, usually when they reach the age of 18. Although, with the exception of the state of Washington, there is no such legislation in the USA, the Ethics Committee of the American Society for Reproductive Medicine (2013) came out in support of disclosure about the use of donor gametes to persons conceived in this way. In no country is it mandatory for parents of donor-conceived children to tell their children that they are donor–conceived. However, in countries where the law permits it, those who are aware of their donor conception are able, in adulthood, to obtain the identity of their donor, should they so wish.

The concern over secrecy in donor conception families has arisen partly from research on adoption, which has shown that adopted children benefit from information about their biological parents and that some children who are not given such information develop emotional, behavioral and identity problems (Brodzinsky, 2006; Grotevant, 1997; Grotevant, Perry, and McRoy, 2005; Triseliotis, 1973, 1984, 2000). It is now generally accepted that open communication between adoptive parents and their children, such that children are given developmentally appropriate information about their adoption and feel free to discuss adoption-related issues as they arise, is important for positive parent–child relationships and the psychological well-being of adopted children (Brodzinsky and Pinderhughes, 2002; Rueter and Koerner, 2008; Wrobel, Harold, Berge, et al., 2003).

The family therapy literature also points to the potentially negative psychological consequences of keeping children's origins secret (Imber-Black, 1998; Papp, 1993). From a family therapy perspective, secrets are believed to be detrimental to family functioning because they create boundaries between those who are party to the secret and those who are not (Bok, 1982; Karpel, 1980; Vangelisti and Caughlin, 1997) and cause anxiety when topics related to the secret are discussed (Lane and Wegner, 1995; Wegner and Erber, 1992). In examining the particular case of parents keeping secrets from their children, Papp (1993) suggested that children can sense when information is being withheld from them owing to the taboo that surrounds the discussion of certain topics, and that children may become confused and anxious, or even develop symptoms of psychological disorder, as a result. There is a growing body of research that supports the view that children can sense when they are not being told something; parents often give themselves away by their tone of voice, facial expression and body posture, or by abruptly changing the subject when an issue related to the secret arises in conversation (DePaulo, 1992).

In relation to donor conception, it has been argued that keeping children's genetic origins secret interferes with communication between those who know the secret (the parents) and those who do not (the children) (Clamar, 1989). The extent to which donor-conceived children suspect that secrets about their parentage are being kept from them cannot be established, but it is thought that children may "pick up" that they are different in some way (Daniels, Grace, and Gillett, 2011; Ehrensaft, 2008). It is conceivable, for example, that children may become suspicious if their parents change the subject whenever the topic of whom they look like comes up. Parents of donor-conceived children have reported difficulties in responding to comments or questions about family resemblances (Becker, Butler, and Nachtigall, 2005) and, in a qualitative study of adults who were aware of their donor insemination, some reported that, as children, they suspected that something was amiss (Turner and Coyle, 2000). Moreover, a study of donor-conceived adults found that those whose parents were perceived as avoiding the topic of donor conception reported poorer family functioning (Berger and Paul, 2008; Paul and Berger, 2007). As this was a cross-sectional study, it cannot be concluded that poor communication about the donor conception caused impaired family functioning; instead, it is possible that impaired family functioning may have resulted in poor communication about donor conception. Either way, it seems that open communication about donor conception and positive family functioning may go hand in hand.

ABSENCE OF GENETIC RELATIONSHIPS

The idea that the absence of genetic connections between parents and children may be detrimental to positive family functioning also arises from studies of adoptive families, in which both parents are genetically unrelated to their adopted children. As discussed in greater detail in Chapter 7, there is now a large body of research showing that adopted children, on average, show higher rates of emotional and behavioral problems than do non-adopted children (Palacios and Brodzinsky, 2010). This has been found to be the case in studies of children of different ages and from different populations, ranging from children referred for psychiatric treatment to community samples. Although higher rates of adjustment problems among children referred for treatment may simply reflect adoptive parents' greater tendency to seek help when their children show difficult behavior, the elevated rates of psychological problems among adopted children in the community who have not been referred for treatment indicate that this is a genuine finding. Nevertheless, recent meta-analyses have shown the differences in psychological problems between adoptive and non-adoptive children to be small, with the large majority of adopted children functioning within the normal range (Juffer and van IJzendoorn, 2005, 2007). Moreover, child adjustment problems appear to be largely related to factors associated with the adoption, such as children's experiences of abusive or neglectful parenting and multiple caretakers in the years before the adoption takes place, rather than the absence of a biological link between adoptive parents and their children (Dozier and Rutter, 2008; McCall, 2011; Palacios and Brodzinsky, 2010). Thus, the older children are when they are adopted, the more likely they are to have experienced adverse circumstances in their early years and the greater their risk of psychological disorder. As donor-conceived children are not exposed to the adverse experiences associated with psychological problems in adopted children (such as abuse, neglect or multiple caretakers), they would not be expected to show increased rates of psychological problems resulting from these factors.

Although the absence of a biological link between children and their adoptive parents does not, in itself, appear to be a major factor in the increased rates of psychological problems shown by adopted children, the transition to adolescence presents specific challenges for adopted children with respect to identity formation (Brodzinsky, 2011; Grotevant and Von Korff, 2011; Grotevant, Rueter, Von Korff, et al., 2011). These issues may also be of relevance to adolescents who have been conceived by gamete donation. It has been shown that adopted adolescents need to integrate their experiences of being adopted into a meaningful narrative in order to develop a secure sense of identity. As part of this process, adopted adolescents often gather information about their past, including information about their birth parents, and some search for – and make contact with – members of their birth family (Howe and Feast, 2000).

Children conceived by gamete donation differ from adopted children in that they have a genetic link to one parent (their father in egg donation families and their mother in donor insemination families) and are born into the families in which they are raised; they are not relinquished by, or removed from, their biological parents. However, the absence of a genetic connection to one parent is considered by some to create significant similarities between donor-conceived and adopted children (Cahn, 2009; Crawshaw, 2002; Feast, 2003), which may have implications for children's identity development, psychological adjustment and relationships with parents.

Research on stepfamilies, in which one parent is genetically unrelated to the child, has also given rise to the idea that the absence of a genetic link between parents and children may have an adverse effect on family relationships. Stepfamilies, like adoptive families, are associated with raised levels of psychological problems for children (Dunn, Davies, O'Connor, et al., 2000, 2001;

Dunn, Deater-Deckard, Pickering, et al., 1998; Hetherington and Clingempeel, 1992; Hetherington and Stanley-Hagan, 2002). This finding appears to be more marked in stepmother than in stepfather families (Dunn, Davies, O'Connor, et al., 2000; Hetherington and Stanley-Hagan, 2002; O'Connor, Dunn, Jenkins, et al., 2001). As with adoption, the younger the child when making the transition to a step-family, the lower the risk of adjustment problems (Hetherington and Clingempeel, 1992). However, even children who grow up in step-families from an early age are more likely to show psychological dif-ficulties than those who are raised by their biological parents (Dunn, Deater-Deckard, Pickering, et al., 1998; Dunn, Davies, O'Connor, et al., 2000; Dunn, Davies, O'Connor, et al., 2001). Once again, these difficulties appear to result from associated factors, such as the dis-ruption of the relationship with an existing parent and the acquisi-tion of new family members, rather than the absence of a biological link between the stepparent and the child. It is interesting to note, however, that Dunn, Davies, O'Connor, et al. (2000) reported that parents in families comprising both step and biological children were less affectionate toward, and less supportive of, their step than their biological children.

RATES OF DISCLOSURE IN DONOR-CONCEIVED FAMILIES

Until recently, the majority of parents who gave birth to donor-conceived children did not tell their children about their genetic origins. In the European Study of Assisted Reproduction Families, not one set of the participating 111 donor insemination par-ents from Italy, Spain, the Netherlands and the UK had disclosed the donor conception to their children by the time their children were at early school age (Golombok, Cook, Bish, et al., 1995; Golombok, Brewaeys, Cook, et al., 1996), less than 10 percent of parents had done so by the time their children were in early adolescence (Golombok, MacCallum, Goodman, et al., 2002; Golombok, Brewaeys, Cook, et al., 2002), and a follow-up study of the UK sample found that no further children had been told by the time they were 18 years old

(Owen and Golombok, 2009). A similar pattern was found for egg donation families in the UK (Golombok, Murray, Brinsden, et al., 1999; Murray, MacCallum, and Golombok, 2006) and in Finland (Söderström-Anttila, Sajaniemi, Tiitinen, et al., 1998). With respect to embryo donation, MacCallum and Golombok (2007) found that only 9 percent of parents of preschool children born through embryo donation had begun to talk to their children about their biological origins, rising to only 18 percent by the time the children were in middle childhood (MacCallum and Keeley, 2008). This was in stark contrast to the comparison groups of adoptive parents (all of whom had disclosed the adoption to their children) and IVF parents (almost half of whom had told their children about their conception by IVF) (MacCallum and Keeley, 2012). Even in Sweden, where legislation giving donor offspring the right to obtain information about the donor's identity came into force in 1985, more than a decade later, only 11 percent of parents were found to have informed their children of their donor conception (Gottlieb, Lalos, and Lindblad, 2000; Lindblad, Gottlieb, and Lalos, 2000). Investigations in the USA have produced comparable findings, with rates of disclosure to children reported to range between 14 percent and 30 percent (Amuzu, Laxova, and Shapiro, 1990; Klock and Maier, 1991; Leiblum and Aviv, 1997; Nachtigall, Tschann, Szkupinski Quiroga, et al., 1997; Schover, Collins, and Richards, 1992).

When asked about their reasons for secrecy, parents of children born through egg, sperm and embryo donation have said they were worried that their children would be upset, shocked and confused by the knowledge that they were not genetically related to one parent (or both parents) (Cook, Golombok, Bish, et al., 1995; Golombok, Murray, Brinsden, et al., 1999; MacCallum, Golombok, and Brinsden, 2007). The parents were also concerned about jeopardizing the positive relationship that existed between the non-genetic parent(s) and the child, fearing that their child would no longer love the non-genetic parent(s) if they were to find out. As one mother said about her husband, "He doesn't want our daughter not to love him. I know it wouldn't make a difference. But he feels he doesn't want her to know in case it changes her feelings toward him." Another mother said: "I would hate for her to retaliate and say to her dad in an argument, 'You're not my real father anyway'. I would be mortified if she said that."

Another mother described the problem of the children's lack of physical resemblance to their father:

> Occasionally people say to my husband "Oh the boys don't look like you," which is, you know, quite – quite upsetting, because we know the facts and they don't. They're saying it innocently, you know, men tease and stuff ... He deals with it a lot better than he used to. I can see he's less hurt by it now than he used to be. But, you know, you have to quickly change the subject when that happens.

Some parents felt that they had left it too late: "I think we've left it too late. I think if you're going to tell them, we'd have to have done it when he was very young. It's too late now he's six." In addition, they did not know how to tell their children and, as the donors were anonymous, they were concerned about not being able to answer their child's inevitable question: "If you are not my biological parent, then who is?"

Rates of disclosure to children appear to be higher among parents who feel able to be open with other family members about the involvement of a donor in the conception of their child (Shehab, Duff, Pasch, et al., 2008). However, many parents who share this information with family or friends at the time of fertility treatment do not go on to tell their children, which creates the possibility that their children will find out by accident through the indiscretion of a or friend or family member (Golombok, Brewaeys, Cook, et al., 1996; Golombok, Lycett, MacCallum, et al., 2004; Golombok, Murray, Jadva, et al., 2006; Lalos, Gottlieb, and Lalos, 2007; Readings, Blake, Casey, et al., 2011).

In recent years, there has been a rise in the number of parents intending to tell their children that they were born through donated gametes (Daniels, Gillett, and Grace, 2009; Godman, Sanders, Rosenberg, et al., 2006; Hahn and Craft-Rosenberg, 2002; Hargreaves and Daniels, 2007; Lalos, Gottlieb, and Lalos, 2007). In spite of these intentions, many parents do not actually disclose this information. In a longitudinal study of children born in the UK in 2000 (the UK Longitudinal Study of Assisted Reproduction Families), 46 percent of parents of infants conceived by donor insemination and 56 percent of parents of infants conceived by egg donation planned to tell their children about their donor conception. However, only 28 percent of donor insemination parents and 41 percent of egg donation parents actually did so by the time their children were 7 years old (Readings, Blake, Casey, et al., 2011), the age by which most adopted children are told about their adoption. Moreover, some parents who reported that they had told their children had discussed the use of fertility treatment, but not the more fundamental issue of the use of donated eggs or sperm (Readings, Blake, Casey, et al., 2011). Many parents of children conceived by embryo donation have been found to similarly give only partial information about the nature of the conception to their children (MacCallum and Keeley, 2012).

There is anecdotal evidence that the removal of donor anonymity in some countries has resulted in an increase in the proportion of parents who tell their children about their donor conception. However, there is little systematic data on the impact of the removal of donor anonymity on disclosure rates. In a 5-year follow-up of the Swedish sample mentioned above, 61 percent of parents were found to have disclosed the donor insemination to their children (Lalos, Gottlieb, and Lalos, 2007). However, the participation rate in this study was very low and likely to have been biased toward families in which parents had disclosed. A larger Swedish study of both egg and sperm recipients found that 90 percent were in favor of disclosure (Isaksson, Skoog Svanberg, Sydsjö, et al., 2011), which suggests a shift toward greater openness; nonetheless, only 16 percent of parents had begun the process of disclosure by the time their children were 4 years old (Isaksson, Sydsjö, Skoog Svanberg, et al., 2012). In New

Zealand, where disclosure has been encouraged since 1985 and legislated since 2004, a study found that only 35 percent of young adults who had been conceived by donor insemination had been told about the nature of their conception (Daniels, Gillett, and Grace, 2009). However, a study of New Zealand families with younger children found that one-third of the parents had told their children about their donor conception, and, of the parents who had not told, three-quarters intended to do so (Rumball and Adair, 1999). It seems that social and legislative changes may have resulted in parents' greater openness with their donor-conceived children about their biological origins, but it remains the case that a substantial proportion of parents still choose not to tell.

FAMILY FUNCTIONING IN NON-DISCLOSING FAMILIES

In spite of the growing number of families formed through donor conception and the concerns that have been raised regarding the potentially negative consequences for parent–child relationships and child adjustment, few studies have investigated the functioning of these families. The European Study of Assisted Reproduction Families (see Chapter 3) included a group of 111 families with 4- to 8-year-old children who had been conceived through donor insemination, and found the quality of parenting in these donor insemination families to be similar to that of IVF families and superior to that of natural conception families (Golombok, Brewaeys, Cook, et al., 1996; Golombok, Cook, Bish, et al., 1995). This suggests that the couples who conceived children through donor insemination became highly effective parents, and the absence of a genetic connection between the fathers and their children did not prevent the development of positive relationships between them. The families were followed up when the children approached adolescence (Golombok, Brewaeys, Giavazzi, et al., 2002; Golombok, MacCallum, Goodman, et al., 2002). Although the donor insemination families no longer showed higher levels of parenting quality relative to the natural conception families, they were characterized by high levels of warmth between parents and children, accompanied by appropriate levels of discipline and control. In a follow-up study of the UK families when the children were 18 years old, higher levels of warmth and discipline were shown by donor insemination mothers than by IVF mothers, which suggests greater engagement with their children as they reached early adulthood; no differences were found between fathers in both groups (Owen and Golombok, 2009).

A sample of egg donation families was also recruited in the UK and compared with the donor insemination families in terms of parenting quality (Golombok, Murray, Brinsden, et al., 1999). The only difference to emerge was that mothers and fathers of young children who had been conceived by egg donation reported lower levels of stress associated with parenting than did parents of donor insemination children. The egg donation families, like the donor insemination families, were found to be functioning well. Again, few differences in parenting were identified when the children reached adolescence, although the egg donation mothers showed lower levels of sensitive responding and were less likely to be emotionally over-involved with their children than were the donor insemination mothers (Murray, MacCallum, and Golombok, 2006).

In terms of child adjustment, no differences in emotional or behavioral problems between children conceived by either sperm donation (Golombok, Brewaeys, Cook, et al., 1996; Golombok, Brewaeys, Giavazzi, et al., 2002; Golombok, Cook, Bish, et al., 1995; Golombok, MacCallum, Goodman, et al., 2002) or egg donation (Golombok, Cook, Bish, et al., 1995; Murray, MacCallum, and Golombok, 2006) and comparison groups of IVF, natural conception and early adopted children were found in childhood or early adolescence. This suggests that in families in which children are unaware of their donor conception, the absence of a genetic link (with fathers in donor insemination families and mothers in egg donation families) is not associated with raised levels of child adjustment problems.

In the only study of parenting and child development in families formed through embryo donation, families were found to be functioning well when the children were of preschool age (MacCallum, Golombok, and Brinsden, 2007) and in middle childhood (MacCallum and Keeley, 2008). The parents differed from comparison groups of adoptive and IVF parents only in terms of greater emotional over-involvement with their children. Although emotional over-involvement is sometimes associated with emotional difficulties in children, the degree of over-involvement shown by parents represented moderate, rather than pathological, levels. The children were not found to be at increased risk of psychological problems either in their preschool (MacCallum, Golombok, and Brinsden, 2007) or their early school years (MacCallum and Keeley, 2008).

In an investigation that used parent questionnaires to compare sperm donation, egg donation and embryo donation families with families created by assisted reproductive procedures using the parents' own gametes, no differences in the psychological adjustment of 5- to 9-year-old children were found (Shelton, Boivin, Hay, et al., 2009). Although no information was obtained on the proportion of children who were aware of the nature of their conception, most had been born in the 1990s and were thus unlikely to have been told. A further questionnaire-based study compared donor insemination families with naturally conceived two-parent families, single-mother families and stepfather families in terms of parental psychological distress, parental relationship quality, general family functioning, parenting quality and quality of parent–child relationships (Kovacs, Wise, and Finch, 2013). The children ranged in age from 5 to 13 years. Where differences were identified between the donor insemination families and the other family types, these reflected more positive functioning in the donor insemination families. Of particular interest are the more positive findings for donor insemination fathers than for stepfathers, which suggest that the intention to become non-genetic parents, and the age of children at the time at which these fathers become non-genetic parents, may be important factors in the quality of the relationship between fathers – and possibly mothers – and their genetically unrelated children. Further support for this possibility comes from the finding of Dunn, Deater-Deckard, Pickering, et al. (1998) that many stepparents do not view their step-children as their "own" children. However, with the exception of the donor insemination families in the Kovacs, Wise and Finch (2013) study, the response rates were low. Although one-third of the parents reported having disclosed the donor conception to their children, the impact of disclosure was not explored.

FAMILY FUNCTIONING IN DISCLOSING FAMILIES

Parents who talk to their young children about their donor conception generally begin to do so by the time their children are 4 years old. These parents tend to tell their children stories about needing help to have a baby, rather than giving detailed explanations of the reproductive process (Blake, Casey, Readings, et al., 2010; Mac Dougall, Becker, Scheib, et al., 2007). Contrary to parents' concerns, it appears that children who are told about their donor conception in their preschool years respond neutrally, or with curiosity, rather than distress (Blake, Casey, Readings, et al., 2010; Leeb-Lundberg, Kjellberg, and Sydsjö, 2006; Lindblad, Gottlieb, and Lalos, 2000; Mac Dougall, Becker, Scheib, et al., 2007; Rumball and Adair, 1999). However, children appear to have little understanding of egg or sperm donation by age 7 (Blake, Casey, Readings, et al., 2010), the age by which most adopted children understand what it means to be adopted (Brodzinsky and Pinderhughes, 2002). It is not until age 10 that most donor-conceived children are able to give clear accounts of the nature of their conception (Blake, Casey, Jadva, et al., 2013). In a study of the thoughts and feelings of adolescents who had grown up with the knowledge that they were donor conceived, the majority reported feeling comfortable about their donor conception and felt that learning about their donor conception had not had a negative impact on their relationships with their parents (Scheib, Riordan, and Rubin, 2005). It is note-worthy that parents do not appear to regret telling their children that they were donor conceived (Lindblad, Gottlieb, and Lalos, 2000; Mac Dougall, Becker, Scheib, et al., 2007; Scheib, 2003).

The experience of those who are told or find out about their donor conception in adolescence or adulthood, as opposed to early childhood, can be strikingly different. Participants in qualitative studies have reported that secrecy about the nature of their conception caused them severe psychological harm, and many have reported feeling deceived by their parents and angry toward them (Blyth, 2012; Franz and Allen, 2001; Turner and Coyle, 2000). Moreover, in a survey of 165 donor-conceived adolescents and adults who were members of the Donor Sibling Registry, a website that helps donor-conceived persons search for their donor and donor siblings (see below for further details of this study), those who had found out about their donor conception in adolescence or beyond were more likely to report feeling upset, angry, shocked and confused than were those who had been told in childhood (Jadva, Freeman, Kramer, et al., 2009). It is important to point out, however, that the participants in these studies had either joined a support group for donor conceived offspring or had joined the Donor Sibling Registry, and thus the extent to which they were representative of individuals aware of their donor conception is not known. Also, all had been conceived by donor insemination; no data are yet available on the feelings and experiences of adolescents and young adults conceived by egg or embryo donation.

In order to investigate the psychological consequences for families of openness with children about their donor conception, a longitudinal investigation of families created by donor insemination and egg donation, the UK Longitudinal Study of Assisted Reproduction Families, was initiated at the millennium. Phase 1 was conducted when the children were at age 1 year (Golombok, Lycett, MacCallum, et al., 2004), Phase 2 was conducted at age 2 years (Golombok, Jadva, Lycett, et al., 2005), Phase 3 was conducted at age 3 years (Golombok, Murray, Jadva, et al., 2006), Phase 4 was conducted at age 7 years (Casey, Jadva, Blake, et al., 2013; Golombok, Readings, Blake, et al., 2011) and Phase 5 was conducted at age 10 years (Golombok, Blake,

Casey, et al., 2013). In the preschool years, the differences identified between family types pointed to more positive parent–child relationships in families created by gamete donation than in the comparison group of natural conception families, with no differences in the quality of family relationships according to whether the children lacked genetic connections to their fathers (in the case of donor insemination) or mothers (in the case of egg donation) (Golombok, Jadva, Lycett, et al., 2005; Golombok, Lycett, MacCallum, et al., 2004; Golombok, Murray, Jadva, et al., 2006). The donor-conceived children were found to be functioning well, but, in spite of their parents' highly involved parenting, did not show higher levels of adjustment than their counterparts from natural conception families. These findings replicated those obtained in the European Study of Assisted Reproduction Families conducted 15 years earlier.

In contrast to the more positive outcomes for the donor conception families in the preschool years, greater difficulties emerged when the children were 7 years old (Golombok, Readings, Blake, et al., 2011), the age by which children show an understanding of biological inheritance (Gregg, Solomon, Johnson, et al., 1996; Williams and Smith, 2010; Richards, 2000) and the meaning and implications of the absence of a biological connection to parents (Brodzinsky, 2011; Brodzinsky and Pinderhughes, 2002; Brodzinsky, Schechter, and Brodzinsky, 1986; Brodzinsky, Singer, and Braff, 1984). The gamete (egg and sperm) donation mothers who had kept their children's origins secret showed higher levels of emotional distress than did those who had been open with their children about their origins. Whether or not secrecy contributed to the distress is not known. However, keeping secrets has been shown to produce psychological problems (Lane and Wegner, 1995; Wegner and Lane, 2002) which may explain the higher levels of distress shown by non-disclosing mothers.

With respect to the relationship between parents and children, interview and observational assessments of mother–child interaction revealed less positive interaction in the donor-conceived families in which parents had not disclosed the method of conception to the children than in the natural conception families (Golombok, Readings, Blake, et al., 2011). There were no differences for fathers, apart from higher negativity shown by donor insemination children during an observational assessment of interaction with their fathers (Casey, Jadva, Blake, et al., 2013). It is important to note that the differences identified when the children were aged 7 years were not indicative of dysfunctional family relationships, but, instead, reflected variation within the normal range. It is interesting to note that, in spite of predictions to the contrary, the divorce rate among the parents of donor-conceived children did not differ from that of parents who conceived their children naturally, and was lower than the divorce rate for parents with children of a similar age in the UK (Blake, Casey, Jadva, et al., 2012).

In terms of child adjustment, the absence of a genetic connection to either the mother or the father was not associated with emotional or behavioral problems when the child was aged 3, 7 or 10 years (Golombok, Blake, Casey, et al., 2013), unless the mother herself was experiencing emotional problems and the children were aware of their donor conception, in which case the children showed higher levels of difficulties at the age of 7. At the age of 10, the children were interviewed about their relationships with their parents; those who were aware of their origins were asked about their feelings about having been donor-conceived (Blake, Casey, Jadva, et al., 2013). The large majority of donor-conceived children perceived their relationships with their mothers and fathers as warm and involved; the absence of genetic relationships did not appear to affect children's feelings of closeness to their parents. Some remembered feeling shocked or surprised when they were told about their donor conception. One child recalled: "I was quite amazed because I never knew about all that." Another child said: "Just a little bit shocked really. Yeah I just didn't realize that it was like that. I thought it was just the normal way of people getting made." Most had positive feelings about their donor conception. As one child put it: "I'm fine. I'm not,

I don't feel any differently, I'm just carrying on with my life. I don't really think about it much, because there's much more like, special on my mind, like cooler things. So I don't really care about it much." Another child said about their donor: "I'm very grateful for him, and I'm very thankful for him, and but it's weird that we can't ever meet him, because I thought we could be like friends ... be like my mum and dad's friends." However, the children tended not to discuss their donor conception with friends and family, and some reported feeling embarrassed when talking about the subject.

As the children studied so far have been preadolescent, the longer-term outcomes of the awareness of donor conception for parent–child relationships and child adjustment are not yet known. Because adolescence is the developmental stage at which issues relating to identity become salient and difficulties in parent–child relationships are more likely to arise (Steinberg, 2001; Steinberg and Morris, 2001; Steinberg and Silk, 2002), adolescence may present particular challenges to donor conception families.

SEARCHING FOR DONOR RELATIONS

As discussed above, the wish to obtain information about birth families is characteristic of adopted children at adolescence (Brodzinsky, 2011; Grotevant and Von Korff, 2011; Wrobel and Dillon, 2009), and it has been argued that research on adoption can provide valuable insight into how donor-conceived offspring may feel about searching for and contacting their genetic relations (Cahn, 2009; Crawshaw, 2002; Feast, 2003). The main reason given by adopted individuals for searching for birth relatives is to gain a more complete understanding of their family history in order to enhance their own sense of identity (Brodzinsky, Smith, and Brodzinsky, 1998; Wrobel, Grotevant, Samek, et al., 2013). In a study of the experiences of adopted individuals who had found information about their origins (Howe and Feast, 2000), the majority reported that this had helped them gain a better sense of self and had improved their psychological well-being. Although some of those who had made contact with birth parents had experienced disappointment, the reunions had generally had positive outcomes for those involved. Interestingly, adopted persons' experiences of finding and meeting birth siblings appear to have been more consistently and unambiguously positive than their experiences of finding and meeting birth parents (Humphrey and Humphrey, 1989).

There is growing evidence that similar processes are at play for children born through gamete donation, although, so far, the available data come from studies of those who have been conceived through donated sperm, rather than donated eggs or embryos (Freeman, Bourne, Jadva, et al., 2014). Increased openness has been accompanied by a growing interest in searching for donor relatives. In the years to come, children conceived using donated gametes in countries where donor anonymity has been removed (such as the UK) will become adults and gain the legal right to request their donor's name. This is already possible in Sweden, where legislation enabling donor-conceived people to obtain the identity of their donor was enacted in 1985, and in the Australian state of Victoria where a donor-linking service is in place. Although no such legislation exists in the USA, parents and donor offspring in the USA are themselves beginning to search for their donor relatives.

In 2000, the Donor Sibling Registry – an internet site designed to facilitate the search for donors as well as families who share the same donor – was established in the USA by a donor-conceived boy and his mother. Since that time, 44,000 people have registered with this website and more than 11,000 matches between donor offspring, donors and donor siblings have been made. Thus, it appears that knowledge of biological origins is important for the identity formation of some donor-conceived persons, just as it is for some adopted persons. Nevertheless, the proportion of donor-conceived people who search for their donor and donor siblings is not known.

In 2007, a survey of Donor Sibling Registry members that included 791 mothers of donor-conceived children (Freeman, Jadva, Kramer, et al., 2009) and 165 donor-conceived adolescents and adults, ranging in age from 13 to 61 years (Jadva, Freeman, Kramer, et al., 2010) was carried out to examine why people seek out their donor relatives and what happens when they are found. The mothers' main reasons for searching were curiosity and for their children to have a better understanding of who they were. As one mother said, "I think, down the line, it will be very beneficial for my son to know his background more fully ... He only has half the information about who he is. I think as he gets older, it will always nag at him." Like their mothers, the offspring also searched out of curiosity and to find out more about themselves:

> I am an only child, with step-siblings and one half-sibling ... I suppose the best description of my reasoning is curiosity, but it is also, if I can put this poetically, a call from my blood. I know there is a certain affinity with genetic family that is different from any other.

Most of those who made contact with their donor were pleased to have done so:

> I am so glad that I met him, and would not trade the world for the experience I had. We communicate in some form or another at least every other day, and he is one of the most important people in my life.

> I used to think of the donor as a sort of super-human ... Perfect in a lot of ways (based on knowing he was chosen out of a catalog). Now I know he's just a normal guy.

Mothers were also generally pleased about the outcome:

> She always wanted to meet her biological father since she was two years old ...When he sent his picture my daughter was so happy to see that she looked exactly like him ... They have so much in common ... She likes the fact that he has made her feel welcome with his family and now we have a larger extended family. She can complete the other side of her family tree.

But it was not always happy ever after:

> I did not meet my biological father. I only exchanged a few letters
> with him. His responses were clear that although he's glad I was
> born, he is not proud to have participated in donor conception ...
> It's a pretty bad feeling that my life has been such a source of
> shame and embarrassment, through no fault of my own, by the
> people who brought me into the world.

Although many of the offspring wished to meet their donor, few had
actually done so, and no one gave the desire to form a relationship
with him as their main reason for searching.

The most striking finding was of just how many donor siblings
were found. Donor siblings are genetic half-siblings who have been
born from the same donor but raised in different families. Half of
the families found at least five donor siblings, with many finding
more than 10 and one sibling constellation numbering 55! Since that
time, donor sibling networks of more than 100 have been identified
through the Donor Sibling Registry (Freeman, Bourne, Jadva, et al.,
2014). Unexpectedly, some families with a child born from the same
donor experienced a strong emotional bond when they met, and they
viewed each other not as new acquaintances, but as family. As one
mother put it:

> I was actually just curious about what the sibs might be like
> (personalities, looks etc.). After connecting with the other moms
> it turned out to be a more wonderful experience than I'd ever
> imagined ... We've become a family of sorts of our own and
> share a special bond. It wasn't why I sought the sibs but it was a
> completely wonderful surprise.

Another mother said:

> I felt very maternal toward my son's brother and sister. What
> really surprised me was just how strongly I felt towards them ...

> I know that genetically I have no relationship to them but they
> are my family, they are a part of me. They mean the world to me.

Mothers also described their children's relationships with their donor
siblings as familial, and often referred to the donor siblings as broth-
ers and sisters:

> My kids love the idea of having more siblings, and the
> relationships they have formed are great. It is like they have a
> bond even though they did not grow up together, and they are
> amazingly similar in a lot of ways.

> My daughter ... is clearly attached to them [her donor siblings]
> and they are to her ... There are special bonds that she is forming
> with them that look like nothing else I've seen with friends of
> hers ... The fact he is her sibling draws them together like bees to
> honey ... I thinks she feels very full and good about herself as her
> experience of "family" grows and deepens.

The children themselves reported similar feelings, with 85 percent
describing the experience of meeting their donor siblings as positive.
As a 16-year-old boy succinctly said, "It's like we have known each
other all our lives even though we did not grow up together."

A surprising result was that the families were more interested
in forming relationships with the donor siblings than with the donor.
They generally wanted to meet the donor to find out what he was
like, but it was the siblings with whom they particularly wanted to
stay in touch. Some children were also in touch with the donor's
family, including the donor's children and parents, who were effectively their half-siblings and grandparents (Jadva, Freeman, Kramer,
et al., 2010).

Adolescents with identity-release sperm donors were studied by Scheib, Riordan and Rubin (2005). Identity-release sperm
donors are donors who have agreed, at the time of donation, for any
children born from their donation to be given their identity upon

request, after reaching the age of 18. Again, the large majority of donor-conceived children were found to be curious about what their donor was like as a person. Most planned to request the identity of their donor upon reaching the age of 18 and to pursue contact with him. However, only 10 percent reported that he was an important person in their life and only 6.9 percent wanted a father–child relationship with him. Regarding contact among families who shared the same identity-release donor, Scheib and Ruby (2008) reported that parents' principal motivations for seeking contact were curiosity and to create a family for their child. As found with the Donor Sibling Registry study reported above, families with the same donor felt connected to each other and reported a sense of family relatedness between donor siblings. Few of the families had met the donor in person.

Studies of donor-conceived families that have included lesbian and single-mother families have found that children are more likely to have been told about their donor conception – and to have been told at an earlier age – than their counterparts from two-parent heterosexual families (Freeman, Jadva, Kramer, et al., 2009; Jadva, Freeman, Kramer, et al., 2009, 2010; Sheib and Ruby, 2008; Vanfraussen, Ponjaert-Kristoffersen, and Brewaeys, 2001). This is not surprising, given that the mothers in these families have to address their children's questions about their father. The majority of parents who search for donor relations are also lesbian couples or single mothers, particularly single mothers, which suggests that these families are more interested in searching for their children's donor relatives than are traditional heterosexual families (Freeman, Jadva, Kramer, et al., 2009; Scheib and Ruby, 2008). It is interesting to note that 89 percent of donor-conceived offspring from lesbian mother families in the Donor Sibling Registry study had told their non-biological mothers that they were searching for their donors, whereas only 29 percent of those from two-parent heterosexual families had told their fathers (Jadva, Freeman, Kramer, et al., 2010). This suggests that children in heterosexual families wish to avoid upsetting their fathers.

Studies are beginning to emerge of lesbian mother and single heterosexual mother families created using known sperm donors. In a qualitative study of 11 young adults in the USA who had been conceived by lesbian mothers using known donors, some viewed the donor strictly as a donor and not as a member of the family, others saw him as a member of their extended family but not as a parent, and yet others saw him as a father (Goldberg and Allen, 2013). In the US National Longitudinal Lesbian Family Study, only 13 percent of the 27 children with known donors saw their donors regularly, and a further 14 percent saw him occasionally (Gartrell, Rodas, Deck, et al., 2006). Comparable diversity was found in the UK (Tasker and Granville, 2011). In a study of 11 children with lesbian mothers, two had no contact with the donor whereas four had a father-like relationship with him, with the others falling between these two extremes. A study of single mothers by choice in the USA identified a similar pattern (Hertz, 2002). Whether children in lesbian families were conceived using known or unknown donors did not appear to influence their psychological adjustment in adolescence (Bos and Gartrell, 2011).

CONCLUSIONS

Although children and young adolescents who are unaware of their donor conception show positive relationships with their parents and high levels of psychological adjustment, little is known about older adolescents or adults in this situation. Moreover, there will always be a risk of accidental disclosure. Children whose parents begin to talk to them about their donor conception from an early age appear to integrate this information into their developing sense of identity, whereas some donor offspring who find out about their donor conception in adolescence or adulthood report enduring psychological distress. Moreover, evidence is emerging from longitudinal research of more positive functioning in families in which parents have disclosed the child's donor conception, although it cannot necessarily be assumed that the more positive functioning is a direct result of the disclosure; disclosing families may show more open communication generally. Taking these findings together, openness with children in the preschool years seems to be optimal in terms of the emotional well-being of donor offspring. Those who are aware of their donor conception may search for their donor and donor siblings, generally because they are curious and wish to find out about their ancestral background in order to incorporate this information into their life story. Whilst most donor offspring who search for their donor do not wish to form a parental relationship with the donor, some do wish to form a fraternal relationship with their donor siblings. It seems that a new phenomenon is taking place – family relationships based on genetic connections between children who were not previously aware of each other's existence are being created across multiple family units. Many of these children have lesbian or single heterosexual mothers. As a consequence, family networks are being created with different family types – traditional two-parent families, lesbian mother families and single heterosexual mother families – who are discovering that they are related.

5 Surrogacy families

In 1986, the case of "Baby M" in the USA caught the world's attention when her surrogate mother, Mary Beth Whitehead, refused to give up the baby to William and Elizabeth Stern, a couple who had paid her $10,000 to carry their child. Although Mary Beth Whitehead had signed a legal contract stating that she would relinquish the baby, she felt unable to let her go, which resulted in a high-profile legal battle between the surrogate mother and the intended parents that has influenced the practice of surrogacy to this day. This was the first surrogacy dispute in the USA and it centered on who should have custody of the child. Mary Beth Whitehead had conceived Baby M using her own egg and the intended father's sperm, a practice known as traditional or genetic surrogacy, and a key argument of her legal team was that it was not in the child's best interest to be separated from her biological mother. On the side of the intended parents, the argument focused on whether or not a surrogacy contract was enforceable by law. Custody was awarded initially to the intended parents in a New Jersey court. On appeal, however, the New Jersey Supreme Court ruled that the surrogacy contract was invalid on the grounds that payment to a surrogate mother was "Illegal, perhaps criminal, and potentially degrading to women," and that the surrogate mother and the intended father were the legal parents of the child. Although custody was awarded to the Sterns – as this was considered to be in the best interest of Baby M – Mary Beth Whitehead was given visitation rights. As a result of this case, many American states and countries around the world banned commercial surrogacy.

Another notable case took place in the UK in 1985. Britain's first commercial surrogate mother, Kim Cotton, gave birth to a baby girl for a childless couple. As with Baby M, the surrogate mother had been inseminated with the sperm of the intended father. When it was reported that the surrogacy arrangement had involved a payment to Kim Cotton of £6,500, the authorities intervened, taking the baby into the care of the state. When the surrogate then sold her story to the press for more than double the amount she had received for having the baby, a media frenzy ensued, focusing on the apparent callousness of the surrogate mother. As the *Guardian* newspaper on July 1, 1985, put it, "How will baby Cotton feel when she learns that her unknown mother did not give her up sadly, out of necessity, but gladly, for money?" In the court case that followed, the judge awarded custody of the baby, known as "Baby Cotton," to the intended parents. As a result of this case, legislation was rushed through the British Parliament to outlaw commercial surrogacy. In the UK, surrogate mothers are entitled to obtain only genuine expenses associated with the pregnancy. In practice, though, the definition of what counts as a genuine expense remains unclear in law, and it is not unusual for payments of up to £15,000 to be made to surrogate mothers by intending parents. Such a sum is not very far removed from that which is paid to surrogates in the USA in commercial surrogacy arrangements. However, unlike the USA, the UK maintains unenforceable surrogacy contracts; the surrogate mother and her husband (if she is married) are always the legal parents of the child – even in cases of gestational surrogacy (see below) – until legal parenthood is transferred by court to the intended parents.

The introduction of egg donation in 1983 paved the way for another form of surrogacy, gestational surrogacy, whereby the child is conceived using the egg of the intended mother (or an egg donor) and the sperm of the intended father (or sperm donor) and the resulting embryo is implanted in the surrogate mother. Thus, the surrogate hosts the pregnancy but does not have a genetic connection to the child. In a Californian legal case in 1990, a gestational surrogate was refused custody of a child to whom she had given birth on the grounds that she had simply hosted the pregnancy. This set the scene for the upsurge in gestational surrogacy in the USA that we see today. No one knows exactly how many babies have been born through gestational surrogacy worldwide, but estimates point to more than 1,000 per year in the USA, alone (Armour, 2012). Although not every American state allows surrogacy, some do, and some allow surrogates to be paid, with surrogates commonly earning around $30,000 for their services.

In many other countries, any form of surrogacy remains illegal. However, in recent years, there has been a dramatic rise in the number of people traveling abroad for surrogacy. This is owing to the prohibitive cost of surrogacy, with agencies in the USA, for example, often charging more than $100,000, and also to the difficulties involved in finding surrogates in countries where payment is not permitted. Countries such as India, Russia, Mexico, Poland, Thailand and Ukraine are just some of the destinations that have become popular for surrogacy, with those who can afford it also traveling to the USA.

Although gestational surrogacy is a recent phenomenon, traditional surrogacy dates back to biblical times. As described in the

Old Testament, Sarah, who was infertile, encouraged her husband Abraham to embark upon a sexual relationship with her maid Hagar, with the intention of producing a child to be raised as Sarah's own. In due course, Hagar gave birth to a son. However, as highlighted by Haberman (2014), the difficulties that ensued between Hagar and Sarah paralleled those experienced more than 4,000 years later between Mary Beth Whitehead and the Sterns. Other problems may also arise today, especially when intended parents and surrogate mothers take matters into their own hands, as occurred in the case of Amy and Scott Kehoe, who found an egg donor, a sperm donor and a surrogate mother through the Internet who gave birth to twins in the USA in 2009. One month later, the twins were removed from them by court order after it transpired that Amy Kehoe had been diagnosed with a severe psychiatric disorder and had previous drug charges. The surrogate mother was so concerned about the welfare of the twins that she took legal steps to recover them (Ghevaert, 2010). There have also been instances of intended parents changing their mind. In 2011, a 20-year-old genetic surrogate mother, who already had two children of her own, was abandoned with twins after the intended parents split up (thestar.com; Vukets, 2011). And in Thailand in 2014, a scandal erupted when an intended couple returned home to Australia with a healthy twin, leaving the other twin, who had Down Syndrome, with the surrogate mother.

Although surrogacy has become more widespread – and attitudes toward it have become less negative – surrogacy remains the most controversial form of assisted reproduction, raising a number of ethical concerns. Those opposed to surrogacy have argued that surrogacy is unacceptable because the child is treated as a commodity to be bought and sold, with payment to a surrogate viewed by some as tantamount to baby selling. Another objection to surrogacy is the potential for exploitation inherent in a situation in which economically disadvantaged women have babies for women who are more affluent than themselves; this is particularly seen to be true in cases in which the decision to embark upon surrogacy is driven largely by payment. Surrogacy also raises questions relating to pro-creative liberty: should women who wish to host a pregnancy for another woman be allowed to do so? It is interesting to note that feminist thought on surrogacy is divided, with some viewing surrogacy as the ultimate exploitation of women and others insisting that women should have autonomy over their reproductive lives and thus be free to act as paid surrogates should they so wish. Cross-border surrogacy has raised additional ethical concerns regarding the potential exploitation of surrogate mothers living in poverty in developing countries. In India, for example, where commercial surrogacy was legalized in 2002, Western couples access surrogates from poor backgrounds, who enter into surrogacy arrangements because of the large financial incentives involved. For couples seeking surrogacy in India, the cost can be as little as one-quarter of the US rate (DasGupta and DasGupta, 2014). Although the surrogate is paid only a small proportion of the fee charged by the clinic, it is equivalent to 10 years' income for her (Pande, 2009), enough to educate her children or buy a house, which would not otherwise have been within the realms of possibility for her family (DasGupta and DasGupta, 2014). Indian surrogates often live in "surrogacy houses" away from their family during the pregnancy, and rarely meet the couple whose child they gestate.

An issue that has been of principal concern and is of particular relevance to this book is whether or not surrogacy has an adverse effect on the well-being of children born in this way (Brazier, Campbell, and Golombok, 1998). As discussed in Chapter 4, developments in assisted reproductive technologies have resulted in new family forms in which genetic parenthood is dissociated from social parenthood. Children conceived by egg donation lack a genetic relationship with their mother, children conceived by sperm donation lack a genetic relationship with their father and children conceived by embryo donation are genetically unrelated to both parents. However, these children are born to the parents who raise them. With surrogacy, the mother who gives birth to the child and the mother who parents the child are not the same. Furthermore, in the case of genetic surrogacy, in which the surrogate mother's egg is used, the surrogate mother is not only the gestational mother, but also the genetic mother of the child.

It may be expected from the findings of research on families created by egg, sperm or embryo donation that the outcomes for parents and children in surrogacy families are equally positive. However, surrogacy differs from other types of assisted reproduction in ways that could conceivably result in greater problems for surrogacy families than for families created by more traditional assisted reproduction procedures involving gamete or embryo donation. First of all, intended parents must live through the 9 months of pregnancy with the uncertainty of whether or not the surrogate mother will relinquish the child. Furthermore, as the intended mother is not, herself, pregnant, prenatal bonding with the child may be absent or diminished. Secondly, the intended parents must establish a mutually acceptable relationship with the surrogate mother during the pregnancy and ensure that this relationship does not break down. Not only is this situation likely to produce anxiety in the intended parents, but it may also put a strain on their relationship, especially if one partner is more in favor of the surrogacy arrangement than the other. From the perspective of the intended mother, who is unable herself to give birth, the relationship with the fertile and (often younger) surrogate mother, to whom she is indebted, may result in feelings of inadequacy, depression and low self-esteem. Thirdly, there is a great deal of prejudice against the practice of surrogacy, and intended parents may experience disapproval from family, friends and their wider social world. Unlike other forms of assisted reproduction, in which the mother experiences pregnancy and thus it is not essential for the parents to be open about the circumstances of their child's conception, couples who become parents through surrogacy have to explain the arrival of their newborn baby.

All these factors have the potential to impact negatively on not only the psychological well-being of the intended parents but also the way in which they parent their children. Moreover, the need to resort to surrogacy, in itself, may interfere with the intended parents' quality of parenting. Couples whose children are born through surrogacy may view the process as an inferior route to parenthood or may feel less confident as parents. Specific aspects of the surrogacy arrangement may also influence intended couples' psychological well-being and parenting quality. Greater difficulties may arise in situations in which the surrogate mother is the genetic mother of the baby, because intended mothers, who are neither the genetic nor the gestational mother of their children, may feel greater insecurity in their mothering role. This is sometimes the experience of adoptive mothers (Grotevant and Kohler, 1999). Whether the surrogate mother is known or unknown to the commissioning parents prior to embarking upon the surrogacy arrangement may also impact on parenting. Better outcomes may be expected when the surrogate mother is a relative or a friend, because of the longevity and closeness of the relationship. However, this may blur relationships within the family, such that a sister who becomes a surrogate mother may become unduly involved with the child and thus weaken the status of the intended mother. A further factor that may influence parenting is whether the surrogate mother remains in contact with the family as the child grows up. It has been suggested that contact with the surrogate mother may benefit the child by providing the child with a greater understanding of his or her origins. However, the ongoing involvement of the surrogate mother with the family may have an undermining effect on the parenting of the intended couple. The most crucial question of all is how the children will feel about having been relinquished by the surrogate mother, especially in cases in which she is their genetic mother, and in cases in which she has received a large sum of money in return.

In the studies described below, the term "surrogacy family" refers to the family in which a child born through surrogacy grows up, and "surrogacy parents" and "parents" are used interchangeably to describe the parents who raise a child born through surrogacy, irrespective of whether or not they are the genetic parents of that child. The term "gestational surrogate" is used when the surrogate mother hosts the pregnancy and has no genetic link to the child. The term "genetic surrogate" is used when the surrogate mother's egg is used in the child's conception and thus she has a genetic link to the child. The children born as a result of surrogacy are referred to as "surrogacy children," and the surrogate mothers' own children are referred to as "surrogates' children."

STUDIES OF SURROGACY FAMILIES

In spite of the contentious nature of surrogacy and the adverse publicity it has attracted around the world, surprisingly little empirical research has been conducted to determine its impact on surrogate mothers, surrogacy parents and, most importantly, children. In a questionnaire-based study of the psychological adjustment of children in different types of assisted reproduction families, Shelton, Boivin, Hay, et al. (2009) compared a group of 21 5- to 9-year-old children born through gestational surrogacy with 378 children born through IVF, 182 through donor insemination, 153 through egg donation and 27 through embryo donation. The questionnaires completed by mothers and fathers ranged from those designed to assess conduct problems and attention deficit hyperactivity disorder to measures of anxiety, depression, peer problems and pro-social behavior. The children born through surrogacy did not differ from children in the other types of assisted reproduction families, for any of the measures. Neither did they show raised levels of conduct or peer problems when their scores were compared with general population norms.

In the only in-depth investigation, a group of 42 families created by surrogacy was included in the UK Longitudinal Study of Assisted Reproduction Families (see Chapter 4 for further discussion of this study). The families were recruited when the children were around 1 year of age through the General Register Office of the UK Office for National Statistics, which keeps a record of all families formed through surrogacy when legal parentage is granted to the intended parents. In order to reach families in which legal parentage had not yet been granted, those families with children of the same age who were members of the only UK surrogacy agency in existence at the time (known as Childlessness Overcome Through Surrogacy [COTS]) were also asked to take part. Although it was not possible to calculate an exact participation rate, it was estimated that more than 60 percent of the eligible surrogacy families with 1-year-old children throughout the UK were recruited to take part in the research. Approximately two-thirds of the families had used a genetic surrogate, with the remaining third having used a gestational surrogate. Around 70 percent of the surrogates had been unknown to the intended parents prior to the surrogacy arrangement, whereas the other surrogates had been relatives or friends. The surrogacy families were compared with a matched group of 51 egg donation families (who had been recruited through fertility clinics) and a matched group of 80 natural conception families (who had been recruited through maternity wards), all of whom had had planned pregnancies. For both of these family types, all eligible families were asked to take part and more than 70 percent agreed. The egg donation families were included as a comparison group (in addition to the natural conception families), in order to control for the experience of female infertility and the involvement of a third party in the birth of the child.

The first assessment was carried out at around the time of the child's first birthday and focused on three aspects of family functioning using in-depth, standardized interviews and questionnaires: the parents' psychological well-being and marital satisfaction; the quality of their parenting; and the temperament of their children (Golombok, Murray, Jadva, et al., 2004). Both mothers and fathers took part in the research. Contrary to the concerns that have been expressed about the potentially negative consequences of surrogacy for family functioning, the differences identified between the surrogacy families and the other family types indicated greater psychological well-being and adaption to parenthood by the mothers and fathers of children born

through surrogacy than by the comparison group of natural conception parents. Both mothers and fathers in surrogacy families reported
lower levels of stress associated with parenting than did those with
naturally conceived children, and mothers also showed lower levels
of depression. With respect to parent–child relationships, the findings were again more positive for the surrogacy parents than for the
natural conception parents. Mothers and fathers in surrogacy families showed greater warmth and attachment-related behavior toward
their infants, and greater enjoyment of parenthood, than did natural
conception parents. The surrogacy fathers were also more satisfied
with the parental role. The only exception to this positive pattern of
findings was that the surrogacy mothers and fathers showed higher
levels of emotional over-involvement with their infants. However,
this reflected only a slight degree of over-involvement, rather than
a dysfunctional level. Interestingly, the egg donation parents were
similar to the surrogacy parents in terms of the quality of their relationships with their children. However, the egg donation mothers,
like the natural conception mothers, showed higher levels of depression than did the surrogacy mothers, possibly owing to physical consequences of the pregnancy. No differences in infant temperament
were identified between the three family types.

Aspects of the surrogacy arrangement were also examined.
An important question is whether it makes a difference if the surrogate mother is also the genetic mother of the child. It appears not,
as no differences were found in the quality of the surrogacy parents'
parenting according to whether or not the surrogate was the genetic
mother of the child. However, the nature of the relationship between
the surrogacy parents and the surrogate mother did seem to make
a difference. When the surrogate mother was a relative or a friend,
as opposed to someone who was unknown to the surrogacy parents
prior to the surrogacy arrangement, the surrogacy mothers showed
more positive parenting.

The families were revisited when the children were aged
2 years (Golombok, MacCallum, Murray, et al., 2006). Once again,

the focus of the research was on the psychological well-being of the parents, the quality of the parent–child relationships and the psychological development of the children. At this phase of the study, the quality of parent–child relationships was examined using the Parent Development Interview (Slade, Belsky, Aber, et al., 1999), an interview technique designed to assess the nature of the emotional bond between a parent and the child. In line with the findings when the children were 1 year old, the surrogacy mothers appeared to have more positive thoughts and feelings about their toddlers than did the natural conception mothers. They showed higher levels of pleasure in their children and greater feelings of competence as parents, and lower levels of anger, guilt and disappointment with their children. No differences were found between the surrogacy and natural conception fathers in terms of their relationships with their children. However, the surrogacy fathers reported lower levels of parenting stress. The egg donation mothers and fathers were similar to the mothers and fathers in surrogacy families in terms of their thoughts and feelings about their children, although the surrogacy fathers again showed lower levels of parenting stress. The surrogacy children did not differ from either the natural conception children or the egg donation children with respect to their social, emotional or cognitive development.

The families were followed up for a third time when the children were 3 years old (Golombok, Murray, Jadva, et al., 2006). The findings were consistent with those of the earlier phases of the study. Where differences in parent–child relationships were identified, these showed more positive relationships in terms of both warmth and interaction among mothers in surrogacy families than among their counterparts in natural conception families. Once again, the egg donation mothers were similar to the surrogacy mothers with respect to the quality of their relationships with their children. The children showed positive psychological adjustment, with no differences between children born through surrogacy, egg donation or natural conception.

The next phase of the study took place when the children were aged 7 years (Golombok, Readings, Blake, et al., 2011), the age by which children develop a more sophisticated understanding of the absence of a genetic or gestational link to their parents (Gregg, Solomon, Johnson, et al., 1996; Williams and Smith, 2010; Richards, 2000). In the earlier phases of the study, the children were too young to be fully aware of the circumstances of their birth. In addition to an interview assessment of mother–child relationships, an observational assessment of mother–child interaction was carried out at this phase of the research to examine the quality of dynamic interactions between mothers and children that could not be captured by interview or self-report. No differences were found in the quality of mother–child relationships between the surrogacy families and either the natural conception or the egg donation families, as assessed by interview. However, the surrogacy mothers showed less positive interaction with their children in the observational assessment than did the natural conception mothers. Once again, the egg donation mothers were similar to the surrogacy mothers on this measure. Thus, the more positive parent–child relationships shown by the surrogacy, than by the natural conception, mothers when the children were in their preschool years was no longer apparent when the children were 7 years old. Nevertheless, the surrogacy families were not experiencing difficulties. They did not show more negative parent–child relationships than did the natural conception families. Instead, the differences identified reflected more subtle differences in patterns of mother–child interaction.

The psychological adjustment of the children was measured when the children were aged 7 years, and again at the age of 10, using the Strengths and Difficulties Questionnaire completed by mothers and the children's teachers (Goodman, 1994, 1997, 2001), and the surrogacy children's scores compared with those of children conceived by gamete donation (i.e. the scores of the egg donation children were combined with those of the donor insemination children described in Chapter 4 [Golombok, Blake, Casey, et al., 2013]). At

7 years of age, the surrogacy children showed higher levels of adjustment problems than did the children conceived by gamete donation as rated by mothers but not teachers. Interestingly, this finding parallels that of internationally adopted children at the age of 7 (Stams, Juffer, Rispens, et al., 2000), which Juffer and van IJzendoorn (2005) attributed to internationally adopted children's need to struggle with identity issues earlier than domestically adopted children, due to their difference in appearance from their parents. Surrogacy children may similarly face identity issues at an early age: not only are they born to a surrogate mother, which makes them different from other children, but they may also remain in contact with their surrogate mother as they grow up. It is important to emphasize, however, that the surrogacy children in this study were generally well-adjusted at the age of 7, with scores within the normal range. Also, the raised levels of psychological problems shown by the surrogacy children disappeared by the age of 10, which, again, was consistent with the decline in difficulties shown by internationally adopted children by adolescence.

The sample sizes in this study were relatively small and may have been biased toward the inclusion of well-functioning families. Furthermore, some families were lost over time. However, the study also had a number of advantages, including an in-depth, multi-method approach involving interview, observational and questionnaire measures, as well as data collection from mothers, fathers, children and teachers; thus, the potential for participants to present the family in an artificially positive light was reduced. Moreover, almost 80 percent of the surrogacy families who enrolled in the research were still taking part 10 years later. As the first study worldwide to investigate parenting and child development in surrogacy families, the results must be replicated – ideally in other countries and cultures – before general conclusions can be drawn. Nevertheless, the findings of this initial study are reassuring and indicate that some of the fears that have been expressed about the consequences of surrogacy for children are based on speculation, rather than fact.

A question that often crops up whenever surrogacy is discussed is how the parents and surrogate mother get on with each other during the pregnancy and after the child is born. The most commonly voiced concern is that the surrogate mother will refuse to hand over the baby. In fact, this rarely occurs. The cases that have hit the headlines have given a false impression of the frequency with which surrogate mothers change their minds. As part of the UK Longitudinal Study of Assisted Reproduction Families, intended parents were interviewed about the nature of their relationship with the surrogate mother at all five phases of the research; that is, when their children were aged 1 year (MacCallum, Lycett, Murray, et al., 2003) until their children were aged 10 (Jadva, Blake, Casey, et al., 2012). When the children were aged 1 year, the 42 sets of parents were asked to report on their relationship with the surrogate mother both during the pregnancy and after their children were born. During the pregnancy, the large majority of intended mothers saw the surrogate mother at least once per month – often accompanying her to medical appointments – with intended fathers having less contact. This is in line with the findings of Ragoné (1994), who found, in a study in the USA, that the role of the intended father during pregnancy was de-emphasized, whereas the intended mother formed a strong bond with the surrogate mother and was very involved in the pregnancy. For the most part, intended parents in the UK study reported a harmonious relationship with the surrogate mother. Where this was not the case, there was minor conflict or a lack of communication, rather than major conflict or hostility. Most of the intended mothers (but only one-third of the intended fathers) were present at the birth. In spite of concerns to the contrary, all of the surrogate mothers relinquished the baby to the intended parents without difficulty, with the exception of one woman who did so after some hesitation. Likewise, all of the intended mothers had no difficulty accepting the baby, although one woman reported minor problems initially.

In the year following the birth, almost all of the mothers and fathers met with the surrogate mother at least once, and most described their relationship with her in positive terms. However, the frequency of contact between the parents and the surrogate mothers decreased over time, particularly in cases in which they had not known each other prior to the surrogacy arrangement and the surrogate mother's egg had been used to conceive the child. By the time the children were 10 years old, 60 percent of the parents were still in contact with the surrogate mother and, for the large majority, this relationship remained positive. As one mother put it: "In my experience it's been extremely positive. I've got a lovely friend that you know ... words can't express how I feel about [surrogate mother] because she's just been brilliant the whole way through." Thus, fears were allayed that difficulties would develop between the parents and the surrogate mother as the child grew up, or that the involvement of the surrogate mother would interfere with the mother's confidence as a parent. However, those who had lost contact may have done so intentionally as a result of difficulties between the surrogate mother and the family.

The nature of the relationship between surrogate mothers and their surrogacy children was of particular interest, especially in cases in which the surrogate mother had been the genetic mother or a friend or relative of the family. In the year following the birth, three-quarters of the surrogate mothers saw the baby. Although most of the parents were happy about this, a few had mixed feelings. Where there was no contact between the surrogate mother and the baby, this was usually by mutual agreement or because the surrogate mother did not want contact. There were no reported cases of contact being denied by the parents. Not surprisingly, the frequency of contact between the children and their surrogate mothers mirrored that of their parents and declined as they grew older, with 60 percent of children remaining in contact with their surrogate mothers by the age of 10. Interestingly, children who were genetically related to their surrogate mother were less likely to keep in touch with her than were those who lacked a genetic link. This may have been deliberate on the part of the parents, in order to distance the surrogate mother from the child.

Surrogacy parents are much more open with their children about the circumstances of their birth than are parents of children conceived by egg, sperm or embryo donation. All of the parents in the UK Longitudinal Study of Assisted Reproduction Families planned to tell their children about the surrogacy (MacCallum, Lycett, Murray, et al., 2003), and the large majority did so by the time their children reached 7 years of age (Jadva, Blake, Casey, et al., 2012). However, by the child's age of 7, the majority of parents whose children had been born through genetic surrogacy had told their children that they had been carried by another woman, but had not disclosed the use of the surrogate mother's egg (Readings, Blake, Casey, et al., 2011); almost half of these parents had still not disclosed this information by the time their children turned 10 (Jadva, Blake, Casey, et al., 2012). Thus, these children were unaware that their surrogate mother was also their genetic mother. As one mother put it, "We've made it like bread in the oven, 'she just kept you warm until you were ready to come out,' so no, it hasn't come up that biologically she's not mine."

Some mothers were worried about rejection by their children. As one mother said:

> I think the one thing that is in the back of my mind and haunts me slightly is if ever one of my girls might turn around and say to me 'You're not my mum.' I think that would cut very, very deep. But that hasn't happened so far ... and I don't believe that they would say that ... because we have a very good relationship ... a very close relationship so I don't think it would enter their mind but it's in my mind ... rightly or wrongly.

When children were interviewed at the age of 7 years and at the age of 10, the majority showed some understanding of surrogacy, at least to the extent that they had been born to a woman who was not their mother. As one child put it, "Well my mum's womb, I think ... well it was broken, so [surrogate mother] carried me instead of my mum." Most of the children who were in contact with their surrogate mother said that they liked her, describing her as "nice" or "kind." For example, one child said "She was really kind about ... like carrying me in her tummy" and another said, "I think she is kind and she's lovely and funny." Two-thirds wished to see her more often and the remainder felt that the level of contact was just right, with the exception of only one child, who wished to see her less. Despite the widespread opinion that children would be distressed by the knowledge that they had been born through surrogacy, this did not appear to be a big issue for the children in the study, with the majority feeling neutral or indifferent about this. The view of this 10-year-old was typical of the other children in the study: "I feel fine. I don't feel bad or cross in any way. It's just pretty much nature so I can't do anything about it. I wouldn't like to do anything about it." Nevertheless, the oldest children in the study were only 10 years old. They may feel differently as they grow up.

Some of the children also understood their relationship to the surrogate mother's own children. One father described it as follows:

> Since he was very young, he understood that the surrogate's children were his half siblings. He has known that. He has so absolutely known that. In fact, when he did a family tree at school, he put a little dog leg and [surrogate mother and children] as part of his family tree. And even more interestingly ... the surrogate's child also put him as her half-brother.

As yet, no studies have been carried out of the views of older children born through surrogacy. It remains to be seen how children will feel as they enter adolescence, when issues relating to identity become more significant, and whether payment to the surrogate mother for her services will make a difference to the reactions of the child. The situation may become even more complex for children whose surrogate mother lives in a different country or speaks a different language, as is becoming increasingly common with the growing use of surrogate mothers in India and other countries.

STUDIES OF SURROGATE MOTHERS AND THEIR FAMILIES

Some of the most contested ethical questions regarding surrogacy relate to the surrogate mother. Is the surrogate mother in a position to give truly informed consent if she has never done this in the past and is therefore unaware of what it feels like to relinquish a baby she has carried for 9 months and who may also be her genetic child? Do surrogate mothers feel regret once they have handed over the baby? Do they experience psychological distress or long-term psychological problems? What is the impact of surrogacy on the surrogate mother's own family, including her partner and her children?

In order to examine the psychological consequences of surrogacy for surrogate mothers, 34 women who had given birth to a surrogacy child in the UK were administered a standardized interview one year after the birth of the child and completed a questionnaire assessment of post-natal depression (Jadva, Murray, Lycett, et al., 2003). More than 70 percent of those who were asked to participate agreed to do so. None of the women reported experiencing any doubts about handing over the baby to the intended parents. When asked to recollect their feelings and experiences, around one-third of the women reported feeling upset in the weeks following the hand-over, although only one woman described feeling severely depressed. One year later, only two women (6 percent) reported psychological difficulties arising from their experiences of surrogacy, and none obtained a score on the post-natal depression questionnaire that was indicative of clinical depression. Neither was there a difference in depression scores between the genetic and gestational surrogate mothers, which suggests that the surrogate mothers did not experience long-term psychological problems, even in cases in which they were genetically related to the surrogacy child. Thus, the psychological difficulties experienced by surrogate mothers were not severe and tended to dissipate with time; this lends little support to the expectation that surrogate mothers will experience psychological problems following the relinquishment of the child. The study found a great deal of variation in the frequency of contact between the surrogate mother and the baby following the hand-over. Whereas one-third of the surrogate mothers had seen the baby at least once a month, one-quarter had not had any contact. Not one of the surrogate mothers felt as if the surrogacy child was their own – a factor that might have helped them to relinquish the baby to the intended parents. For almost two-thirds of the surrogate mothers, information was also available from the parents, as they were participants in the UK Longitudinal Study of Assisted Reproduction Families. Interestingly, the accounts of the surrogate mothers were almost identical to those of the parents, thus validating the parents' reports of positive relationships with the surrogate mothers.

In the only investigation of the long-term outcomes of surrogacy for surrogate mothers and surrogate mothers' own children, 34 surrogate mothers (20 of whom had taken part in the previous study 1 year after the birth of the surrogacy child) and 36 of their children (aged 12 to 25 years) were interviewed between 5 and 15 years after the mother had given birth to a surrogacy child (Jadva and Imrie, 2014a, b; Jadva, Imrie and Golombok, 2014; Imrie and Jadva, 2014). The findings challenged the widespread expectation that difficulties would arise in the relationship between the surrogate mother and the intended parents as time went on, and instead painted a largely positive picture of the relationships formed between surrogate mothers and the families they helped to create. In three-quarters of surrogacy arrangements, the surrogate mothers had stayed in touch with the children they had carried for another couple, and generally saw them once or twice a year. In addition, almost half of the surrogate mothers' own children were in contact with the surrogacy child, whom many described as a sibling or half-sibling, irrespective of genetic relation. However, others did not appear to ascribe any significance to their genetic or gestational relatedness to the surrogacy child, and yet others created their own terminology to describe this new form of relationship, including "surrosister" and "tummy-sister" (Jadva and Imrie, 2014b).

Only half of the surrogate mothers' children were interviewed, and thus the views of the other half are not known. This is partly because the children were asked to participate by their mothers and some mothers felt disinclined to ask children who had left home. However, this is the first study to examine surrogacy from the perspective of surrogate mothers' own children, and it sheds light on their experiences and views. Despite fears to the contrary, it appears that these children were not adversely affected by their mothers' involvement in surrogacy. Indeed, the large majority were positive about this and felt proud of their mother for helping a woman who was unable to have children, herself. As a child of a genetic surrogate mother said: "I think it's amazing … It's quite, I dunno, it's like … it's difficult for a woman to like give away a child that she's given birth to and I just think it's … fantastic that my mum can, and make people so happy." Similarly, a child of a gestational surrogate mother stated: "I think it's a really nice thing to do for someone, obviously if they can't have children and they really want a child that's a bad thing, so if someone else is able to do that for you and help you through it then it's something that is compassionate really."

CONCLUSIONS

Surrogacy is not without its difficulties. Although uncommon, the surrogate mother may change her mind and decide to keep the baby, as occurred in the case of Baby M. Intended parents may also change their mind and leave surrogates, literally, holding the baby. Nevertheless, the findings from the few studies of surrogacy that currently exist indicate that families formed in this way are generally functioning well, suggesting that the absence of a gestational link between the parents and the child does not jeopardize the development of positive family relationships or positive child adjustment. It is interesting to note that surrogacy and egg donation families appear to show similarly positive outcomes. As the key distinguishing factor between these two family types (especially in the case of genetic surrogacy) is whether or not there is a gestational relationship with the child, this provides further support for the conclusion that a gestational link is not essential for positive family functioning. Moreover, there is evidence that harmonious relationships can ensue between surrogate mothers' families and the families these surrogates help to create. What is not yet known is how these relationships will play out over time and, crucially, how children born through surrogacy will feel about their origins later in their lives.

6　Solo mother families

Assisted reproductive technologies were initially developed to enable infertile heterosexual couples to have children and create families that are indistinguishable from the traditional nuclear family – a family comprising a mother, a father and a singleton child or siblings. However, these technologies have increasingly been used for social, rather than medical reasons; that is, because of the absence of an opposite-sex partner rather than the presence of infertility. As described in Chapter 2, the use of donor insemination enables lesbian women to become pregnant without the involvement of a male partner. This chapter focuses on a different type of family created without the involvement of a male partner: families headed by single heterosexual mothers, also known as "single mothers by choice" or "solo mothers" (Weinraub, Horvath, and Gringlas, 2002).

The terms "single mother by choice" and "solo mother" refer to a woman who actively chooses to parent a child without a partner. Women who decide to parent alone have a range of possibilities available to them for becoming pregnant, and not all these involve assisted reproduction. Some women have sexual intercourse with a man who will not act as a father to the child, some adopt a child, some undergo self-insemination with a donor who may be known to them or anonymous, and some receive fertility treatment with donor sperm (Bock, 2000; Graham and Braverman, 2012; Hertz, 2006; Jadva, Badger, Morrissette, et al., 2009; Weinraub, Horvath, and Gringlas, 2002). Although single women who wish to become mothers opt for different methods – according to their circumstances and beliefs – donor insemination at a clinic appears to be an increasingly popular route to motherhood. Donor insemination is favored over adoption by those who wish to experience pregnancy and have a genetically related child, and is favored over sexual intercourse by women who do not wish to have casual sex or to deceive a man in order to become pregnant (Graham, 2014; Hertz, 2006; Jadva, Badger, Morrissette, et al., 2009; Weinraub, Horvath, and Gringlas, 2002). For those who choose donor insemination, most prefer to use an anonymous or identity-release donor (a donor whose identity can be requested by the child upon reaching adulthood) rather than a known donor, to avoid the potential complications of the donor's involvement with the family as the child grows up (Jadva, Badger, Morrissette, et al., 2009). Many also prefer to attend a fertility clinic, in countries where this is permissible, than to embark upon self-insemination. Clinics offer single women greater legal protection than is possible with self-insemination, as sperm donors have no parental rights over children conceived at a clinic. Clinics also offer greater medical protection, as a result of the stringent screening process required of sperm donors. However, some women find sperm donors independently of clinics, either through personal contacts, advertising or matching websites such as Pride Angel in the UK and Family by Design in the USA, which connect men who wish to donate sperm with women looking for sperm donors. Sperm donors are also being found through Facebook. Whereas single lesbian women and single heterosexual women may become single mothers by choice, existing research has largely focused on single heterosexual women (Graham, 2012, 2014; Zadeh, Freeman, and Golombok, 2013).

Although little is known about the characteristics of single mothers by choice, women who choose to parent without men have received a negative press. The past condemnation and denigration by the media of single mother families in general (in that they are often blamed for society's ills) has been extended to include single mothers by choice – with the added reproach that single mothers by choice are selfish. As a journalist in the UK *Sunday Times* newspaper wrote (in an article entitled "Selfish women rule in an era that doesn't need men," on July 15, 2001):

> Apart from the risks of mucking around with the gene pool,
> this is turning us into a society of repellently selfish women.
> It is promoting the belief that children are merely the means
> for (predominantly) female self-fulfillment rather than the
> embodiment of a society's contract between the past, present
> and future ... women are choosing to produce fatherless children
> by way of sperm banks ... no taboo, however ancient, can now
> frustrate a woman's science-sanctified right to create a child for
> her personal gratification.

In response to an article in the UK *Daily Mail* newspaper with the headline "Daddies be damned!", which reported on the rise in the number of single women in the UK who were having children by donor insemination, a reader suggested that these women should "Spend their money on another Prada handbag ... not a person with feelings and needs" (Graham and Braverman, 2012). Similarly, a *New York Times* article entitled "First comes the baby carriage" stated on October 13, 2005: "Many single women still find the choice to get pregnant met with incomprehension or even hostility from friends, family and some strangers. The most common accusation is that they are selfish, because of the widely held belief that two-parent homes are best for children."

So, who are single mothers by choice? As highlighted by Graham and Braverman (2012, p. 197), they are perceived by their critics as: "Selfish career women who wanted the latest, must have accessory; a baby." But are they really so different from other women who wish to have a child? As one single mother by choice described it: "I think I wanted to have a child because of the same reason that everybody wants to. I wanted to be a mum, I wanted to have that experience, I wanted to feel that kind of love, I wanted to see how good I'd be at it, and have a sort of meaning behind everything."

Studies have shown that single mothers by choice are generally, but not always, well-educated, financially secure women in professional occupations who become mothers in their late thirties or early forties (Bock, 2000; Graham, 2012, 2014; Graham and Braverman, 2012; Jadva, Badger, Morrissette, et al., 2009; Murray and Golombok, 2005a; Weinraub, Horvath, and Gringlas, 2002). Contrary to popular belief, these women have thought long and hard about having a child alone, have consulted with friends and family and have ensured that they have the financial resources and social support they need. They are also concerned about the absence of a father from their children's lives and many have actively sought out relatives or friends to be male role models (Jadva, Freeman, Kramer, et al., 2009; Murray and Golombok, 2005a).

In spite of the way in which they are portrayed, the majority of women who decide to go it alone as mothers do so not from choice, but because they do not have a current partner and feel that time is running out for them to have a child (Graham, 2012; Graham and Braverman, 2012; Hertz, 2006; Jadva, Freeman, Kramer, et al., 2009; Murray and Golombok, 2005a). As a mother of a young child said:

If I'd been in a long term relationship, one that I thought would be going a long way, and settled, I'd have had children much, much younger. In my little world, when I was a teenager, I was going to get married when I was about 20, and have my first child when I was about 21, 22, and then I was thinking of maybe 4 children. How naïve is that – isn't it? But it was never my intention to have children so late. I just hadn't met the person.

Indeed, many single mothers by choice report that they would have rather had their children within a traditional family setting, but could not wait any longer because of their increasing age and associated fertility decline; because they wanted to be mothers, they did not actually have a choice (Graham, 2014; Murray and Golombok, 2005a; Zadeh, Freeman, and Golombok, 2013).

In an in-depth qualitative study of women thinking about and embarking on single motherhood through the use of donor sperm, Graham (2014) found that the decision to pursue single motherhood was based on a deep-seated desire to become a mother, and that the potential child's well-being was at the forefront of women's minds as they decided upon whether to proceed, what route to take to achieve motherhood and what process they should use to select a sperm donor. Many, but certainly not all, hoped to have a relationship with a man in the future – not just for themselves, but also for their child to have a father. So, contrary to popular perceptions, single mothers by choice do not take the decision to have a child lightly; they want the best for their child, and many would prefer to raise their child with a man. As one mother put it:

I get a real bee in my bonnet, I never ever want someone to think that he was a mistake, or a result of a fling, or that he wasn't wanted, so I would much rather people knew how I became pregnant and my reasons – to know that he was completely wanted. I would hate for someone to think that I just messed up my life by having him, because this was the whole plan, and this is what I wanted.

In recent decades, there has been a dramatic increase in the number of single-parent families. In the USA in 2008, 29.5 percent of households with children were headed by single parents (US Census Bureau, 2012a). Similarly, in the UK in 2007, 30 percent of children aged up to 14 years were living in single-parent households (Lloyd and Lacey, 2012b). These figures compare with less than 10 percent in the USA and the UK at the beginning of the 1970s. However, single mothers are not a homogenous group. Single-mother families are formed in a number of ways, each with different implications for children. Parental divorce or separation is the most common reason for children to be raised in single-mother families. There has also been a rise in the number of children born to single unmarried mothers as a result of unplanned pregnancies. As described above, the small but growing number of single mothers by choice has resulted from quite different origins. However, the concerns that have been voiced about the children of single mothers by choice have arisen from research on children in single-mother families that have been created by divorce or unplanned pregnancies. How relevant are the experiences of children in these single-mother families to children raised by single mothers by choice? In order to address this question, research on the outcomes for children of being raised by divorced and unmarried single mothers will be examined to establish whether growing up under these circumstances is psychologically harmful for children and, if so, why this is the case. This will be followed by consideration of the extent to which findings relating to the children of divorced and unmarried single mothers can be extrapolated to children of single mothers by choice. The findings of the few empirical studies that currently exist of the development and well-being of children of single mothers by choice will also be discussed.

DIVORCED SINGLE MOTHERS

Since the 1970s, there has been an increase in the proportion of marriages ending in divorce. Approximately 40 to 50 percent of married couples in the US divorce (Kazdin, 2000), with around 5 percent of US marriages ending in divorce in 2008 (US Census Bureau, 2012b). In the UK, the proportion of married couples who have divorced before reaching their fiftieth wedding anniversary has increased by around one-third since 1979, reaching 45 percent in 2005 (Lloyd and Lacey, 2012a). As noted in Chapter 1, divorce statistics do not tell the whole story as there are no official registries of relationship breakdown among cohabiting couples, and thus of the number of children who experience the separation of cohabiting parents (Amato, 2000).

There is now a large body of research on the psychological consequences of divorce for children. These studies have consistently shown that children whose parents divorce are more likely to show emotional and behavioral problems and are less likely to perform well at school than are children in intact families (for reviews see Amato, 2000, 2001, 2005; Amato and Keith, 1991; Coleman and Glenn, 2009; Hetherington and Stanley-Hagan, 1999; Pryor and Rodgers, 2001; Rodgers and Pryor, 1998). One of the most highly regarded of these studies was conducted by Mavis Hetherington and her colleagues in the USA. The researchers followed up 4-year-old children from the time of their parents' divorce and compared these children to a group of children whose parents were happily married and also to a group of children whose parents had remained together in spite of marital problems. The behavior of the children in all three family types was assessed over a period of 6 years. In the first year, the children from divorced families not only showed higher levels of conduct problems than did the children whose parents were happily married, but also than those whose parents were in conflict but remained together. This was found to be the case both at home and at school. By the end of the second year, however, the behavioral difficulties shown by the children of divorced parents had declined, although the boys still showed higher levels of conduct problems than did the boys from happy two-parent homes (Hetherington, Cox, and Cox, 1982). The findings were similar 6 years following the divorce. Compared with children in non-divorced families, girls whose mothers had not remarried remained well-adjusted. Sons also showed more positive adjustment than they had previously, although they still showed a tendency toward higher rates of conduct problems (Hetherington, 1988).

As most studies of children in single-parent families have investigated families formed by divorce, it is difficult to conclude whether it is having only one parent that is psychologically harmful for children, or whether children's difficulties result from other aspects of the divorce. One factor that has consistently been shown to be related to children's adjustment problems is conflict between parents (Amato, 1993, 2000, 2005; Pryor and Rodgers, 2001; Rodgers and Pryor, 1998). It is interesting to note that longitudinal studies have found that children whose parents divorce can develop psychological problems years before their parents separate – sometimes even before they have considered separation (Cherlin, Furstenberg, Chase-Lansdale, et al., 1991). This suggests that the psychological problems shown by children in single-parent families may not result from the absence of a parent, but instead may arise from conflict and hostility between parents before the divorce takes place.

The financial hardship that is often experienced by single-parent families following divorce is another factor that has been found to be associated with children's psychological problems (Amato, 1993, 2000, 2005; Hetherington and Stanley-Hagan, 2002; Pryor and Rodgers, 2001; Rodgers and Pryor, 1998). From their detailed examination of four large, nationally representative samples in the USA, McLanahan and Sandefur (1994) concluded that the lower and sudden drop in income that results from single parenthood is the most important factor in the underachievement of young people from single-parent homes. They found that adolescents who had lived apart from one parent during some period of their childhood were twice as likely to drop out of high school, twice as likely to have a child before the age of 20 and 1.5 times more likely to be out of work in their late teens or early twenties than were those from comparable backgrounds who had grown up with two parents at home. Similar findings were reported from an earlier study of 16,000 children born in England and

Wales in one week in March 1958 (Elliot and Vaitilingam, 2008; Ferri, 1976). A comparison between the children in single-parent families and the children in two-parent families around the time of their eleventh birthday showed that those in single-parent families were more likely to show emotional and behavioral problems, as well as poorer academic achievement. However, the difficulties experienced by children in single-parent families were explained almost entirely by the low income associated with single parenthood, rather than the absence of a parent. When family income was controlled for in the statistical analyses, children with single parents were not found to differ from children with two parents in the family home. Rodgers and Pryor (1998) reviewed more than 200 studies of the effects of divorce on children and concluded that the low socio-economic status of single-parent families was largely responsible for the lower educational achievement of children whose parents had divorced. As well as the direct effects of low income, the financial hardship experienced by many single parent families following divorce often necessitates a move to a poorer neighborhood and a change of school, each of which is associated with negative outcomes for children (Amato, 2000, 2005).

In addition to financial support, social and emotional support are often lacking for single mothers. As Hetherington and Stanley-Hagan (2002) pointed out, it is not unusual for mothers to feel anxious, depressed, lonely and lacking in confidence when they divorce. At the same time, children become more demanding, less compliant, more aggressive and more withdrawn. For newly single mothers, the demands of looking after difficult children while in a poor emotional state can impair their ability to function as effective parents. They may be less affectionate, less communicative, less consistent, more irritable and more punitive in disciplining their children than before, which may exacerbate their children's difficulties (Hetherington and Clingempeel, 1992). A number of studies have demonstrated a link between parental depression, poor parenting and negative child outcomes in single-parent families following divorce (Amato, 2000; Dunn, Deater-Deckard, Pickering, et al., 1998; Hetherington and Stanley-Hagan, 2002). However, improvement in the emotional well-being of single mothers following divorce is associated with improvement in children's adjustment. Two years after-divorce, three-quarters of divorced women reported that they were happier in their new situation than they had been in their final year of marriage, and most felt that it was easier to raise their children alone than in partnership with a disengaged, undermining or acrimonious husband (Hetherington and Stanley-Hagan, 2002).

Although divorce has consistently been found to have an adverse effect on children's functioning, the differences between children in divorced and intact families are relatively small (Amato, 2000, 2001, 2005; Amato and Keith, 1991). Not all children whose parents divorce experience problems, and some show improved functioning (Amato, 2000, 2001, 2005; Amato and Keith, 1991). Of those who do exhibit problems, some experience short-term distress, which may last from a few months to 2–3 years, whereas others face long-term difficulties (Amato, 2001; Hetherington, 1989). Whether or not children develop problems, and how quickly they recover, depends on a number of factors – the most significant of which appears to be the effect of divorce on the relationship between their parents (Amato, 2000, 2001, 2005; Amato and Keith, 1991; Coleman and Glenn, 2009; Hetherington and Stanley-Hagan, 1999; Rodgers and Pryor, 1998). When parents remain in conflict after divorce, children are more likely to continue to have problems, especially if they are drawn into their parents' disputes. However, if parents are able to cooperate, children are more able to cope.

In addition to the quality of the relationship between parents, the quality of the relationship between children and parents following divorce has also been found to be influential in children's psychological well-being, with a warm and supportive relationship with at least one parent acting as a protective factor for the child (Amato, 2000; Amato and Gilbreth, 1999). Where children remain with the mother, there is growing evidence for the psychological benefits of a positive relationship with the non-resident father (Dunn, 2004, 2008; Dunn, Cheng, O'Connor, et al., 2004).

Whether or not the gender of the child or the age at which the child makes the transition into a single-parent family makes a difference to the impact of divorce on children remains inconclusive (Amato, 2000, 2001; Amato and Keith, 1991; Hetherington and Stanley-Hagan, 1999; Rodgers and Pryor, 1998). Although boys seem to be more vulnerable than girls, it has been suggested that girls may show distress in different ways. In terms of children's age at the time of divorce, adolescence is often considered an especially difficult time. However, few studies have identified a clear link between children's age at the time of divorce and psychological outcomes (Amato, 2000).

An important question is whether the difficulties experienced by children in single-parent families following divorce result from selection effects, rather than the divorce, itself. Individuals with psychological problems may be more likely to marry each other and to transmit psychological problems to their children through inheritance or poor parenting, irrespective of marital breakdown. Parents' psychological problems may also contribute to marital breakdown. Thus, the difficulties shown by children may not be directly related to divorce. Amato (2000) concluded from his review that the negative outcomes for children whose parents had divorced had resulted largely from marital breakdown, rather than selection effects, and, to the extent that pre-existing factors were involved, divorce exacerbated these difficulties.

A further issue that is often raised regarding children in single-mother families is whether the absence of a father results in less typical gender role behavior, particularly for boys. More specifically, are boys less masculine in their identity and behavior, and girls less feminine, than are boys and girls who grow up with a mother and a father in the family home? Although early studies produced contradictory results, a meta-analysis by Stevenson and Black (1988) concluded that there were no effects for boys or girls when the highest quality studies were examined. In an investigation of 5- to 12-year-olds in the USA, no differences in sex-typed preferences were identified according to the presence or absence of a father in the home (Serbin, Powlishta, and Gulko, 1993). Similarly, in a study of 3-year-old children participating in the Avon Longitudinal Study of Pregnancy and Childhood, a large epidemiological study in the UK, no differences in gender role behavior were found between father-absent and father-present families for either boys or girls (Stevens, Golombok, Golding, et al., 2002). The children in single-mother families had not lived with their father since they were 12 months old or younger. Taken together, these studies suggest that growing up in a single-mother family does not influence children's gender development.

UNMARRIED SINGLE MOTHERS

In addition to the increasing number of children raised by divorced single mothers, there has been a sharp rise in the number of children raised by unmarried single mothers, many of whom have had unplanned pregnancies. Today, around 20 percent of babies in the USA (McLanahan, 2012) and 15 percent of babies in the UK (Kiernan, 2006) are born into single-mother families. In contrast, in the 1960s, the proportion of children born to single mothers was less than 5 per cent. In the USA, the rates are highest for children born to African American mothers. However, there has been an increase in single mother families across many ethnic–racial groups. Whereas in the UK the large majority of unmarried single mothers are white, a higher proportion of black Caribbean mothers are single at the time of their child's birth, relative to mothers from other ethnic groups (Kiernan and Mensah, 2010). Rather than race or ethnicity, the factor most associated with the rise in single unmarried mothers is social disadvantage. Whereas college-educated women continue to have children in the context of marriage, women who have not received an education beyond high school are much more likely to have children as single unmarried mothers (Kiernan, 2006; McLanahan, 2012).

Although single at the time of their children's birth, many unmarried mothers experience transitions in and out of cohabiting relationships, rather than remaining stably single (Kiernan and Mensah, 2010; McLanahan, 2012).

An influential study of the consequences of unmarried single-motherhood for children is the Fragile Families Study, a longitudinal investigation of approximately 5,000 children born between 1998 and 2000 in the USA. The study recruited participants in medium to large cities, and included an over-sample of births to single and cohabiting unmarried mothers ("fragile families") (Reichman, Teitler, and McLanahan, 2001). In-depth data have been obtained on children's cognitive development and behavior problems. More negative cognitive and mental health outcomes have been found for children born to single unmarried mothers than to married parents, even after differences in parental resources have been adjusted for (Waldfogel, Craigie, and Brooks-Gunn, 2010). The more negative outcomes in terms of cognitive development appear to have resulted from a high level of family instability, rather than single motherhood, in itself, whereas growing up with a single mother seems to have mattered more than family instability for children's emotional and behavioral problems. As discussed above, in relation to single-mother families formed by divorce, a number of possible mechanisms have been identified to account for the more negative outcomes for these children, including economic disadvantage, parental mental health problems and poor parenting quality. Again, selection effects may have also operated such that the pre-existing characteristics of parents might have led to poorer outcomes for children of unmarried single mothers. The extent to which each of these factors shapes children's outcomes in single unmarried mother families is, as yet, uncertain (Waldfogel, Craigie, and Brooks-Gunn, 2010).

In the UK, the Millennium Cohort Study (Hansen, Johnson, Joshi, et al., 2008), a longitudinal investigation of a nationally representative sample of approximately 18,000 children born at the turn of the century, has also provided data on children of unmarried single mothers. The study includes an over-sample of disadvantaged families, and 15 percent of the children in the sample were born to unmarried single mothers. In a comparison between children born to single mothers, cohabiting mothers and married mothers over the first 5 years of life, children born to single mothers who did not marry the child's biological father and children born into cohabiting families in which the parents have since separated have shown the highest rates of behavioral and emotional problems (Kiernan and Mensah, 2010). The single mothers have also experienced the highest levels of economic disadvantage and poorest mental health. After the family's socio-economic status and the mothers' levels of depression have been taken into account, no significant differences have been found across family types for children's emotional problems. However, although reduced, raised levels of behavioral problems have remained for the children of single mothers.

SINGLE MOTHERS BY CHOICE

How relevant are the findings of research on the psychological adjustment of children in single-mother families created by divorce or unplanned pregnancy to the children of single mothers by choice? Unlike divorced or unmarried single mothers, single mothers by choice make an active decision to parent alone, and thus differ from those who unintentionally find themselves in this situation. The studies examined above show the children of divorced and unmarried single mothers to be at greater risk of developing emotional and behavioral problems than are their counterparts from two-parent families. However, the more negative outcomes for children in single-parent families formed as a result of divorce or unplanned pregnancy appear to be largely associated with parental conflict, socio-economic disadvantage, maternal depression and lack of social support – none of which is characteristic of families formed by single mothers by choice. Children of single mothers by choice have not been exposed to parental conflict or separation from fathers with whom they have shared their daily lives. Neither have they experienced the economic disadvantage, lack of social support or maternal psychological problems that commonly accompany marital breakdown or unplanned single parenthood (Hertz, 2006; Jadva, Badger, Morrissette, et al., 2009; Murray and Golombok, 2005a). Nevertheless, they grow up without fathers from the start and, perhaps more significantly, do not know their father's identity, unless a known donor was used. Even in countries where the use of anonymous donors is prohibited, children are not able to discover the identity of their donor until adulthood. This makes them distinct from most other children of single mothers, whose fathers may be absent but whose identity is known.

There is, as yet, little research on the development and well-being of children raised by single mothers by choice. The two controlled studies that exist have focused on families created by donor insemination at a clinic, rather than by sexual intercourse, adoption or self-insemination. In one study, conducted in the UK, a comparison was conducted between 27 single heterosexual mother families and 50 married heterosexual parent families, all with a 6- to 12-month-old infant who had been conceived by donor insemination (Murray and Golombok, 2005a). The mothers were administered an interview designed to assess their quality of parenting, which produced standardized ratings of expressed warmth toward the infant, emotional over-involvement with the infant, interaction with the infant, sensitive responding to the infant's signals, enjoyment of motherhood and social support. They also completed questionnaire assessments of anxiety, depression, feelings of attachment to the infant and stress associated with parenting. No differences were identified between the two family types in terms of mothers' psychological well-being, adaptation to motherhood, expressed warmth, emotional involvement or bonding with their infants. However, the single mothers showed lower levels of interaction and sensitive responding to their infants than did the married mothers, possibly because the presence of a partner allowed the married mothers more time with their babies. The differences between the two family types did not indicate parenting problems in the single-mother families but, instead, reflected a difference between "moderate" and "good" mother–child interaction and "average" and "above average" sensitive responding for the single and two-parent families, respectively. It was concluded that, in the child's first year of life, the single mother families were generally functioning well.

The families were followed up at the child's second birthday. By the age of 2, children have fully established attachment relationships to parents and understand that they are members of a family (Edwards and Liu, 2002). At this age, children also show an increase in resistant and angry behavior – often described as "the terrible twos" – which has been associated with parenting difficulties (Belsky, Woodworth, and Crnic, 1996). The mothers were administered the Parent Development Interview (Slade, Belsky, Aber, et al., 1999), an in-depth interview assessment of the emotional bond between parents and their children that produces ratings on variables such as joy, anger, guilt, overprotectiveness and disappointment in the child. Mothers also completed questionnaire assessments of anxiety, depression and stress associated with parenting, as well as a questionnaire measure of the socio-emotional problems and competencies of their children, the Brief Infant–Toddler Social and Emotional Assessment (Briggs-Gowan, Carter, Irwin, et al., 2004). The families continued to function well as the children reached 2 years old (Murray and Golombok, 2005b). With 2-year-old children, the single mothers were no more likely to be experiencing parenting stress, anxiety or depression than were the married mothers. Although mothers from both types of family showed positive relationships with their children, the differences that were identified between the single and the married mothers indicated greater joy among the single mothers and less anger toward their children, accompanied by a perception of their children as less clingy. Thus, in direct contrast to the concerns raised about the quality of parenting of single mothers by choice, the findings showed more positive and less negative maternal feelings toward their children. With respect to the children, those with single mothers showed fewer emotional and behavioral problems than did those with married mothers. This suggests that the use of donor insemination to have a child as a single mother does not adversely affect children's socio-emotional development. However, it is important to remember that, at age 2, the children of single mothers were too young to understand the meaning of their non-traditional family structure; they were unaware of the social significance of not having a father.

In the study of 7-year-old children conceived by donor insemination discussed in Chapter 2, comparisons were carried out between the single mother (heterosexual and lesbian) families and the two-parent (heterosexual and lesbian) families (Chan, Raboy, and Patterson, 1998). Parents completed questionnaire assessments of depression, self-esteem and stress associated with parenting, and parents and teachers completed questionnaire assessments of children's social competence and behavioral adjustment. No differences in conduct or emotional problems, social competence or adaptive functioning were identified between the children of single and partnered mothers. Moreover, when compared with a large, normative sample, the children were found to be well adjusted, as rated by parents and teachers, and, when compared with a clinical sample, they showed higher social competence and lower behavioral problems. Growing up with a single mother by choice was not associated with greater behavioral problems for children. Instead, children's behavioral problems were associated with greater parenting stress, irrespective of family type.

At present, no studies have been carried out on the adjustment of the children of single mothers by choice beyond the age of 7 years. As noted in Chapter 4, it is at the age of 7 years that children acquire a more complex understanding of family relatedness (Gregg, Solomon, Johnson, et al., 1996; Richards, 2000; Williams and Smith, 2010), and it is at adolescence that issues associated with identity become more relevant and relationships with parents may become more difficult (Steinberg, 2001; Steinberg and Morris, 2001; Steinberg and Silk, 2002). Thus, it cannot necessarily be assumed that the apparent absence of problems in parent–child relationships or child adjustment in the families of single mothers by choice that have been studied so far will continue as the children grow older. A qualitative study of 35 stable single-mother families with 38 children aged between 8 and 17 years sheds some light on the nature of mother–child relationships in families in which the mother has been parenting alone continuously from early in the child's life, though not all of the families in this study were headed by single mothers by choice (Nixon, Greene, and Hogan, 2012). The children were interviewed about various aspects of their relationship with their mother, including communication, conflict, confiding and perceived obligations, and about what it was like to be raised in a single-parent household. Mothers were interviewed about their experiences of parenting alone and their relationship with their children – again, in relation to communication, conflict, confiding and perceived obligations. The children described having a close emotional bond with their mother, characterized by open communication, shared activities and trust. The majority of mothers described their relationship with their children as intense and exclusive, but did not always view this as positive – particularly when boundaries between the parent and child roles became blurred. These findings suggest that mothers and children may be more dependent on each other in stable single-parent families, although firm conclusions cannot be drawn in the absence of a comparison group of two-parent families.

As discussed in Chapter 2, a study that included a group of children raised in stable single-mother families from infancy – although not necessarily by single mothers by choice – followed up children from early childhood (Golombok, Tasker, and Murray, 1997) through early adolescence (MacCallum and Golombok, 2004) to early adulthood (Golombok and Badger, 2010). Although the focus of the study was on comparisons between lesbian mother families and the other family types, the families headed by single heterosexual mothers were found to be functioning well. The majority of young adults who grew up with single heterosexual mothers said they did not miss having a father, with comments such as: "I am very happy in my life and my mum's been 2, 3, 4 parents to me, she's been everything"; "I still got all the love I needed really, still always had enough support"; and "I am just happy, I don't feel like I missed out. I don't feel like I need anything from him." However, reflecting on their childhood, some did recollect times when they missed having a father: "There are vague memories of school on Father's day ... when you are really young it's kind of like 'well why don't I have that'"; "I've never done father–son things that other people have done"; and "I think there is a lot I haven't learned just from not having a dad around, I missed out on the relationship between a son and a father."

A crucial question regarding children born to single mothers by donor insemination is how they will feel about not knowing the identity of their biological father. How best to respond to children's questions about their father is a major concern of single mothers by choice (Jadva, Badger, Morrissette, et al., 2009; Mattes, 1997). In a study of single mothers by choice with children aged between 4 and 8 years, the mothers reported that their children had begun to ask about their father from the age of about 2 to 3 years (Zadeh, Freeman, Smith, et al., unpublished data). One mother said:

> When he was about two and a half, and he was just saying to me ... she's got a daddy... she's got a daddy, and she's got a daddy and I haven't, and I just said that's right, and he said why? So that was probably the first time that we had any sort of discussion.

Another mother recalled the first time her son asked about his father:

> He was about three, and we were coming home from swimming and this little voice in the back of the car said "Mummy, why don't I have a daddy?" ... And so I said, "You don't have a daddy," and I reiterated all the people he does have and stuck with that, and then he asked "What's for lunch?"

For other mothers, conversations with their children focused on the sperm donor, rather than the absence of a father:

I said to my friend, what am I gonna say, what are the words that I'm gonna use, and she said, "your dad's a donor." ... and she [child] used to think I was saying donut, I think, at the beginning, and we used to laugh whether it was a chocolate one or a jam one. And I said no, don-or, don-or, and we'd explain about a kidney donor or a blood donor, well this was a, a seed donor.

For another mother:

The conversation was along the lines of why can't he know the sperm donor that we used, and I sort of had to explain that he was anonymous ... I was explaining that we know that the sperm donor is a very kind man, and his comeback was how do you know? You've never met him, which I thought was very sensible. And he also said if he was so kind and nice, why can't you just marry him?

Some mothers felt that their child was upset by not having a father (Blake, Zadeh, Statham, et al., 2014). As one mother said, "She does ask for a daddy ... it is a hole. But it's not a constant thing. She only tends to mention it when she's spent some quality time with someone else's daddy." Another mother said:

She has been upset that she hasn't got a daddy. That started when she was in nursery. They often have circle time and they'll talk about, you know, daddy or what my daddy is and I think she probably just felt a bit left out that she couldn't say "my daddy does this" or "my daddy does that," and so she would make up things that her daddy did.

However, other mothers reported that their children were quite matter-of-fact about it:

I didn't really know what effect the story was having on him until a little girl his age said to him, "Where's your dad?" And I wasn't sure what he would respond, and he turned around and said, "I don't have one." And I was looking at him, and he said it really blasé, really matter of fact, and he wasn't bothered in the slightest, and I think that, at that moment then I thought, well that's good, because it's not something that he feels he needs to feel sad about. He was so matter of fact about it.

One mother described her daughter announcing in public that she was donor-conceived:

We were on the London underground. This drunkard man came up to us. We were taking photographs, me and my mum, at the time. And he was really drunk, he sort of came over and he said don't you ever fall out, don't you ever lose touch with your father. He obviously had children problems. And she went, "My dad's a donor," like that, and the whole carriage heard, and swung round and me and my mum just chuckled to each other. It was brilliant.

Another mother reported a similar experience with her son:

It's really funny actually because we went to a local park with typical east London ladies who started chatting with [child], and one said I bet your daddy really dotes on you, and [child] turns to her and goes, no, I've got a donor daddy, and the face, I mean I just wish I had a picture, she just looked and asked what, what did he just say? And I said he has a donor daddy. She goes oh, one of those! But we're really friendly with her now, she says hi and everything but it obviously kind of threw her rather.

Single mothers have been found to be more likely than heterosexual couples to be open with their children about their use of donor insemination (Murray and Golombok, 2005a, b). This is not surprising, as single mothers must explain the absence of a father to their children. They are also more likely to tell their children about their donor conception at an earlier age. In the study discussed in Chapter 4 of 165 adolescents and adults who were searching for their donor and donor siblings through the Donor Sibling Registry, a website designed to help donor-conceived people find their donor and donor siblings, 87 percent of participants from single-mother families had been told about their donor conception by the age of 7 years, compared with only 25 percent of those from two-parent heterosexual families. Moreover, all of those who had not found out about their donor conception until adulthood were from families headed by heterosexual couples (Freeman, Jadva, Kramer, et al., 2009). In a later study of 741 donor-conceived adolescents and adults who were members of the Donor Sibling Registry, disclosure was again found to have occurred earlier in single-parent than in two-parent heterosexual families, with 75 percent of respondents from the former stating that they had always known they had been donor-conceived, compared with only 24 percent from the latter (Beeson, Jennings, and Kramer, 2011).

The extent to which children of single mothers by choice feel the need to know the identity of, have information about or even form a relationship with their donor as they grow older is unknown, as no studies of representative samples have been carried out. However, donor-conceived adolescents and adults with single mothers appear to be more likely than those with two heterosexual parents to seek out their donor and donor siblings. A study of 29 adolescents aged 12 to 17 years with identity-release donors found those from single-mother families to be more likely than their counterparts from two-parent families to plan to request the identity of their donor at the age of 18 (Scheib, Riordan, and Rubin, 2005). This suggests that finding out about donor relations is more important to adolescents from single-mother families than it is for adolescents from two-parent families. Furthermore, the study reported above of adolescents and adults who were searching for their donor relations through the Donor Sibling Registry found differences in the reasons donor-conceived persons gave for searching between those from single-parent and those from two-parent homes; those from single-mother families were more likely to give the wish to find new family members as their main reason for searching (Jadva, Freeman, Kramer, et al., 2010). Similar findings have been reported from data obtained from their parents. Scheib and Ruby (2008) found that single mothers were the most interested in contacting other families with children who had been conceived with the same identity-release donor, and wished to do so to create a sense of family for their child. Furthermore, in the study of 791 parents who were members of the Donor Sibling Registry discussed in Chapter 4 (Freeman, Jadva, Kramer, et al., 2009), single mothers formed the largest group of parents in the sample and were the most likely to state that they wished to search for donor relations in order to enhance their child's sense of identity. However, like those with two parents, the majority of donor-conceived adolescents and adults who had been born to single mothers by choice searched for their donor because they were curious, and not because they wanted a father-like relationship with him (Beeson, Jennings, and Kramer, 2011; Jadva, Freeman, Kramer, et al., 2010; Mahlstedt, LaBounty, and Kennedy, 2010).

SINGLE FATHERS

In addition to single mothers, single fathers are also on the rise. In 2013, a ninefold increase in single fathers since 1960 was reported in the USA, with almost one-quarter of single parent households headed by single fathers, rather than single mothers (Pew Research Center, 2013). Although the study defined single fathers as single men living with their own children – and included those living with a partner – more than half of the single fathers identified lived alone with their children. Single-father families are most likely to be formed following parental separation or divorce, or, less commonly, following the death of the mother (Weinraub, Horvath, and Gringlas, et al., 2002). Although it is unusual for a father to be awarded sole custody of his children following divorce, this is becoming more widespread – often because the mother is unable to care for the children herself. There are also small but growing numbers of unmarried single-father families.

Little research has been conducted on the quality of parenting shown by single fathers or the consequences of single fatherhood for children's psychological adjustment. As Biblarz and Stacey (2010) pointed out in their review of existing studies, comparisons between single-father and single-mother families have been confounded by the very different processes that select men and women into single parenthood. Studies have shown that single-father households are more likely to have been recently formed through children switching custody arrangements owing to difficulties in their relationships with their mother or their mother's new partner. Moreover, children in this situation are more likely to be boys, to be older and to have behavioral problems. The few existing studies of single fathers have shown that most are committed and competent parents. However, where differences have been identified, single mothers have tended to show more positive parenting than have single fathers, in terms of closeness, involvement, communication, supervision and control, and their children have shown more positive outcomes in terms of behavior and achievement (Biblarz and Stacey, 2010). The different pathways to single parenthood for men and for women are likely to have influenced these findings, but the extent to which they have done so is currently unclear.

The new phenomenon of "single fathers by choice" was first reported in 2012. Like their female counterparts, single fathers by choice are men, both heterosexual and gay, who actively choose to parent alone. The most common route for them to achieve this is adoption. Although inconceivable just a few years ago, single men are also beginning to have children through surrogacy and egg donation. An article in *Men's Health* magazine entitled "You don't need a woman to have a child" told the story of single men who had enlisted egg donors and surrogate mothers in order to become fathers. As yet there is no research on single fathers by choice, so it is not known to what extent they differ from single mothers by choice in terms of their motivations and experiences.

CONCLUSIONS

Although children in single-mother families formed by divorce are more likely to show lower levels of psychological well-being and lower levels of academic achievement than their counterparts in two-parent families, their difficulties appear to be largely associated with aspects of the divorce, rather than single-parenthood per se. Several factors appear to be involved, including parental conflict before, during, and sometimes after the divorce, financial hardship, maternal depression and poor parenting, all of which may interact with and exacerbate each other. Although some children are adversely affected by divorce, most recover over time, especially where divorce improves family relationships. Similar processes appear to be at play in families headed by unmarried single mothers. The higher levels of behavioral and emotional problems, and lower levels of cognitive development, of children raised by unmarried single mothers appear to be largely associated with socioeconomic disadvantage, mothers' mental health problems and parenting difficulties, with each adversely influencing the other. Studies of single mothers by choice provide an opportunity to examine the impact of single-motherhood on children in the absence of these risk factors, and will be informative in the future in addressing the question of whether being raised by single mothers, in itself, has negative consequences for children. A potential risk factor for these children is not knowing the identity of their fathers. Little research has been conducted on children in single-father families and nothing is yet known about the children of single fathers by choice.

7   Gay father families

Research on the psychological development and well-being of children raised by same-sex parents has focused almost entirely on families headed by lesbian mothers, rather than gay fathers. As discussed in Chapter 2, children with lesbian mothers do not differ from children in traditional families with respect to psychological adjustment or sex-typed behavior. However, children with gay fathers are different from children with lesbian mothers in that they are raised by men, rather than women. As it is widely believed that mothers are better suited to parenting than are fathers, the findings from studies of lesbian mother families cannot necessarily be extrapolated to families headed by gay men. This chapter will explore whether children who grow up with gay fathers may be expected to differ from children with lesbian mothers, and will examine the findings of the small but growing number of studies that have investigated parenting and child development in gay father families.

Although gay men are often assumed to be uninterested in, or actively opposed to, becoming parents, an increasing number of gay men are raising children, and many young gay men now expect to raise children when they are older (D'Augelli, Rendina, and Sinclair, 2008). Using data from the Gallup Daily Tracking Study in 2012, it was estimated that 20 percent of gay men aged 50 or younger who were living alone or with a spouse or partner were raising children under 18 years old, and estimates from the American Community Survey showed that 10 percent of gay couples were raising children under the age of 18 (Gates, 2013).

Is it the case that mothers make better parents than do fathers? Research on fathering has shown that heterosexual fathers influence their children in similar ways to mothers (Lamb, 2010, 2013; Pleck, 2010). In terms of attachment, for example, an analysis of 14 different investigations of infants' attachment to their mothers and fathers, involving almost 1,000 families, found the proportion of children who were classified as securely attached to their father almost identical to the proportion classified as securely attached to their mother (van IJzendoorn and De Wolff, 1997). It also appears that the more fathers are involved with their infants, the more likely the infants are to form secure attachments to them. This was demonstrated in an early study by Cox, Owen, Henderson and Margand (1992), who investigated fathers' relationships with their babies – first when they were aged 3 months and again at the age of 1 year. The fathers who took delight in their 3-month-old infants and who were affectionate and encouraging to them were most likely to later have securely attached 1-year-olds. Since that time, many studies have shown that fathers and mothers influence children in similar ways, and that the aspects of parenting that matter most for children's psychological well-being, such as warmth, responsiveness and sensitivity, are the same for fathers as they are for mothers (Lamb, 2010, 2013; Lamb and Lewis, 2011; Pleck, 2010). From a detailed analysis of the research literature on fathering, Pleck (2010) established that it is the quality of fathers' relationships with their children – rather than their male gender or their masculine behavior – that is important. It was also concluded that the influence of fathering on children is equivalent to, and interchangeable with, that of mothers (Pleck, 2010). As Lamb (2012) put it, most parenting skills are learned "on the job," and when men spend more time on the job, they become as skillful as mothers. Although fathers interact differently with their children in some ways, particularly in terms of more boisterous play, there is no evidence that this has an adverse effect on children's psychological adjustment (Lamb, 2012).

Might it be expected that gay fathers can provide as positive a parenting environment for children as families with mothers present? If there is nothing unique about mothering, then gay fathers who show warm, sensitive and responsive parenting should promote positive child development. However, mothers are still generally believed to be more nurturing than are fathers (Biblarz and Stacey, 2010). Moreover, the wider social environment can have a marked impact on children's psychological well-being, and children with gay fathers may be exposed to greater prejudice and discrimination than are children with lesbian mothers, because gay father families possess the additional non-traditional feature of being headed by men (Golombok and Tasker, 2010). Regarding children's gender development, it has been suggested that children with gay fathers may differ from children with lesbian mothers or heterosexual parents owing to the presence of two male parents and the absence of a female parent from the home. Goldberg, Kashy and Smith (2012) postulated that children with gay fathers may show less sex-typed behavior than do children with heterosexual parents as a result of coming from a less sex-typed family environment, and girls in gay father families may show less sex-typed behavior than do girls in lesbian mother families, due to the absence of a female role model.

ROUTES TO PARENTHOOD

Gay men may become fathers through several routes. Although a large number of gay men are fathers as a result of having had children through heterosexual relationships, it is only in recent years that children have grown up in gay father families. A small proportion of previously married gay fathers are raising their children following divorce. However, by far the largest proportion of gay father families have been formed through adoption (Gates, 2013). In addition, some gay men co-parent with lesbian or heterosexual women. In these co-parenting arrangements, the child is usually raised in separate households, with varying degrees of involvement by gay fathers – ranging from occasional visits to shared parenting, with the child spending equal amounts of time in each family home. Finally, an increasing number of gay men are having children through surrogacy. The Ethics Committee of the American Society for Reproductive Medicine (2006) stated that requests for assisted reproduction should be treated without regard for sexual orientation, and, in the UK, gay couples who become fathers through surrogacy may become the joint legal parents of their child. Gay fathers usually opt for gestational, rather than genetic surrogacy, which involves both an egg donor and a surrogate mother.

A number of studies have examined what motivates gay men to bring up children, how gay men choose from among the various routes to parenthood and what factors influence their decisions. Goldberg, Downing and Moyer (2012) set out to examine motivations for parenthood in a qualitative study of 35 gay couples in the USA who had begun the process of adopting their first child. Many of their reasons for wanting to have children were identical to those of heterosexual couples: their valuing of family relationships, their enjoyment of children and their feeling that raising children is a natural part of life.

As part of a study of parenting and child development in adoptive gay father families in the UK (see below for further details), fathers were asked about their reasons for wanting to become parents and why they had opted for adoption in preference to surrogacy or co-parenting (Jennings, Mellish, Casey, et al., 2014; Mellish, Jennings, Tasker, et al., 2013). Many had thought that it would never be possible for them to become parents, in spite of their strong desire to do so. As one father said, "I always presumed I'd be a dad, and one of the hardest things to come to terms with about being gay, was the assumption that I wouldn't have children." Unlike heterosexual adoptive parents, who often experienced years of unsuccessful infertility treatment before turning to adoption, adoption was often the first choice for gay men who wished to become parents. Some favored adoption for moral reasons: "Once we'd talked about being parents this was the only thing we were really interested in because we didn't want to create another child ... with children needing adoption that was the only thing ... that was the only option that we seriously considered really, we didn't want to do anything else." Another parent remarked, "Paying for a child just seems wrong, to be honest." Others had weighed up the advantages and disadvantages of adoption versus surrogacy and co-parenting and had decided upon adoption to avoid the potential complication of the involvement of other people in their children's lives:

> We've come with a no for everything else, because surrogacy doesn't work for two men, in my opinion, because whoever the birth mother is, you can't just exclude them and then expect a child as they grow up to understand why that person has been excluded, it just doesn't work, so then you're involving that person and what level do you involve that person in? If we want to be the parents, then we want to be the parents, you know.

Co-parenting was considered a particularly unattractive option by some fathers, who gave examples of co-parenting arrangements that had broken down as circumstances changed or when the parents disagreed on how to parent. It was important to the adoptive gay fathers to have autonomy, as parents. Although some remained in contact with the child's birth family, this was viewed as less threatening than the involvement of surrogate mothers or co-parents. A further reason given by gay fathers for choosing adoption was that neither parent would be the genetic father. In this way, they could avoid an imbalance between the biological and non-biological father in the nature of their relationships with their child and the possible problems that this could bring: "We wanted it to be equal ... I think in an argument you could potentially bring it up and some things you can't take back." Moreover, adoption is free of charge in the UK. This motivated some fathers to choose adoption in preference to international surrogacy, which was unaffordable for some.

Although gay men who become parents through adoption tend not to place great importance on biological links to their children, for other gay men, biological links to their children are considered essential. In a study of gay co-parents in Belgium, the wish for a genetically related child was the primary reason for parents to choose co-parenting as a route to fatherhood (Herbrand, 2008). These fathers wanted their children to be raised by both biological parents, albeit in different households. In cases in which the biological parents had a partner, only the biological mother and father were called "mum" and "dad."

The motivations of gay couples who had chosen surrogacy as a route to fatherhood were studied in Spain (Smietana, 2011). All of the fathers had undergone gestational surrogacy in the USA. Like gay fathers who had opted for adoption, those who had become parents through surrogacy sought to become the only legal and de facto parents of their children. They wished to create what they described as "normal families," in which they could live with their children and raise them together on a daily basis.

In a comparative appraisal of gay men's perceptions of the advantages and disadvantages of the different routes to parenthood available to them (Smietana, Jennings, Herbrand, et al., 2014), it was concluded that biological parenthood was most important to those who opted for co-parenting, less so to those who chose surrogacy and not important to those who adopted. Surrogacy and adoption were considered to have several common advantages; they allowed both fathers to be the legal parents of their children, to be their primary caregivers and to live permanently with them. A further perceived advantage of surrogacy was that it enabled fathers to raise their children from birth. These findings in Europe closely paralleled those of Goldberg's study of gay adoptive couples in the USA (Goldberg, 2012).

ADOPTIVE GAY FATHER FAMILIES

Heterosexual adoptive families

Although the aim of adoption is to improve the lives of children whose birth parents are unable to look after them, adoption is not without its challenges. As discussed in Chapter 4, adopted children are more likely than non-adopted children to experience psychological problems, which can make parenting more difficult for adoptive than for biological parents. Although it has been suggested that the higher levels of psychological difficulties shown by adopted children may simply reflect adopted parents' greater tendency to seek professional help, it has now been established that there is a genuine difference between the rates of psychological disorder shown by adopted children and their non-adopted peers (Brodzinsky, Smith, and Brodzinsky, 1998). This holds true not only in terms of the higher proportion of adopted children who are referred for psychiatric treatment relative to non-adopted children, but also in community studies, in which the rates of psychological disorder among adopted and non-adopted children in the general population are compared, irrespective of whether or not their parents have sought professional help (Palacios and Brodzinsky, 2010). The psychological problems shown by adopted children are primarily behavioral, rather than emotional, in nature (Brodzinsky, Smith, and Brodzinsky, 1998), and include conduct problems such as hyperactivity, impulsivity, oppositional behavior and substance abuse, rather than anxiety or depression. Adopted children are also more likely than their non-adopted peers to show learning problems at school (Brodzinsky, Smith, and Brodzinsky, 1998). However, not all adopted children experience psychological problems. As discussed in Chapter 4, in a meta-analysis of studies that compared the psychological adjustment and self-esteem of adopted and non-adopted children, Juffer and van IJzendoorn (2005, 2007), found no differences in self-esteem between the two groups of children. They also found the overall difference in adjustment problems between adopted and non-adopted children to be quite small, with the higher overall levels of adjustment problems shown by adopted children reflecting severe difficulties in a small proportion of adopted children rather than greater difficulties in the majority. It was concluded that the psychological adjustment of most adopted children fell within the normal range. It is interesting to note that children adopted from other countries showed fewer adjustment problems than did those adopted domestically. This was attributed to their lower likelihood of maltreatment in their early years.

Why is it that adopted children are at risk for psychological problems? A number of factors associated with their pre-adoption experiences appear to be involved (Dozier and Rutter, 2008; Palacios and Brodzinsky, 2010). Even before birth, adopted children are often exposed to less favorable circumstances than are non-adopted children. Their birth mothers are more likely to abuse alcohol or drugs, live in poverty and experience high levels of stress, all of which may affect the developing fetus and result in poorer cognitive and behavioral outcomes for children. Adopted children are also more likely to have experienced physical or sexual abuse or neglect in their early years. Whereas maltreatment, in itself, can be severely damaging to psychological well-being, a further consequence is that these children may be placed in foster care and may be moved from one foster home to another. Although foster care can be advantageous – in that it removes children from a harmful family environment – the benefits depend not only on the quality of foster care that children receive, but also on the number of foster homes that they live in (Dozier, Zeanah, and Bernard, 2013). The greater the number of foster care placements that children experience, the less opportunity they have to form secure attachment relationships and the greater their risk of psychological disorder.

As many children enter their adoptive families with a history of traumatic early experiences, it is important to understand the factors that contribute to positive and negative outcomes for children in their new adoptive homes. Research on children who have spent their early years in institutions has not only demonstrated the advantages of adoption in terms of cognitive, emotional and social development, but has also shed light on the legacy of their adverse early life experiences (Bakermans-Kranenburg, McCreery, Dobrova-Krol, et al., 2012). A study of children who lived in severely deprived Romanian orphanages at the time of the Ceauşescu dictatorship and who were later adopted into families in the UK underlines the benefits of adoption for children who have experienced extreme adversity in their first years of life (Rutter, Beckett, Castle, et al., 2007). These children showed remarkable catch-up in physical, cognitive, language, socio-emotional and behavioral development. However, some continued to show significant psychological problems as they grew up, including autistic-like behavior, indiscriminate friendliness with strangers, hyperactivity and impaired cognitive development. Similar findings were reported from a study of children from Romanian orphanages adopted by Canadian parents (Chisholm, 1998; Morison, Ames, and Chisholm, 1995). It was concluded from these studies that adoption is immensely beneficial for children who have experienced early adversity, but that lasting psychological difficulties may remain.

In addition to the demands of raising children with psychological problems, adoptive parents are confronted by tasks that biological parents do not have to tackle (Brodzinsky, 2011). Although adoption used to be conducted in secrecy, it is now well-established that secrecy about children's adoption and lack of information about their birth family is associated with identity and mental health problems in adopted children (Brodzinsky, 1987, 2006; Treseliotis, 1973, 1984, 2000). Thus, adoptive parents are now encouraged to begin to talk to their children about their adoption from an early age. As first described by Kirk (1964), adoptive parents must acknowledge the difference between adoptive parenthood and biological parenthood in order to communicate openly with their children about their adoption and promote positive family relationships. It was later advised that adoptive parents should neither overemphasize nor under-emphasize these differences, but instead should acknowledge them and create a family environment that supports their children's curiosity about their origins and maintains open communication about adoption issues (Brodzinsky, 2011; Brodzinsky and Pinderhughes, 2002). Adoptive parents face further challenges when their children reach adolescence. Greater conflict has been found between adoptive parents and adopted adolescents than between non-adoptive parents and non-adopted adolescents (Rueter, Keyes, Iacono, et al., 2009). Moreover, poor communication about adoption has been associated with more negative relationships between parents and adopted adolescents (Brodzinsky and Pinderhughes, 2002; Passmore, Foulstone, and Feeney, 2007; Rueter and Koerner, 2008).

A further issue that adoptive parents may have to consider is whether or not to maintain contact with their children's birth parents – an arrangement often referred to as "open adoption" – and the nature and extent of such contact. This may range from an exchange of letters once per year to frequent face-to-face contact. In a longitudinal study of the consequences of different types and levels of contact, parents and children in adoptive families who had contact with the children's birth family were found to be more satisfied than were those who did not. Moreover, satisfaction with contact arrangements – rather than whether or not contact took place – was found to be predictive of fewer behavioral problems in adopted adolescents (Grotevant, McRoy, Wrobel, et al., 2013; Grotevant, Rueter, Von Korff, et al., 2011), although what constituted satisfactory contact changed over time (Grotevant, 2009). In this study, the children's birth mothers had voluntarily put them up for adoption as infants. Children removed from their birth family because of maltreatment may have different experiences (Grotevant, McRoy, Wrobel, et al., 2013). A distinction has been made between "open adoption," whereby there is an exchange of information or contact between the adoptive and the birth family, and openness of communication about adoption within the adoptive family, irrespective of contact. Brodzinsky (2006) found open communication to be more predictive of adopted children's psychological well-being than whether or not the adoption was open. In line with this finding, Von Korff and Grotevant (2011) showed that contact is associated with more frequent adoption-related family conversations, which in turn is associated with adoptive identity development.

A key question regarding adoption is whether adopted children are less likely to form secure attachment relationships with their adoptive parents than are non-adopted children with their biological parents. It has been suggested that experiences of institutional care or maltreatment in birth families will decrease the likelihood of children forming secure attachment relationships with their adoptive parents. In order to examine this issue, a meta-analysis of observational studies of attachment security was conducted by van den Dries, Juffer, van IJzendoorn and Bakermans-Kranenburg (2009). Children who had been adopted before the age of 1 year were found to be just as likely to be securely attached as were their non-adopted peers, whereas those adopted after their first birthday were more likely to show insecure attachment relationships. Two possible explanations for these findings were proposed. First of all, children who were placed with their adoptive parents before the age of 1 year may have experienced deprivation for a shorter period of time. Secondly, it may have been easier for younger children to form secure attachments with their adoptive parents because they received sensitive parenting in infancy, when attachments were still being formed. Irrespective of their age at the time of adoption, the adopted children showed higher rates of disorganized attachment, which was attributed to harmful experiences before the adoption took place.

Researchers have also examined the parenting processes that promote well-being in adopted children. The Leiden Longitudinal Adoption Study, which investigated the development of children who had been adopted from abroad within the first 6 months of life, provided an opportunity for examining the influence of adoptive parenting on the adjustment of children who had not experienced severe early adversity (Juffer and van IJzendoorn, 2009). It was found that higher levels of maternal sensitivity in infancy and middle childhood were directly associated with more positive socio-emotional development in middle childhood (Stams, Juffer, and van IJzendoorn, 2002), and indirectly associated with more positive socio-emotional development in adolescence (Jaffari-Bimmel, Juffer, van IJzendoorn, et al., 2006). Maternal sensitivity was also associated with attachment security in adolescence (Beijersbergen, Juffer, and Bakermans-Kranenburg, et al., 2012) and early adulthood (Schoenmaker, Juffer, van IJzendoorn, et al., 2014). Furthermore, adoptive mothers' representations of their attachment relationships with their own parents appear to influence the security of attachment of their adopted children. In a study of adopted children who had experienced maltreatment in their early years, it was found that adoptive mothers' mental states regarding attachment, as assessed using the Adult Attachment Interview, influenced the attachment security of their adopted children, as assessed using a story-completion task designed to elucidate children's expectations of the relationship between parents and children (Steele, Hodges, Kaniuk, et al., 2003). Specifically, children whose adoptive mothers were classified as secure by the Adult Attachment Interview were more likely to show representations of security on the story-completion task 3 months after placement. Thus, there is growing evidence that the nature of parenting in adoptive families plays a part in the well-being of adopted children.

From the perspective of adopted children, a key task is to develop an understanding of their adoption. Although children acquire a rudimentary knowledge of adoption in their preschool years, as mentioned previously, it is not until they reach the age of around 7 years that they show awareness of biological inheritance (Gregg, Solomon, Johnson, et al., 1996; Richards, 2000; Williams and Smith, 2010) and the meaning and implications of the absence of a biological connection to their adoptive parents (Brodzinsky, 2011; Brodzinsky and Pinderhughes, 2002; Brodzinsky, Schechter, and Brodzinsky, 1986; Brodzinsky, Singer, and Braff, 1984). A primary task for all adolescents is to develop a sense of identity; that is, to answer the question "Who am I?" As highlighted by Grotevant and Von Korff (2011), adopted adolescents are faced with the additional questions of "Who am I as an adopted person?", "What does being adopted mean to me?" and "How does this fit into my understanding of my self, relationships, family and culture?". For adopted adolescents, integrating the experience of being adopted into a life story is important for the development of a secure sense of identity (Brodzinsky, 2011; Dunbar and Grotevant, 2004; Grotevant, 1997, 1999; Grotevant, Dunbar, Kohler, et al., 2000; Grotevant and Von Korff, 2011). As part of this process, they may search for information about their birth family and try to contact them. The development of a coherent adoptive identity is considered an influential factor in the psychological well-being of adopted adolescents, with problems in adoptive identity development often resulting from a lack of information about themselves and their origins. However, there is much variation in the extent to which being adopted is central to an adolescent's identity (Grotevant and Von Korff, 2011). Thus, searching for birth relatives may be important to some but viewed as irrelevant by others. Adolescents who are highly preoccupied with their adoption have been found to report greater alienation from their adoptive parents (Kohler, Grotevant, and McRoy, 2002), although the direction of effects is unclear.

Although there is strong evidence that adoption benefits children whose birth parents are unable to raise them – and many children are in need of adoptive families – there has been considerable objection to the idea of gay men becoming adoptive parents. It has been argued that this would add a further layer of complexity to an already risky situation. Adoption is difficult – why make it even more so? But, is it the case that children adopted by gay fathers experience greater problems than do children adopted by lesbian mothers or heterosexual parents? Are gay fathers less competent parents? Although research on gay father families is still very new, empirical studies of parenting and child development in gay father families have begun to address these questions.

Studies of adoptive gay father families

Studies of the functioning of adoptive gay father families began to appear in 2005. A series of papers was based on a group of gay and lesbian parents with adopted children of early school age (Erich, Leung, and Kindle, 2005; Erich, Leung, Kindle, et al., 2005; Leung, Erich, and Kanenberg, 2005) and a group of gay and lesbian parents with adopted adolescents (Erich, Hall, Kanenberg, and Case, 2009; Erich, Kanenberg, Case, et al., 2008). These papers described positive family functioning and well-adjusted children in lesbian and gay families. A survey of adoptive gay and lesbian parents similarly reported high levels of social support and appropriate parenting skills (Ryan, 2007; Ryan and Cash, 2004). A further survey used the Child Behavior Checklist (Achenbach and Rescorla, 2000) to compare the emotional and behavioral problems of large samples of both preschool and school age children with either gay, lesbian or heterosexual adoptive parents, and found that children's psychological problems were not contingent on parental sexual orientation (Averett, Nalavany, and Ryan, 2009). While providing the first insights into the functioning of gay and lesbian adoptive families, the parents in these studies were volunteers recruited through gay and lesbian support groups and internet sites, the children spanned a wide age range, data were obtained by self-report questionnaires only and the findings were not presented separately for gay father and lesbian mother families. Thus, the conclusions that can be drawn from these studies are limited.

The first controlled study of parenting and child development in a systematic sample of gay father families was carried out in the USA (Farr, Forssell, and Patterson, 2010a, b). Twenty-nine families headed by gay couples, 27 families headed by lesbian couples and

50 families headed by heterosexual couples were recruited from five private domestic adoption agencies situated in different geographical locations where adoption by same-sex parents was legally recognized. The different family types were similar in terms of demographic characteristics, although the gay fathers were more likely to have adopted sons whereas the lesbian mothers were more likely to have adopted daughters, and the gay and lesbian parents were more likely than the heterosexual parents to have adopted a child transracially. The children were aged between 1 and 6 years, with an average age of 3 years. All had been adopted at birth or in the first few weeks of their life, and none had experienced prior placements. Parents completed questionnaire measures of relationship satisfaction, stress associated with parenting and the effectiveness of their disciplinary techniques, and no differences were found between family types for any of these measures. Child adjustment was assessed using the Child Behavior Checklist (Achenbach and Rescorla, 2000), as administered to parents, as well as the companion Caregiver-Teacher Report Form. No differences were found in children's behavioral or emotional problems between the gay father families and the other family types, whether assessed by the parents or the children's caregivers or teachers.

Although the gay father families did not differ from the lesbian mother or heterosexual parent families in family functioning or child adjustment, parents who reported greater happiness with their partners, less parenting stress and the use of more effective disciplinary techniques had children with higher levels of adjustment, regardless of parents' sexual orientation. An internet survey of 230 adoptive gay fathers by the same research team examined the factors associated with raised levels of parenting stress among gay men (Tornello, Farr, and Patterson, 2011). In line with the findings of research on heterosexual adoptive parents, gay adoptive fathers with less social support, older children and children who had been adopted at older ages reported more parenting stress. An additional stressor for gay fathers was a less positive identity as a gay man, with fathers who were more sensitive to stigmatization reporting greater parenting stress.

A study of adoptive gay father families was also carried out in the UK, where gay and lesbian couples can become the joint legal parents of their adopted children (Golombok, Mellish, Jennings, et al., 2014). Unlike the USA, where inter-country adoption and transracial adoption are common, more than 95 percent of the children adopted in the UK are adopted from social care, and transracial adoption is discouraged. Forty-one two-parent gay adoptive families, 40 two-parent lesbian adoptive families and 49 two-parent heterosexual adoptive families participated in the study. The families were recruited through adoption agencies that placed children with same-sex parents. The children were aged between 3 and 9 years, and all had been placed with their adoptive families for at least 1 year. As in the study by Farr, Forssell and Patterson (2010a), there was a preponderance of boys adopted by gay fathers and a preponderance of girls adopted by lesbian mothers. A further difference between family types was that the children adopted by gay fathers were older at the time of adoption and had been placed with them for a shorter period of time. Reflecting the difficult backgrounds of the children in the study, around one-third of their birth mothers had experienced mental health problems, more than one-third had been exposed to domestic violence and more than one-third had abused alcohol. In addition, more than one-third of the birth fathers had been convicted of criminal behavior. Regarding the children, two-thirds had experienced neglect, more than one-third had experienced emotional abuse and more than 15 percent had experienced physical abuse. There were no significant differences between family types in the proportion of children who had experienced each of these adversities.

Each parent completed questionnaire measures of anxiety, depression and stress associated with parenting. They also participated in a standardized interview assessment of parenting quality that produced variables relating to warmth, sensitive responding, enjoyment of play, amount of interaction, quality of interaction, frequency of conflict, level of conflict, disciplinary indulgence and disciplinary aggression. Children's adjustment was assessed using the

Strengths and Difficulties Questionnaire (Goodman, 1994, 1997, 2001), which was administered to parents and teachers. In addition, each parent and the child took part in an observational assessment of parent–child interaction. Where differences were identified between the gay father families and the lesbian mother or heterosexual parent families, these indicated more positive functioning in the gay father families. The gay fathers showed lower levels of depression and stress associated with parenting than did the heterosexual parents. In terms of parenting, gay fathers showed higher levels of warmth, higher levels of interaction and lower levels of disciplinary aggression, as assessed by interview, and higher levels of responsiveness, as assessed by direct observation, than did the heterosexual parents. With respect to child adjustment, conduct problems (as rated by parents) were greater among children in heterosexual than in gay and lesbian families. In all family types, the children showed higher rates of psychological disorder than did non-adopted children, as would be expected with adopted children. Regardless of family type, and in line with the findings of Farr, Forssell and Patterson (2010a), parenting stress was found to predict children's conduct problems, with higher levels of parenting stress associated with higher levels of conduct problems. In addition, disciplinary aggression was marginally predictive of children's conduct problems.

The more positive outcomes for gay father families in terms of parental well-being and parent–child relationships may be associated with the characteristics of the parents or the children. As adoption by gay couples is a relatively new phenomenon in the UK that has attracted much controversy, it seems likely that the screening process is especially stringent for gay couples who wish to adopt; this should result in even higher levels of psychological well-being and commitment to parenting among adoptive gay fathers than among adoptive lesbian or heterosexual parents. It is also conceivable, as a result of concerns regarding adoption by gay men, that children with higher levels of psychological problems would be least likely to be placed with gay couples.

The lower levels of child externalizing problems among children with gay fathers found in the above study suggest that this may be the case. However, the children adopted by gay fathers had been adopted at an older age and placed with the adoptive family for a shorter time, and both of these factors have been associated with greater adjustment problems (Dozier and Rutter, 2008; Palacios and Brodzinsky, 2010). Moreover, from the available data on the children's pre-adoption history, it appears that the children who had been placed with gay fathers were no less likely to have experienced serious adversity such as neglect or emotional or physical abuse, than had children placed with lesbian mothers or heterosexual parents. Neither were their birth mothers less likely to have experienced mental health problems, domestic violence or alcohol abuse, or their fathers less likely to have been convicted of criminal behavior. Although research in the USA provides some indication that the most difficult children tend to be placed with same-sex parents (Brodzinsky and Evan B. Donaldson Adoption Institute, 2011; Brooks and Goldberg, 2001; Matthews and Cramer, 2006), this does not currently appear to be the case in the UK – perhaps because almost all adoptions involve children who have experienced adversity in their early years. It appears, therefore, that, rather than adopting less difficult children, gay fathers provide a highly positive parenting environment for their adopted children.

A study that took a different perspective compared the brain activity of heterosexual mothers, heterosexual fathers and adoptive gay fathers, all of whom had young babies (Abraham, Hendler, Shapira-Lichter, et al., 2014). The parents' brain activity while watching a video of themselves interacting with their baby was measured by an MRI scan. Whereas the heterosexual mothers showed heightened activity in areas of the brain associated with emotion processing and the heterosexual fathers had increased activity in areas associated with cognitive processing, the gay fathers showed increased activity in both of these regions. These findings add to the emerging body of research on the psychobiology of fatherhood (Ehlert, 2014) and suggest that gay fathers who are primary caregivers may respond similarly to both heterosexual mothers and fathers.

As with lesbian mother families, a question that is frequently asked in relation to gay father families is whether the children will show less sex-typed behavior than their peers with heterosexual parents. In order to examine this question, children's sex-typed behavior has been measured using the Preschool Activities Inventory, which is completed by parents (Golombok and Rust, 1993a, b). This questionnaire is designed to assess gender role behavior within, as well as between, sexes; that is, to differentiate between boys who show high levels of typically masculine behavior from those who do not, and between girls who show high levels of typically feminine behavior from those who do not. Goldberg, Kashy and Smith (2012) studied a subsample of adoptive families with children aged between 2 and 4 years, all of whom had lived with their adoptive parents for at least 2 years. Thirty-four gay father families, 44 lesbian mother families and 48 heterosexual parent families took part. The girls in the gay father families were found to be no less feminine, and the boys no less masculine, than their counterparts in lesbian mother and heterosexual parent families, and both the girls and the boys showed behavior that was typical of their gender. Similarly, in the study by Farr, Forssell and Patterson (2010b), the children of gay fathers were found to show typical gender development, and no differences were identified between the children of gay fathers and the children from the other family types for either boys or girls. The study by Golombok, Mellish, Jennings, et al. (2014) also found typical gender role behavior among the children of gay fathers, with no differences in sex-typed behavior between children with gay fathers and children with lesbian or heterosexual parents, for either boys or girls.

It is often assumed that gay couples are more likely than heterosexual couples to play an equal part in looking after their children, as they are less susceptible to pressure to conform to prescribed gender roles. The extent to which gay couples share parenting, and whether gay fathers share parenting more or less than do lesbian or heterosexual couples, was studied by Farr and Patterson (2013) as part of their study of parenting and child development in adoptive gay father families (described above). Each parent completed questionnaire measures of the division of childcare labour in their family. The gay couples, like the lesbian couples, were more likely to report sharing parenting tasks evenly than were the heterosexual couples, and most parents in all three family types were satisfied with their childcare responsibilities. The parents and children also took part in an observational assessment of family play (Schoppe, Manglesdorf, and Frosch, 2001), which was coded to produce ratings of supportive interactions (including pleasure and cooperativeness) and undermining interactions (including displeasure and competition). Gay couples were rated as the least supportive in the family play task, but were less undermining than were the heterosexual couples. The extent to which the couple shared parenting was unrelated to child adjustment. Instead, children's behavior problems, as assessed by the Child Behavior Checklist (Achenbach and Rescorla, 2000), were associated with dissatisfaction with the division of childcare responsibilities and an undermining style of parental interaction – particularly competition between the parents – irrespective of parental sexual orientation. In the UK study, only one-fifth of the gay and lesbian couples shared childcare evenly, which suggests that they were less egalitarian than were couples in the USA (Mellish, Jennings, Tasker, et al., 2013).

An important issue for children adopted by gay parents is what, when and whom to tell about their family. Unlike children who are adopted by heterosexual parents, they not only have to explain that they were adopted but they also have to explain that they have gay fathers. In the UK study of 3- to 9-year-old children, nearly all of the parents had spoken to their children about their adoption (Mellish, Jennings, Tasker, et al., 2013). The conversations that gay fathers had with their children about adoption were similar to those held by the lesbian and heterosexual adoptive parents:

> We use the word "adoption." We haven't gone into detail about
> what that means. You know, we've said you were inside mummy
> Lorraine's tummy and she loves you very much but she wasn't
> able to look after you, so then you went to Jill who was her foster
> carer, and then you came to live with us. We wanted a little girl
> and we decided we could look after you. So we talk about it in
> those terms. She doesn't fully understand what adoption means,
> but she knows she has a mummy Lorraine and she talks about
> her from time to time.

Most of the gay fathers had also spoken to their children about having two dads, often in the context of the many different kinds of families that exist:

> We just say it's normal. And we give examples of the fact that
> children live in all sorts of families, one of my nieces live with
> our – with her gran. Four of our nieces and nephews are dual
> heritage and they're Muslim and we're not. You know, diversity is
> everywhere, you can't escape it and actually why would you want
> to? Embrace it because it makes family life more rich. And so
> we've always kind of talked on the fact that there's nothing two
> dads can't do that a mum and a dad can do or two mums can do.
> Just it might be done slightly differently.

As another father put it:

> Well we've just explained things, that there are different
> relationships, that some ... some people have mothers and
> fathers, some people have mothers ... have two mothers, and
> some people have two fathers and so on, so we talk about
> different family relationships.

A small minority of fathers said that their children had been
faced with homophobic comments from their peers at school, such
as: "You're different 'cause you've got two dads"; "It's stupid and
nasty to have two dads"; and "I'm going to get my dad to come and

shoot your dad!". Although the majority of their children's friends were accepting, they were often curious and asked questions about the family:

> We go camping quite a lot in the summer, so the kids are in and out of everybody's tent. So you'll quite often get other kids, and usually one of those kids go: "Where's [child]'s mum?" "Well he doesn't actually have one here." "Why not?" "Well she's not around. He's got two dads." And you can see these kind of kids going, "What? I'm sorry, I don't get that," and then, you know sometimes they'll want to know more, because kids are great in that respect. They just come out and tell you as it is, so you just answer them. You know, in honesty. That's always been our thing. Honesty and it's served us well so far. I think if you're honest and upfront, people can't really argue with you. Or they find it very hard to argue with you.

Many of the parents made a point of trying to instill confidence in their children and prepare them for negative remarks from peers:

> Among his circle of friends there is no issue, but you know, we are also conscious of the fact that not everybody in the wider world sees the world exactly in the same way. So I think part of it is making him feel comfortable with it so that if somebody ever threw it back at him in a mean way, hopefully it would be like water off a duck's back and he would say, "Yeah, I'm aware of that, what else have you got to say to me?" You know, that sort of attitude. So giving him a little bit of resilience around both the adoption process and having two dads.

A qualitative study of older children aged 13 to 20 years in the USA explored how adopted adolescents with gay and lesbian parents disclosed information about their family (Gianino, Goldberg, and Lewis, 2009). The young people found it more difficult to say that they had gay or lesbian parents than to say that they had been adopted. Early adolescence was the time when they were most scared and least likely to tell others that their parents were gay or lesbian. They did not want to be seen as different and were anxious about being teased or bullied. By middle and late adolescence, most had disclosed to friends whom they thought would be accepting and whom they felt they could trust. A particular fear was that their peers would assume that they were also gay and would reject them as a result. It was important to the young people to be in control of whom to tell about their gay parents, and when. As found in the UK study discussed above (Mellish, Jennings, Tasker, et al., 2013), parents held conversations with their children to help prepare them for disclosure.

Gay fathers' experiences of the adoption process in the UK varied enormously (Mellish, Jennings, Tasker, et al., 2013). Whereas some had nothing but praise for the adoption agencies, many encountered difficulties that they perceived to be related to their sexual orientation, and a minority received explicitly negative responses from adoption agency staff. For example, one gay father described having the phone slammed down on him when making an initial enquiry. The staff member asked him what his wife's name was, to which he answered, "Matt": "[The adoption agency member said] 'Y'what? Nat?' I'm like, 'No, not Nat, Matt.' I mean, I ended up literally spelling it out, 'M-A-T-T,' and I went, 'It's a bloke,' and beep, phone went down." Similarly, the experiences of gay men who wished to adopt in the USA ranged from extremely negative, whereby adoption agencies refused to consider them, to highly encouraging and supportive (Goldberg, 2012; Hicks, 2006; Matthews and Cramer, 2006). A further barrier was that some states did not allow same-sex couples to adopt children jointly.

SURROGACY

Of all the new family forms discussed in this book, gay father families with children born through surrogacy and egg donation deviate most from the traditional nuclear family. Such families combine several controversial pathways to parenthood. They differ from the traditional family with respect to the sexual orientation of the parents, the gender of the parents and the children's conception through assisted reproduction, involving both surrogacy and egg donation. Children growing up in gay father families formed through surrogacy may have two fathers and two "mothers" – a genetic father, a social father, a genetic mother and a gestational mother – but no mother in the family home. It is surprising that these families have generated relatively little outrage in the popular press. The announcement in 2010 by the world-famous singer Elton John and his partner David Furnish that they had become the parents of a baby boy born through surrogacy was greeted with congratulations rather than condemnation. Whether because of their celebrity status or as a result of more accepting public attitudes toward new family forms in the new millennium, reaction to the birth of baby Zachary, whose conception had involved IVF, an egg donor and a surrogate mother and who would be raised by two fathers (one of whom was genetically unrelated to him) was exceptionally subdued compared to the furor caused by the birth of Louise Brown to a married heterosexual couple whose own gametes had been used in her conception little more than 30 years previously.

Although limited as yet, the research described above on adoptive gay father families shows that children can flourish in this family environment. But what about children in gay father families that have been formed through surrogacy? Adopted children can learn about their birth parents and the reason for their adoption, and may remain in contact with their birth parents as they grow up. The background of children born to gay fathers through surrogacy is somewhat different. How might they feel about their family and the circumstances of their birth? Will they wish to have a relationship with one or both of the women who helped create them? Will they view their surrogate or their egg donor as their mother? How will they relate to each of their two fathers, one of whom is their genetic parent and the other who is not? Although some of these questions have begun to be addressed in heterosexual families created through surrogacy (see Chapter 5), the reactions of children who have a mother and a father may not be the same as that of children who have two fathers.

A question often asked about gay parents who have children through surrogacy is how they decide who will be the biological father. In a study of 37 gay couples who attended a fertility clinic in Canada, three-quarters had used the sperm of both partners to fertilize the donated eggs, and one embryo from each man had been transferred to the surrogate (Grover, Shmorgun, Moskovstev, et al., 2013). Thus, the majority of prospective fathers decided to leave this to chance. In the majority of cases, only one child resulted from the pregnancy; however, when twins were born, they were genetic half-siblings. In contrast, in an investigation of 15 gay couples seeking gestational surrogacy at a clinic in the USA, 80 percent chose one partner to provide the sperm (Greenfeld and Seli, 2011). In six of these couples it was agreed that the older partner should donate, in two couples the man who did not already have children was chosen, two couples selected the partner who had the greater desire for biological parenthood and two opted for the partner with "better genes." The remaining three couples used one embryo created from the sperm of each partner.

In their analysis of how egg donors were chosen, Greenfeld and Seli (2011) found that the most commonly requested characteristics were that the donor be tall, attractive and educated, and physically resemble the non-genetic father. Grover, Shmorgun, Moskovtsev, et al. (2013) examined whether the gay couples in their study preferred a known or an anonymous egg donor. The majority chose an anonymous donor who was open to being contacted by the child after the age of 18.

Although there has been a dramatic rise in the number of gay men having children through surrogacy, the creation of gay father families through assisted reproductive technologies is such a recent phenomenon that, as yet, there has been little research done on children born in this way. In the first study, 40 couples who had become fathers through gestational surrogacy in the USA were interviewed about their experiences of parenthood (Bergman, Rubio, Green, et al., 2010). The fathers were financially wealthy, although many had experienced a drop in income after becoming parents due to giving up work or working fewer hours. Their children ranged in age from 2 months to 8 years. The fathers reported parenting to be a very positive experience. They felt proud to be parents and valued themselves more. One of the most striking findings was that having children had brought them closer to their own, as well as to their partner's, parents, many of whom were excited to become grandparents. Most had lost friendships with their gay friends who were not parents. However, they had built new friendship with other parents, both heterosexual and gay.

Little is known about the quality of parenting in gay father families created through surrogacy or about the development of children who grow up in them. Currently, the first study to investigate the quality of parent–child relationships and the adjustment of children born to gay couples through surrogacy is focusing on families with children aged between 4 and 8 years living in the USA (Golombok, Blake, Slutsky, et al., unpublished data). As was found in relation to adoptive gay fathers, many fathers with children conceived through surrogacy thought that parenthood would never be possible for them because they were gay:

> It has always been something that I thought would never happen to me ... It was always kind of a sadness. You know, I grew up in the generation of gay men [who felt] that marriage and family was not an option. It was just a reality that it wouldn't happen. And like now, all my dreams have come true. It's incredible.

Preliminary findings from the study indicate that the families often maintain a relationship with the surrogate mother and, sometimes, with the egg donor, as well:

> So we chose people who were open to having a possible relationship ... whatever that might be, just you know, really whatever was organic, felt natural, so we keep in touch with the egg donor ... but have more of an interaction with the carrier.

> Like we see her about once a year ... we've gone there, they've
> come here ... We enjoy that.

Although gay surrogacy families seem more likely to stay in touch
with their surrogate than with their egg donor, this is not always
the case:

> He is too young to really get where babies come from. And
> he hasn't even really been curious about it or asked about it.
> We plan to share everything with him and let him know there
> are no secrets at all. But I kind of, although the surrogate is so
> important, I kind of tend to favor more the genetic connection.
> So if anything, I'd be more interested in him having a relationship
> with the egg donor rather than the surrogate.

Gay fathers cannot hide their children's origins and generally speak
openly with them about their conception and their family structure.
As one father said:

> We're gay men, we came out at a certain point and we've learned
> to live our lives with truth and what we've learned about that is,
> if you tell them the truth from the beginning they won't resent
> it and also then they won't ever feel betrayed that somehow you
> didn't tell them the truth. So telling them that empowers them
> because it gives them their story. We didn't want there to be any
> big surprises. It is what it is. Even now, they understand that a
> man and a woman have to be involved and there is no woman
> here. So, for us, it's just who we are. It's what our value system is
> and we tell them the truth. That's important to us.

And as another father described:

> We don't want to have secrets and we just think like if
> something's taboo that it just backfires on parents ... so that
> he has to go in this like soul searching like who am I where
> am I from like my parents lied to me, you know. So we'll

be very proud to tell him and I think it will also show him eventually he'll realize how hard we fought for him. And how difficult it was, how expensive it was, how many people were involved ... how like it happened way before all these laws like, he'll grow up not knowing that there are all these laws against getting married and having kids and so I think if we start that earlier then when he's older he'll be like wow that's really cool and my fathers did that back before it was like normal.

Conversations with their young children about their non-traditional family structure tend to focus on the many different families that exist today. As one father reported:

There was a period when they were really starting to get into the family structure of who has two moms, who has two dads, who has a mom and a dad, who has one mom who has one dad, whose parents are divorced. I mean we went through all those permutations. And that was, I don't know, six or nine months ago and there was a period of intense kind of scrutiny around every family and now it's kind of moved on.

Another father described his son's response:

Now it is just a matter of fact. It is a fact to him. He will have the conversation with kids. He'll say like, "I have two daddies." Or "I have a Daddy and a Papa." And like they'll say, "Where is your mommy?" And he'll say, "I don't have a Mommy. I have a Daddy and a Papa."

Many of the fathers in the study faced set-backs during the surrogacy process, but all persevered and not one regretted their decision. One father captured the sentiments of the others like this:

I think that it is a leap of faith. You really have to trust and it is important to find the right people and everything like that. But it really is a leap of faith and it is one that I thank God for every day. I wish it was more available to people. I'm just, over the moon.

CONCLUSIONS

Findings from the few empirical studies conducted so far show that gay fathers provide a supportive family environment for their children and that their children flourish. Whereas Farr, Forssell and Patterson (2010b) reported no differences in parenting or child adjustment between adoptive gay fathers and either adoptive lesbian mothers or adoptive heterosexual parents, Golombok, Mellish, Jennings, et al. (2014) reported more positive parenting and child adjustment in adoptive gay father families. The discrepancy between the two studies may have resulted from the larger sample or the use of more in-depth measures of the quality of parent–child relationships in the UK study, or the more recent introduction of gay adoption in the UK resulting in particularly stringent screening of prospective adoptive parents. The lack of difference in sex-typed behavior between children with gay fathers and children with heterosexual parents for either boys or girls is consistent with previous research on children with lesbian mothers. In spite of these findings, it is important to stress that little, as yet, is known about the development and well-being of children in adoptive gay father families as they reach adolescence and beyond. Moreover, the available findings come only from studies of adoptive gay father families. Investigations of parenting and child development in gay father families created through surrogacy have only just begun. It is noteworthy that gay fathers are more likely to adopt boys, whereas lesbian mothers are more likely to adopt girls. Whether this results from a tendency for adoption agencies to gender-match children to same-sex parents, or from same-sex parents' preference for a child of the same gender as themselves, is not known. Anecdotal evidence favors the former explanation, as same-sex parents appear not to express a strong preference regarding the gender of their child.

8   Conclusions

So what can be concluded about the development and well-being of children in modern families? Is it the case that traditional two-parent families are best for children? Or can children do as well, or perhaps even better, in new family forms? It is important to remember that traditional families headed by two heterosexual parents vary enormously in the extent to which they provide supportive environments for children. The same is true of new family forms. Undoubtedly, some children who grow up in new families will experience difficulties, just as some children in traditional families will. The aim of this book is not to focus on individual children but, instead, to examine the consequences of new family structures for parenting and child development, more generally, and to establish what is known about the processes involved.

   It is clear that some types of non-traditional family are more associated with negative outcomes for children than are traditional families. Single-parent families formed as a result of parental separation or divorce, single-parent families headed by unmarried mothers, and stepfamilies are more likely than are traditional families to result in difficulties for children. In contrast, children in new family forms – children with lesbian or gay parents, children born to single mothers by choice and children who were conceived through assisted reproductive technologies – appear to function well. How can these differences be explained? The answer seems to lie in the different circumstances of non-traditional families and new family forms. Whereas non-traditional families generally experience greater adversity than do traditional families in terms of financial hardship, marital or relationship difficulties and mental health problems – all of which are associated with impaired parenting and children's psychological problems – this is less likely to be the case for families formed by same-sex parents or through assisted reproductive technologies. Moreover, parents in new family forms often struggle to have children and do so against the odds. Many experience years of infertility and infertility treatment before achieving parenthood; others become parents in the face of significant social disapproval and still others surmount both hurdles in order to have a child. It seems that those who succeed in overcoming these obstacles become particularly committed parents when their much wanted children eventually arrive.

Although children in lesbian, gay, solo mother and assisted reproduction families are indistinguishable from children in traditional families in terms of psychological well-being, there appear to be differences between these family types in the quality of parenting. Contrary to expectations, these differences generally reflect a higher, rather than a lower, quality of parenting in new family forms. The most likely explanation for this unexpected finding lies in these parents' high motivation to have children; couples who are less motivated to have children are more likely to give up along the way. It may also be relevant that the children in these families are, by necessity, planned. Unlike children in traditional families, these children cannot be conceived unintentionally, and there is evidence to show that planned pregnancies are associated with more positive outcomes for all concerned (Carson, Redshaw, Sacker, et al., 2012; Hayatbakhsh, Najman, Khatun, et al., 2011; Nelson and O'Brien, 2012).

Given the more involved and committed parenting shown by parents in new family forms, it might have been expected that their children would show higher levels of psychological adjustment than would children from traditional families. Why was this not found to be the case? One possible reason is that the measures of child adjustment used were not designed to detect especially high levels of positive functioning. Owing to the prediction that these children would experience psychological problems, researchers generally applied assessments that rated adjustment on scales ranging from "no problems" to "extreme difficulties." They did not use measures that assessed positions at the other end of the continuum, ranging from "no problems" to "extreme well-being." Had they done so, they may well have identified more positive functioning among the children in new family forms. Nevertheless, studies of traditional families have shown that, beyond a certain level, the quality of parenting that children receive makes little difference to their psychological adjustment (Maccoby, 2007; Roberts, 1986; Roberts and Strayer, 1987; Scarr, 1992). This finding is in line with Winnicott's view that all children need is "good-enough" parenting in order to flourish (Winnicott, 1973). In new families, as in traditional families, a particularly high quality of parenting may bestow no additional advantage on children.

Although children raised by same-sex parents and children born through assisted reproduction do not generally show adjustment problems, certain aspects of these family types may present difficulties for children. Some who discover in adolescence or beyond that they were donor conceived are distressed by this information, and some children of same-sex parents experience stigma at school. These problems are associated, at least in part, with a lack of openness and poor communication, both inside and outside the family.

They are also associated with prejudice and discrimination in the wider social world.

FAMILY STRUCTURE

Research on new family forms is of interest, in itself, as it provides empirical data on the psychological consequences for children who grow up in them. However, it is also of broader theoretical interest, as it increases our understanding of how families influence child development more generally. As noted in Chapter 1, new family forms act as "natural experiments" (Rutter, 2007; Rutter, Pickles, Murray, et al., 2001), in that they separate factors that, in traditional families, occur together. In doing so, they enable us to examine the impact of family structure on children's psychological development and the relative importance of family structure and family processes (Biblarz and Stacey, 2010; Patterson, 2006, 2009; Silverstein and Auerbach, 1999). Comparisons of single-parent and two-parent families increase our understanding of the effects of the number and gender of parents in a family; comparisons of two-parent lesbian mother families, two-parent gay father families and two-parent heterosexual families provide information on the role of parental gender and parental sexual orientation; and comparisons of families created by sperm donation, egg donation, embryo donation, surrogacy and natural conception enable us to explore the impact of the absence of a genetic and/or gestational relationship between parents and their children.

Number of parents

A component of the traditional family that is generally considered beneficial for children is the presence of two parents. Is it the case that two parents are better than one? Comparisons of heterosexual single-parent families and heterosexual two-parent families tell us about the outcomes for children of having only one parent. Almost all of these studies have examined single-mother families, as relatively few families are headed by single fathers. If children raised by single mothers do not differ from children raised in families in which both parents are present, then this would suggest that two parents are not essential for children's positive psychological development.

The aspects of child development that are most often considered to be adversely affected by the absence of a parent are psychological adjustment and gender development. In terms of psychological adjustment, the large body of research on single-mother families shows that children from these families are more at risk of psychological problems than are their counterparts from two-parent homes. This is true of single-mother families formed by divorce, as well as those headed by unmarried single mothers. However, this difference is almost entirely accounted for by the adverse factors that commonly accompany single parenthood, noted above, including economic hardship, maternal depression and lack of social support, as well as factors that predate the transition to a single-parent home, such as parental conflict. When these factors are controlled for, differences in psychological adjustment between children with one and two parents largely disappear, indicating that the factors that accompany the absence of a parent, rather than the absence of a parent in itself, are associated with children's psychological problems. Regarding gender development, there is no evidence to suggest that children who are raised by one parent differ from children who live with two parents with respect to gender identity or gender role behavior. Boys in single-parent families are just as masculine in terms of their identity and behavior, and girls are just as feminine, as are boys and girls from two-parent homes. Further studies of children raised by single mothers by choice in the absence of the adverse circumstances commonly associated with single parenthood will increase understanding of the impact of single parenthood per se.

Gender of parents

Single-mother families differ from traditional families not only in the absence of a parent, but also in the absence of a male parent. As the two are confounded, it is not possible to establish whether differences between children in single-parent families and those in traditional two-parent families result from the absence of a parent, in general, or the absence of a male parent, in particular. So, what can be learned from new family forms in relation to the role of parental gender in child development? The question most frequently asked is "Do children need fathers?" However, the increase in gay father families and the emergence of single fathers by choice have led to the additional question "Do children need mothers?" The two new family forms that can shed light on the role of parental gender on child development are lesbian mother and gay father families.

Lesbian mother families provide a better paradigm than do single mother families for examining the outcomes of father absence on child development, as they enable researchers to control for the number of parents in the family: comparisons can be conducted between two-parent lesbian mother families and two-parent heterosexual families. A number of studies have compared donor-conceived children born to lesbian couples with donor-conceived children born to heterosexual couples. This is the most stringent comparison for examining the effects of father absence, as both groups of children are raised by two parents, and thus the potentially confounding effects of single-parenthood are avoided; furthermore, in lesbian mother families created by donor insemination, there is no father present, right from the child's birth. These studies have consistently shown that children raised by lesbian couples do not differ from children raised by heterosexual couples in terms of psychological adjustment. Thus, the findings of these studies suggest that the absence of a male parent is not associated with child adjustment problems when there are two female parents in the family home. What seems to matter for children is the presence of a second parent, regardless of that parent's gender. There are also no differences in sex-typed behavior between children from two-parent lesbian mother families and those from two-parent heterosexual families. These studies show that the presence of a male parent is not essential for positive psychological adjustment or typical gender development. However, this does not mean that fathers are unimportant for the development and well-being of their children. The quality of fathers' relationships with their children, rather than their gender, is what makes a difference. From the discussion of family processes, below, it seems that fathers, similar to mothers, have a positive influence on the psychological adjustment of their children to the extent that they have a warm, committed and involved relationship with them. In contrast, fathers who have dysfunctional relationships with their children may have a negative effect (Jaffee, Moffitt, Caspi, et al., 2003).

Gay father families are interesting because they tell us about the consequences for children of the absence of a mother, addressing the question "Are fathers as good at parenting as are mothers?" To date, this question has been difficult to answer, as few studies have been conducted on children raised by fathers in the absence of a mother in the home. If children raised by gay fathers do not differ from children raised in families with mothers present, then this would indicate that fathers play as important a role in child development as do mothers. Although only a small number of studies have been conducted, the available findings show no evidence of raised levels of childhood adjustment problems or atypical gender development between children from two-parent gay father families and children from either two-parent lesbian mother or two-parent heterosexual parent homes. These findings lead to the controversial conclusion that the presence of a female parent is not essential for children's psychological well-being or their development of sex-typed behavior.

Sexual orientation of parents

Just as it is not possible to establish whether the findings of research on single-mother families result from the absence of a parent, in general, or the absence of a male parent, in particular, it cannot be determined whether any differences between lesbian mother families and heterosexual parent families, or between gay father families and heterosexual parent families, result from differences in the gender of the parents or from differences in their sexual orientation. However, there are no differences to be explained. The large research literature on two-parent lesbian mother families and the small but growing body of research on two-parent gay father families consistently shows that there are no differences in psychological adjustment or gender development between children who grow up with same-sex parents and those who are raised by two heterosexual parents. The only exception to this finding is the higher, rather than lower, level of adjustment found in children adopted by gay fathers than by those raised by adoptive heterosexual parents in the UK; however, this finding may have resulted from selection effects. Had differences been found with respect to children in these families, they might have stemmed from either the gender or the sexual orientation of the parents, or both. However, the absence of differences implies that parental sexual orientation is not a major determinant of child development.

Biological relatedness of parents

The view that the absence of a biological link between parents and their children places children at risk for psychological problems comes from research on adoptive families, in which children lack a biological link to their adoptive parents, and research on stepfamilies, in which children lack a biological link to their stepfather or stepmother. However, research has shown that factors associated with being adopted or living in a stepfamily, such as difficulties in the families in which children were born, account for the greater problems shown by children in these family types.

A better test of the importance of genetic relatedness for children's psychological well-being comes from research on families created by sperm, egg or embryo donation. Children in these families lack a genetic link with one or both parents, but have been raised by them from birth and thus have not experienced the risk factors that commonly accompany adoption and stepparenting. The importance of gestational relatedness can be examined by investigating children born through surrogacy. Although born to a surrogate mother, these children are raised from the outset by their social parents, one or both of whom may also be their genetic parent(s). The research reviewed in this book has shown that children born through reproductive donation (the donation of eggs, sperm or embryos, or surrogacy), and thus who lack a genetic and/or gestational link to their parents, show positive psychological adjustment and do not differ from children who are biologically related to both their mother and their father. It seems, therefore, that a biological link to parents is not necessary for children's psychological well-being.

A reason that has been put forward to explain the difficulties that occur in relationships between stepparents and stepchildren is that stepparents do not see their stepchildren as their "own"; this finding has been attributed to the absence of a genetic link between them (Dunn, O'Connor, and Cheng, 2005; Henderson, Hetherington, Mekos, et al., 1996). However, this is not true of children conceived by gamete or embryo donation; these parents plan their family, go to great lengths to conceive their children and, when their children are born, view them as their "own." The experiences of donor-conception parents show that, while "ownness" may make a difference to parents' feelings toward their children, it is not dependent upon a genetic bond.

One married heterosexual mother said the following in response to a question about the amount of enjoyment she gets from her donor-conceived children:

> Immeasurable, immeasurable. I can't say any more than that. It's wonderful. It's truly the most wonderful thing. We wouldn't have missed it for the world ... You just get so wrapped up in day-to-day life daily life that you forget about it (the donor conception). And then when you do focus and look at what you've got, and look at what we might not have had if we had been unable to work through it, then I think my goodness, we might not ever have had this. And I think the joy that they've brought us is truly life-changing.

Although children born through reproductive donation do not appear to show emotional or behavioral problems, some young people who were conceived by donor insemination search for their sperm donor. This indicates that some children feel it is important to know the identity of, and have information about, their genetic parents, even if they do not have a parental relationship with them. It is interesting to note that the children of single mothers seem more concerned with searching for their donor than are children of lesbian couples, which suggests that the absence of a second parent is more associated with the desire to find the donor than is the absence of a male parent (Freeman, Jadva, Kramer, et al., 2009; Scheib, Riordan, and Rubin, 2005). Children born by donor insemination to heterosexual couples are the least likely to search for their donor and donor siblings. Whereas several factors may be involved, including the lower rates of disclosure in these families, it seems that the wish not to upset their father may be a deterrent for some. Whether or not children born through egg donation, embryo donation or surrogacy will wish to search for their genetic or gestational parents will become apparent as more of these children reach adolescence and beyond.

Assisted conception

In addition to these structural differences between families, families may differ from the traditional family with respect to the method of the child's conception. Does assisted conception result in different psychological outcomes for children than does natural conception? Research on children born through assisted reproductive technologies such as IVF and ICSI, who are biologically related to both of their parents, has shown that these children are well-adjusted and do not differ in levels of adjustment from their naturally conceived peers. As discussed above, the same is true for children born through assisted reproduction procedures involving reproductive donation. So, in spite of early concerns about the potentially negative consequences of assisted reproduction for children's psychological well-being, there is no evidence to suggest that, in themselves, these new reproductive technologies place children at risk.

Conclusions about family structure

Research on single-mother families has shown that the number of parents in a family does not, in itself, have a negative impact on child development, although children in single mother families are more at risk for psychological problems owing to the adverse circumstances associated with single motherhood. Children's gender development does not seem to be affected. Studies of lesbian mother and gay father families have demonstrated that parental gender does not have a major influence on children's psychological well-being or gender development. Studies of lesbian mother and gay father families have additionally shown that heterosexual parents are not essential for the psychological well-being or sex-typed behavior of girls or boys. Moreover, from studies of families created by assisted reproductive technologies, it seems that neither biological relatedness nor natural conception is a prerequisite for children's psychological well-being. Thus, the growing body of research on new family forms leads to the conclusion that family structure – including the number, gender, sexual orientation and genetic relatedness of parents, as well as their method of conception – does not play a fundamental role in children's psychological adjustment or gender development.

FAMILY PROCESSES

If the type of family in which children are reared does not matter for their development and well-being, then what does matter? The answer to this question appears to be the same for new family forms as it is for traditional families. As outlined in Chapter 1, what matters most for children is the quality of family life. The psychological well-being of parents, the quality of their parenting and the social environment of the family interact in complex ways to facilitate or inhibit children's socio-emotional development. Children themselves contribute to this process; their behavior influences the behavior of others toward them, and some are more resilient than others.

Evidence for the greater importance of family processes over family structure for children's psychological well-being in new family forms comes from studies that have directly examined the relative contribution of each (e.g. Bos and Gartrell, 2010; Bos, Gartrell, Peyser, et al., 2008; Bos, Gartrell, and van Gelderen, 2013; Bos and van Balen, 2008; Bos, van Balen, and van den Boom, 2004; Chan, Raboy, and Patterson, 1998; Farr, Forssell, and Patterson, 2010a, b; Golombok, Blake, Casey, et al., 2013; Golombok, Mellish, Jennings, et al., 2014; Wainright and Patterson, 2008; Wainright, Russell, and Patterson, 2004). These studies have shown that the quality of parent–child relationships and of parents' relationships with each other, as well as social attitudes toward their family, are more predictive of children's adjustment than is family structure. For example, in a study of lesbian mother and single heterosexual mother families in the USA, Chan, Raboy and Patterson (2008) found stress associated with parenting and parents' relationship satisfaction to be associated with children's behavioral problems; Bos and van Balen (2008) found stigmatization to be associated with children's emotional and behavioral problems in a study of lesbian mother families in the Netherlands; Farr, Forssell and Patterson (2010a, b) found parents' relationship happiness, stress associated with parenting and parental disciplinary techniques to be associated with child adjustment in a study of gay fathers in the USA; Golombok, Mellish, Jennings, et al. (2014) found parenting stress to be associated with children's behavioral problems in a study of gay father families in the UK; and, in a study of donor-conception families in the UK, Golombok, Blake, Casey, et al. (2013) found mothers' emotional problems to be associated with child adjustment in children who were aware of their genetic origins.

This finding is in line with studies of non-traditional families. Single-mother, stepfather, stepmother, adoptive and traditional two-parent families from the National Survey of Families and Households in the USA were studied by Lansford, Ceballo, Abbey, et al. (2001); also using the National Survey of Families and Households, Demo and Acock (1996) investigated divorced single-mother families, continuous single-mother families, stepfamilies and traditional two-parent families; single-mother, single-father, stepmother, stepfather and traditional two-parent families from the National Longitudinal Survey of Adolescent Health in the USA were studied by Demuth and Brown (2004); single-mother, stepmother, stepfather and traditional two-parent families from the Avon Longitudinal Study of Parents and Children in the UK were studied by Dunn, Deater-Deckard, Pickering, O'Connor and Golding (1998); and single-mother, single-father, stepmother, stepfather, cohabiting and married parents from the Millennium Cohort Study in the UK were studied by Kiernan and Mensah (2010). All of these studies came to the same conclusion: family processes are better predictors of children's psychological adjustment than is family structure. This does not mean that family structure is irrelevant. Although family structure may not have a direct effect on child development, it does have an indirect influence through its impact on parental well-being, family relationships and quality of family life.

In terms of sex-typed behavior, the finding that the gender identity and gender role behavior of both girls and boys are unaffected by the gender or sexual orientation of their parents is consistent with contemporary theories of the processes involved in gender development (Hines, 2010; Maccoby, 1998; Ruble, Martin, and Berenbaum, 2006). From an early age, boys and girls differ in certain aspects of their behavior. One of the most striking differences is their preference for different toys. By their third birthday, girls are much more likely than boys to play with dolls, dollhouses, tea sets, and other domestic toys, whereas boys most often play with guns, swords, cars, trains and trucks. By this age, girls also prefer girls as playmates and boys prefer to play with boys, a phenomenon known as gender segregation that not only involves a preference for same-sex playmates but also the avoidance of playmates of the other sex (Maccoby, 1998). Differences in play styles can also be seen from 3 years of age. Boys tend to play in a more active, rough-and-tumble way than girls, who tend to talk more to each other and be more nurturing than boys, and boys like to play in large groups of other boys whereas girls often prefer the company of one or two female friends. While girls' friendships are characterized by emotional and physical closeness, the friendships of boys are founded on shared activities and interests. Pretend play also differentiates the sexes, with boys acting out heroic roles involving fighting and adventure, and girls preferring to be family members or dressing up in feminine clothes. Not all boys engage in typically male behaviors, and not all girls engage in behaviors that are typical of girls, all of the time. Moreover, there is a great deal of overlap between the sexes with some children behaving in ways that are more typical of the other gender. Although sex differences in behavior are, to some extent at least, socially determined, they are apparent across nationalities and cultures. Children's preference for same-sex playmates, for example, is a universal aspect of growing up (Whiting and Edwards, 1988).

Theories of the processes involved in gender development have largely focused on differences *between* rather than differences *within* the sexes. That is, they have addressed the question, "Why do boys and girls differ from each other in their behavior?" instead of "Why are some boys more typically masculine in their behavior than other boys?" and "Why are some girls more typically feminine in their behavior than other girls?" It is now generally accepted that sex differences in behavior result from an interplay among biological, psychological and social mechanisms from the prenatal period onwards (Hines, 2010; Ruble, Martin, and Berenbaum, 2006). Studies of children who have been exposed to atypical levels of hormones prenatally, either because of genetic disorders, or because of the treatment of pregnant women with hormones to prevent miscarriage, as well as studies of normal variability in prenatal hormones, have shown that prenatal hormones influence children's subsequent sex-typed toy, playmate and activity preferences (Hines, 2010). For example, it has consistently been shown that girls with the disorder congenital adrenal hyperplasia (CAH), which causes the developing foetus to be exposed to unusually high levels of androgens, show higher levels of typically male toy, playmate and activity preferences than unaffected girls. This has led to the conclusion that prenatal androgens influence children's gender development (Hines, 2010). As discussed in Chapter 2, social learning theorists have emphasized two key processes in children's acquisition of sex-typed behavior; the differential reinforcement of boys and girls, and children's modeling of individuals of the same sex as themselves (Bandura, 1977; Mischel, 1966, 1970). Although it used to be thought that parents played an important role in these processes, the view that children acquire sex-typed behavior by directly imitating parents of the same-sex as themselves is now believed to be too simplistic (Bussey and Bandura, 1999). Instead, it seems that children learn which behaviors are considered appropriate for males and which for females by observing many men and women and boys and girls and by noticing which behaviors are performed frequently by males and rarely by females and vice versa. Children then use these abstractions of sex-appropriate behavior as models for their own imitative performance. Thus children observe a wide variety of role models in their daily life, not just their parents, and tend to imitate those whom they see as typical of their gender. Friends, in particular, appear to be important role models (Maccoby, 1998). In addition, friends are important reinforcers of gender-related behaviors; again, it is not just parents who perform this role. From a cognitive developmental perspective, it has been shown that the selective processing of gender-related information by boys and girls based on culturally prescribed gender stereotypes is involved in the acquisition of sex-typed behavior, and that children become aware of gender stereotypes from as early as 2 years old (Martin, Ruble, and Szkrybalo, 2002).

Although theories of gender development have tended to focus on differences between, rather than within, the sexes, the same processes appear to explain why some children show more sex-typed behavior than others (Golombok, Rust, Zervoulis, et al., 2008). Thus, variation in prenatal androgen levels may predispose some children within each gender to be more sex-typed than others. The differential reinforcement of sex-typed behavior in boys and girls, and the extent to which children are exposed to sex-typed models, may also contribute to the variation in sex-typed behavior within each sex, such that children who experience high levels of reinforcement for sex-typed behavior, and whose role models are highly sex typed, may show higher levels of sex-typed behavior themselves. In addition, individual differences in the processing of gender-related information may play a part. Furthermore, these various processes may act together, such that children who are biologically predisposed toward higher levels of sex-typed behavior as toddlers may experience greater exposure to the social and psychological influences that are likely to increase sex-typed behavior even further as they grow up (Golombok Rust, Zervoulis, et al., 2008).

So it is now generally accepted that prenatal factors such as prenatal androgens interact with social and psychological, including cognitive, factors in children's acquisition of sex-typed behavior. The expectation that the sex-typed behavior of boys and girls with single or same-sex parents would differ from that of children in traditional families arose from the view that parents are influential in the gender development of their children, as espoused by psychoanalytic and classic social learning theories, owing to the absence of a male or female parent (and possibly the presence of two male or female parents). Thus it was predicted that boys raised by single or same-sex parents would be less masculine in their identity and behavior, and girls less feminine. However, current theoretical understanding of the processes involved in children's acquisition of sex-typed behavior suggests that parents play only a small, and possibly insignificant, role. The findings of empirical research on the gender development of boys and girls with single and same-sex parents, showing no differences between these and other children, are in line with this view, which leads to the conclusion that neither the gender nor the sexual orientation of parents has a marked influence on the sex-typed behavior of their children. Further evidence comes from studies of lesbian mothers who tried to discourage their daughters from playing with dolls and their sons from playing with guns, or who encouraged their children to play with gender-neutral, or a gender mix, of toys and games. These attempts patently failed suggesting that however hard they try, parents have little influence on the sex-typed behavior of their daughters and sons.

Although less is known about the processes involved in the development of sexual orientation, no single factor appears to determine whether a person will identify as heterosexual, bisexual, lesbian or gay. The current view is that there are a variety of influences from the prenatal period onward that may shape development in one direction or another, and that different people follow different pathways and may change pathways at different periods of their lives. There is growing evidence that prenatal androgens may sometimes be involved (Hines, 2011). For example, there are now a number of studies of the sexual orientation of women with CAH showing that they are more likely to consider themselves to be bisexual or lesbian than are women who do not have this disorder. Hines (2011) highlighted the well-established link between cross-gendered toy, playmate and activity interests in childhood and a non-heterosexual orientation in adulthood and suggested that prenatal androgens may be associated with both childhood sex-typed behavior and adult sexual orientation. However, this does not mean that all adults who identify as lesbian or gay showed cross-gender behavior as children. Neither does it mean that prenatal androgens determine sexual orientation. Instead, prenatal androgen levels may be one of many influential factors.

Although social learning theorists have focused on childhood sex-typed behavior rather than on adult sexual orientation, insofar as sexual orientation results from social learning, the processes of reinforcement and modeling would also apply. From this viewpoint, it could be expected that different patterns of reinforcement are operating in same-sex than in heterosexual families, such that young people in lesbian mother families would be less likely to be discouraged from embarking upon lesbian or gay relationships. Contemporary perspectives on modeling, which focus on the modeling of gender stereotypes rather than the modeling of parents, suggest that children with same-sex parents may hold less rigid stereotypes about what constitutes appropriate male and female sexual behavior than their peers from traditional families, and may be more open to involvement in same-sex relationships themselves. Thus, young people's sexual orientation may be influenced by attitudes toward sexuality in the family in which they are raised.

Cognitive developmental theorists have also focused on the acquisition of sex-typed behavior rather than sexual orientation. To the extent that cognitive processes are contributing to the development of sexual orientation, it would seem that young people seek out information that is in line with their emerging sexual orientation, and they come to value and identify with those characteristics that are consistent with their view of themselves as heterosexual, lesbian or gay. Cognitive developmental theorists would place less emphasis on the role of parental attitudes than on prevailing attitudes in the wider social environment. Thus, the social context of the family, within a wider society that is accepting or rejecting of homosexuality, would be considered to facilitate or inhibit respectively young people's exploration of relationships with partners of the same sex as themselves.

These theories are compatible with the findings of research on the sexual orientation of children raised by lesbian mothers (the children of gay fathers have not yet been studied). The large majority of young people raised by lesbian mothers identify themselves as heterosexual, showing that the sexual orientation of parents does not influence the sexual orientation of their children. However, the daughters of lesbian mothers are more likely than daughters from heterosexual parent families to explore same-sex relationships as they grow up. Thus, parents' sexual orientation may have some influence on the sexual experimentation of their children, most probably by creating a family environment that either encourages children toward heterosexual relationships or allows non-heterosexual relationships to be explored.

LIMITATIONS

There are limitations to the growing body of research on new family forms that must be borne in mind. With some exceptions, the samples studied have tended to be small, and this has limited their statistical power and ability to detect small effects, should these exist. Often, recruitment procedures have relied on volunteers, and the cooperation rates for systematic samples have sometimes been low, resulting in potentially biased samples. Owing to the discrimination faced by lesbian and gay families, parents whose children are experiencing difficulties may decide against participating in research, as negative findings may work against them. Furthermore, parents who have not disclosed their children's donor conception may be concerned that taking part might jeopardize their secrecy. Moreover, those who do participate in research may play down difficulties, as they may wish to present their families in a favorable light, either as a reaction to the stigma associated with their family structure or because they feel they must live up to high expectations of themselves as parents, given the difficulties they may have had to overcome in order to have children. Much of the research that has been conducted on new family forms has focused on preschool and early school-age children. Less is known about children in adolescence and beyond, and there are few longitudinal studies that enable causal factors in children's outcomes to be determined. A further limitation is that many investigations have relied on information from one family member only – usually the mother – rather than different family members and independent reporters outside the family circle, such as children's teachers. There has also been a tendency to use single measures, such as interviews or questionnaires, rather than a multi-method approach, which gives a fuller picture.

It should be emphasized that separating out the different family structure variables in order to draw conclusions about the role of each in influencing child adjustment is not an easy task. However, this approach does shed light on important questions that are otherwise

difficult to answer as a result of the inability to control family structure variables experimentally. This method has proved useful in
increasing our understanding of the impact of factors such as parental gender and number of parents in the family on child development,
thus addressing key issues such as the child's need for a father (Biblarz
and Stacey, 2010; Silverstein and Auerbach, 1999). As Strohschein
(2010) pointed out, it is difficult to isolate the effects of specific variables in practice; for example, married heterosexual parents tend to
be compared with unmarried same-sex parents, so any differences
between them may be confounded by marital status. Goldberg (2010)
further argued that it makes no sense to isolate variables because variables such as gender and sexual orientation, and their broader social,
political and legal contexts, are inextricably linked. Nevertheless,
teasing apart the components of family structure provides some clar-
ity on the mechanisms through which families may influence their
children, and doing so challenges deep-seated assumptions about
what matters for children's well-being and what does not. As such, it
is a worthwhile, if somewhat imperfect, endeavor.

Moreover, little attention has been paid to the positive effects
of new family forms. This is because most research has focused
on negative outcomes in order to establish whether empirical data
supports or refutes the claims that have been made about the negative psychological consequences that will ensue for children in
non-traditional family forms. For example, research on children with
lesbian mothers has concentrated on emotional and behavioral difficulties, peer problems and atypical gender development, as these
issues have been the focus of custody disputes as well as policy and
legislation on adoption, assisted reproduction and same-sex marriage. Nevertheless, researchers are turning to positive aspects of
new family forms, such as the greater tolerance of diversity shown
by children of same-sex parents (Fulcher, Sutfin, and Patterson, 2008;
Stacey and Biblarz, 2001). Attention to the strengths of new family
forms, rather than the putative weaknesses, is set to be a fruitful area
of research with relevance for all types of families.

FUTURE FAMILIES

Historical time and geographical place are central to the experiences of new family forms and highlight the role of societal attitudes in family functioning. In the 1970s, prejudice and discrimination were everyday features of non-traditional family life: lesbian mothers lived in fear of losing custody of their children, donor insemination was shrouded in secrecy and "test-tube" babies were viewed with suspicion. Although prejudice has not been eliminated, today, more positive attitudes generally prevail, and this has created a more favorable environment for children. Since the turn of the century, same-sex marriage has been introduced in several countries, donor-conceived half-siblings growing up in different families have begun to make contact with each other, and "test-tube" babies have become commonplace. Nevertheless, children's experiences depend, to a large extent, on their social environment, which includes their extended families, their communities and the geopolitical context in which they are raised. In many communities and countries, families that do not conform to accepted structures are treated as outcasts, with parents ostracized and even sentenced to death. Same-sex parents are a case in point. In 2013–14, President Goodluck Jonathan of Nigeria signed into law a bill that banned same-sex marriage, gay groups and shows of same-sex public affection; in Uganda, a bill allowing greater punishments for gay people and for those who fail to turn them in to the police – a toned-down version of the original bill that included the death penalty as a punishment for some aspects of same-sex behavior – was passed by the nation's parliament; President Putin of Russia discouraged lesbian and gay people from attending the Winter Olympic Games; and Pope Francis came out against same-sex civil unions and adoption by same-sex couples, stressing "the proprietary right of children ... to count on models of father and mother, to have a dad and a mum" (Follain, 2014). The families that are the focus of this book are based largely in the more liberal of western counties. Nevertheless, they continue to be exposed to prejudice and discrimination in their daily lives. It is important to remember that it is stigmatization outside the family, rather than relationships within it, that creates difficulties for children in new family forms.

The new millennium has brought significant changes in legislation that are supportive of new family forms. The first country to introduce same-sex marriage was the Netherlands in 2001. Since that time, marriage equality laws have been enacted in 17 countries (Argentina, Belgium, Brazil, Canada, Denmark, France, Iceland, the Netherlands, New Zealand, Norway, Portugal, Spain, South Africa, Sweden, the UK, Malta and Uruguay) and in subjurisdictions, including several American states. These new laws are regarded by professional bodies such as the American Psychological Association and the American Academy of Pediatrics as beneficial for children, as they provide the security of two parents in a legally recognized union, as well as the societal benefits that go with it. Legislation has also been enacted in a number of jurisdictions to enable same-sex couples to adopt children jointly.

With respect to assisted reproduction, donor-conceived children are legally entitled to obtain the identity of their donor upon reaching adulthood – or earlier, under some circumstances – in several countries, including Australia, New Zealand, Sweden, Norway, the Netherlands, Switzerland and the UK. Professional bodies such as the American Society for Reproductive Medicine (Ethics Committee of the American Society for Reproductive Medicine, 2013a) and the Nuffield Council on Bioethics in the UK (Nuffield Council on Bioethics, 2013) encourage parents to be open with their children about their donor conception, and the laws that have been enacted to remove donor anonymity enable donor-conceived children to request the identity of their donor, should they wish to.

Legislation has also been introduced that allows single women and same-sex couples to become parents of children through assisted reproduction. Single women have access to gamete donation in Canada, Belgium, Bulgaria, Finland, Greece, Hungary, Latvia, Russia, Spain and the UK (Glennon, 2015). In the UK, the Human Fertilisation and Embryology Act (2008) enables both partners in a lesbian couple to be named on the birth certificate as the legal parents of children conceived by donor insemination at a licensed clinic, and both partners in a gay couple to be the legal parents of children born through surrogacy. In the USA, the Ethics Committee of the American Society for Reproductive Medicine stated that fertility treatment should be offered irrespective of sexual orientation or marital status (Ethics Committee of the American Society for Reproductive Medicine, 2013b), although, in practice, this is up to the discretion of individual clinics (Glennon, 2015). While extremely rare, some babies have three parents named on their birth certificate. This became possible in British Columbia, Canada, following legislation that came into force in 2013. The first baby to be registered with three legal parents was Della Wolf Kangro Wiley Richards, the daughter of Anna Richards and Danielle Wiley, a lesbian couple, and Shawn Kangro, a friend who was their sperm donor and who is involved as a father in Della's life.

These new laws, introduced around the world to enable same-sex couples to marry, single people and same-sex couples to adopt children and become the legal parents of children born through assisted reproductive technologies, and children born through gamete donation to be legally entitled to obtain the identity of their donor, have been the subject of enormous controversy, with opponents basing their arguments on the grounds that the traditional family is best. However, much of this debate has been founded upon myths and false assumptions about the deleterious consequences of new family forms for the children who grow up in them, rather than the findings of empirical research. Some people are, and will remain, against modern families for personal moral or religious reasons. However, for those who are opposed because they believe such families to be harmful to children, it is hoped that the empirical evidence reviewed in this book will encourage second thoughts. Children are most likely to flourish in families that provide love, security and support, whatever their family structure, and prejudice and discrimination are bad for children, whatever their family structure. Legislative changes that support positive family relationships, irrespective of the way in which families are formed, are in the best interests of children.

Research on new family forms has informed policy and practice. The Nuffield Council on Bioethics (Nuffield Council on Bioethics, 2013) has recommended the provision of counseling for parents of donor-conceived children to help them consider the implications of disclosure and non-disclosure to their children. Stonewall, in the UK, has produced guides for schools to increase awareness of the needs of children with same-sex parents and to counter homophobia (Stonewall, 2010). Furthermore, the Donaldson Adoption Institute in the USA has produced recommendations on adoption by lesbian and gay parents (Brodzinsky and Evan B. Donaldson Adoption Institute, 2011). At a time when there are many children waiting to be adopted but a shortage of suitable adopters, lesbian women and gay men constitute a largely untapped pool of potential adoptive parents. All these interventions are evidence based and were designed with the primary aim of enhancing children's well-being.

Family forms that are currently emerging or are still on the horizon will generate new questions about the well-being of children, as well as novel ways of examining family influences on child development and new insights into the interplay between family structure and family processes. Today, not only do we have "diblings," the term used to describe donor siblings who were conceived from the same sperm donor but are growing up in different families, but also "twiblings," a term coined by the media to describe children who were born to separate surrogate mothers from the same batch of embryos, who are not quite twins and not quite siblings. In the case of intra-family donation, whereby one family member donates eggs or sperm to another family member, a child may find that the person they thought of as their aunt was also their genetic mother, and that their cousins, whom they may closely resemble, were their genetic half-siblings (Jadva, Casey, Readings, et al., 2011; Vayena and Golombok, 2012). Of particular ethical concern is the recent phenomenon of children in the United States being born from embryos created by a commercial company using the sperm and eggs of donors who had never met (Klitzman and Sauer, 2014).

A brand new phenomenon involves men and women who were previously unknown to each other using the Internet to create families. Instead of meeting online with the aim of dating, they are meeting online to embark on parenthood. A survey conducted in 2014 of more than 1,000 members of the Pride Angel website shed some light on who the members are and why they wish to have children in this way (Jadva, Freeman, Tranfield, et al., unpublished data). The majority of the members were women wishing to obtain sperm (45 percent) or men wishing to donate sperm (39 percent). However, 6 percent of the men and 4 percent of the women wished to create a family through a co-parenting arrangement; that is, they wanted to raise a child jointly but separately. Co-parenting is a radical departure from the new family forms that are the focus of this book and it potentially lacks a key element of effective parenting – a close, committed relationship between the parents. As yet, little is known about the relationship between co-parents over time, the nature and quality of children's relationships with each co-parent and, crucially, how children will feel about being raised in this way.

In the not-too-distant future, scientific advances will enable children to be born through mitochondrial DNA transfer and, thus, for the first time, with genetic material from three people – a mother, a father and a woman who donates her mitochondrial DNA (Nuffield Council on Bioethics, 2012). This procedure, which involves transferring the nuclear DNA of the intended parents into a donor egg containing healthy mitochondria, is being developed to enable women at risk of having children with serious mitochondrial disease to have healthy children. Moreover, artificial gametes might soon make it possible for women to produce sperm and for men to produce eggs (Hayashi, Ohta, Kurimoto, et al., 2011). Although intended as an infertility treatment, this procedure would allow both partners in same-sex couples to be genetically related to their children. Lesbian couples would produce daughters only, as both sperm and eggs from women would carry an X chromosome; eggs from men could carry an X or a Y chromosome, which, when fertilized with sperm from a man, could produce either daughters or sons (Johnson, pers. comm.). Research is also being conducted on "artificial wombs," which are essentially machines that would simulate the uterus and enable gestation to take place outside the mother's body (Gosden, 2000). Furthermore, the Nobel Prize-winning scientist Sir John Gurdon predicted in 2012 that human cloning would be possible within 50 years (Gurdon, 2012). These rapidly evolving developments have called into question the current regulatory frameworks that govern assisted reproduction around the world and raise the question of whether it is important, or even possible, to regulate effectively the diverse mix of reproductive cultures that extend across international legal jurisdictions (Golombok, Appleby, Richards, et al., 2015).

In the 1970s, when lesbian mother families first attracted media attention and the first IVF baby was born, it was unimaginable that, within 40 years, lesbian and gay couples would be able to marry, adopt children jointly and become the joint legal parents of children born through assisted reproductive technologies; that a woman would be able to give birth to the genetic child of another woman; that, by freezing embryos, individual twins could be born years apart; and that children would be searching online for their genetic half-siblings growing up in many different families. In spite of the methodological challenges described above, 40 years of research on the families at the forefront of these changes has failed to support the assertion that the traditional family is necessarily the best environment in which to raise children. Families come in all shapes and sizes. Whether children have one parent or two, whether their parents are male or female, whether their parents are of the same sex or the opposite sex, whether they have a genetic or gestational link to their parents, and whether they have been conceived naturally or through assisted reproduction, seem to matter less for children than does the quality of family relationships, the support of their community and the attitudes of the society in which they live.

References

Abraham, E., Hendler, T., Shapira-Lichter, I., Kanat-Maymon, Y., Zagoory-Sharon, O., and Feldman, R. (2014). Father's brain is sensitive to childcare experiences. *Proceedings of the National Academy of Sciences*, 1–6. doi:10.1073/pnas.1402569111

Achenbach, T. M., and Rescorla, L. A. (2000). *Manual for the ASEBA preschool forms profiles*. Burlington, VT: University of Vermont, Research Center for Children, Youth, and Families.

Adamson, D. (2012). *ICMART world reporting: Preliminary 2008 data*. 28th ESHRE Annual Conference, Istanbul.

Ainsworth, M. D. (1985). Patterns of infant–mother attachments: Antecedents and effects on development. *Bulletin of the New York Academy of Medicine*, 61(9), 771–791.

Ainsworth, M., Blehar, M., Waters, E., and Wall, S. (1978). *Patterns of attachment: A psychological study of the strange situation*. Hillsdale, NJ: Lawrence Erlbaum.

Ainsworth, M. D. S., and Wittig, B. A. (1969). Attachment and exploratory behavior of one-year-olds in a strange situation. In B. M. Foss (ed.), *Determinants of infant behaviour* (vol. IV, pp. 113–136). London: Methuen.

Allen, D. W. (2013). High school graduation rates among children of same-sex households. *Review of Economics of the Household*, 11(4), 635–658.

Allen, M., and Burrell, N. (1996). Comparing the impact of homosexual and heterosexual parents on children. *Journal of Homosexuality*, 32(2), 19–35. doi:10.1300/J082v32n02_02

Amato, P. R. (1993). Children's adjustment to divorce: Theories, hypotheses, and empirical support. *Journal of Marriage and Family*, 55, 23–28.

Amato, P. R. (2000). The consequences of divorce for adults and children. *Journal of Marriage and the Family*, 62, 1269–1287.

Amato, P. R. (2001). Children of divorce in the 1990s: An update of the Amato and Keith (1991) meta-analysis. *Journal of Family Psychology*, 15, 355–370.

Amato, P. R. (2005). The impact of family formation change on the cognitive, social, and emotional well-being of the next generation. *The Future of Children*, 15(2), 75–96.

Amato, P. (2014). The demography of contemporary fatherhood. In M. Lamb and L. Ahnert (eds.), *Men as fathers: Interdisciplinary perspectives on fatherhood in the context of the family.* Zurich: The Jacobs Foundation.

Amato, P. R., and Gilbreth, J. G. (1999). Nonresident fathers and children's well-being: A meta-analysis. *Journal of Marriage and Family*, 61(3), 557–573.

Amato, P. R., and Keith, B. (1991). Parental divorce and the well-being of children: A meta-analysis. *Psychological Bulletin*, 110(1), 26–46.

Amuzu, B., Laxova, R., and Shapiro, S. S. (1990). Pregnancy outcome, health of children, and family adjustment after donor insemination. *Obstetrics and Gynecology*, 75(6), 899–905.

Armour, K. L. (2012). An overview of surrogacy around the world: Trends, questions and ethical issues. *Nursing for Women's Health*, 16(3), 231–236. doi:10.1111/j.1751-486X.2012.01734.x

Averett, P., Nalavany, B., and Ryan, S. (2009). An evaluation of gay/lesbian and heterosexual adoption. *Adoption Quarterly*, 12(3–4), 129–151. doi:10.1080/10926750903313278

Bakermans-Kranenburg, M. J., McCreery, B., Dobrova-Krol, N. A., Engle, P., Fox, N. A., Garner, G., et al. (2012). The development and care of institutionally reared children. *Child Developmental Perspectives*, 6(2), 174–180.

Bandura, A. (1977). *Social learning theory.* New York: General Learning Press.

Baran, A., and Pannor, R. (1993). *Lethal secrets. The psychology of donor insemination. Problems and solutions* (2nd edn.). New York: Amistad.

Barnes, J., Sutcliffe, A. G., Kristoffersen, I., Loft, A., Wennerholm, U., Tarlatzis, B. C., Kantaris, X., Nekkebroeck, J., Hagberg, B. S., Madsen, S. V., and Bonduelle, M. (2004). The influence of assisted reproduction on family functioning and children's socio-emotional development: Results from a European study. *Human Reproduction*, 19(6), 1480–1487. doi:10.1093/humrep/deh239

Baumrind, D. (1971). Current patterns of parental authority. *Developmental Psychology Monograph*, 4(1, Pt. 1), 1–103.

Baumrind, D. (1989). Rearing competent children. In W. Damon (ed.), *Child development today and tomorrow* (pp. 349–378). San Fransisco, CA: Jossey-Bass.

Baumrind, D. (1991a). Current patterns of parental authority. *Developmental Psychology Monographs*, 4(1, Pt. 2).

Baumrind, D. (1991b). Parenting stlyes and adolescent development. In R. M. Lerner, A. C. Petersen, and J. Brookes-Gunn (eds.), *Encyclopedia of adolescence* (Vol. II., pp. 746–758). New York: Garland.

Becker, G., Butler, A., and Nachtigall, R. D. (2005). Resemblance talk: A challenge for parents whose children were conceived with donor gametes in the US. *Social Science and Medicine*, 61(6), 1300–1309.

Beeson, D. R., Jennings, P. K., and Kramer, W. (2011). Offspring searching for their sperm donors: How family type shapes the process. *Human Reproduction*, 26(9), 2415–2424.

Beijersbergen, M. D., Juffer, F., Bakermans-Kranenburg, M. J., and van IJzendoorn, M. H. (2012). Remaining or becoming secure: Parental sensitive support predicts attachment continuity from infancy to adolescence in a longitudinal adoption study. *Developmental Psychology*, 48(5), 1277–1282. doi:10.1037/a0027442

Belsky, J., and Cassidy, J. (1994). Attachment: Theory and evidence. In M. Rutter and D. Hay (eds.), *Development through life: A handbook for clinicians* (pp. 373–402). Oxford: Blackwell.

Belsky, J., Woodworth, S., and Crnic, K. (1996). Trouble in the second year: Three questions about family interaction. *Child Development*, 67(2), 556–578. doi:10.1111/j.1467-8624.1996.tb01751.x

Berger, R., and Paul, M. (2008). Family secrets and family functioning: The case of donor assistance. *Family Process*, 47(4), 553–566.

Bergh, T., Ericson, A., Hillensjö, T., Nygren, K. G., and Wennerholm, U. B. (1999). Deliveries and children born after in-vitro fertilisation in Sweden 1982–95: A retrospective cohort study. *The Lancet*, 354(9190), 1579–1585.

Bergman, K., Rubio, R. J., Green, R.-J., and Padrón, E. (2010). Gay men who become fathers via surrogacy: The transition to parenthood. *Journal of GLBT Family Studies*, 6(2), 111–141. doi:10.1080/15504281003704942

Biblarz, T. J., and Stacey, J. (2010). How does the gender of parents matter? *Journal of Marriage and the Family*, 72(1), 3–22. doi: 10.1111/j.1741-3737.2009.00678.x

Blake, L., Casey, P., Jadva, V., and Golombok, S. (2012). Marital stability and quality in families created by assisted reproduction techniques: A follow-up study. *Reproductive BioMedicine Online*, 25(7), 678–683.

Blake, L., Casey, P., Jadva, V., and Golombok, S. (2013). "I was quite amazed": Donor conception and parent–child relationships from the child's perspective. *Children and Society*. doi:10.1111/chso.12014

Blake, L., Casey, P., Readings, J., Jadva, V., and Golombok, S. (2010). "Daddy ran out of tadpoles": How parents tell their children that they are donor conceived, and what their 7-year-olds understand. *Human Reproduction*, 25(10), 2527–2534. doi:10.1093/humrep/deq208

Blake, L., Zadeh, S., Statham, H., and Freeman, T. (2014). Families created by assisted reproduction: Children's perspectives. In T. Freeman, S. Graham, F. Ebethaj, and M. Richards (eds.), *Relatedness in assisted reproduction: Families, origins and identities*. Cambridge University Press.

Blyth, E. (2002). How it feels to be a child of donor insemination. *British Medical Journal*, 234, 797.

Blyth, E. (2004). The UK: Evolution of a statutory regulatory approach. In E. Blyth and R. Landau (eds.), *Third party assisted conception across cultures. Social, legal and ethical perspectives* (pp. 226–245). London: Jessica Kingsley.

Blyth, E. (2012). Genes r us? Making sense of genetic and non-genetic relationships following anonymous donor insemination. *Reproductive BioMedicine Online,* 24(7), 719–726.

Bock, J. (2000). Doing the right thing? Single mothers by choice and the struggle for legitimacy. *Gender and Society,* 14, 62–86.

Bok, S. (1982). *Secrets.* New York: Pantheon.

Bonduelle, M. (2003). Developmental outcome at 2 years of age for children born after ICSI compared with children born after IVF. *Human Reproduction,* 18(2), 342–350. doi:10.1093/humrep/deg061

Bonduelle, M., Joris, H., Hofmans, K., Liebaers, I., and Van Steirteghem, A. (1998). Mental development of 201 ICSI children at 2 years of age. *The Lancet,* 351(9115), 1553. doi:10.1016/S0140-6736(98)24021-9

Bonduelle, M., Ponjaert, I., Van Steirteghem, A., Derde, M. P., Devroey, P., and Liebaers, I. (2003). Developmental outcome at 2 years of age for children born after ICSI compared with children born after IVF. *Human Reproduction,* 18(2), 1–9.

Booth-LaForce, C., and Roisman, G. I. (2014). The Adult Attachment Interview: Psychometrics, stability and change from infancy, and developmental origins. *Monographs of the Society for Research in Child Development.* P. J. Bauer (ed.), serial no. 314, 79(3), 1–185.

Bornstein, M. H. (ed.) (2002). *Handbook of parenting* (2nd edn., 5 vols.). Mahwah, NJ: Lawrence Erlbaum.

Bornstein, M. H. (2006). Parenting science and practice. In W. Damon and R. M. Lerner (series eds.) and I. E. Sigel and K. A. Renninger (vol. eds.), *Handbook of child psychology,* vol. IV: *Child psychology in practice* (6th edn., pp. 893–949). New York: Wiley.

Bos, H., and Gartrell, N., van Balen, F., Peyser, H., and Sandfort, T. (2008). Children in planned lesbian families: A cross-cultural comparison between the United States and the Netherlands. *American Journal of Orthopsychiatry,* 78(2), 211–219. doi:10.1037/a0012711

Bos, H., and Gartrell, N. (2010). Adolescents of the USA National Longitudinal Lesbian Family Study: Can family characteristics counteract the negative effects of stigmatization? *Family Process,* 49(4), 559–572. doi:10.1111/j.1545-5300 .2010.01340.x

Bos, H., and Gartrell, N. (2011). Adolescents of the US National Longitudinal Lesbian Family Study: The impact of having a known or an unknown donor on the stability of psychological adjustment. *Human Reproduction,* 26, 630.

Bos, H., Gartrell, N., and van Gelderen, L. (2013). Adolescents in lesbian families: DSM-oriented scale scores and stigmatization. *Journal of Gay and Lesbian Social Services*, 25(2), 121–140. doi:10.1080/10538720.2013.782456

Bos, H. M. W., Gartrell, N. K., Peyser, H., and van Balen, F. (2008). The USA National Longitudinal Lesbian Family Study (NLLFS): Homophobia, psychological adjustment, and protective factors. *Journal of Lesbian Studies*, 12(4), 455–471. doi:10.1080/10894160802278630

Bos, H. M. W., Gartrell, N. K., van Balen, F., Peyser, H., and Sandfort, T. G. M. (2008). Children in planned lesbian families: A cross-cultural comparison between the United States and the Netherlands. *American Journal of Orthopsychiatry*, 78(2), 211–219.

Bos, H., and Sandfort, T. G. M. (2010). Children's gender identity in lesbian and heterosexual two-parent families. *Sex Roles*, 62(1–2), 114–126. doi:10.1007/s11199-009-9704-7

Bos, H., and van Balen, F. (2008). Children in planned lesbian families: Stigmatisation, psychological adjustment and protective factors. *Culture, Health and Sexuality*, 10, 221–236. doi:10.1080/13691050701601702

Bos, H. M. W., van Balen, F., and van den Boom, D. C. (2004). Experience of parenthood, couple relationship, social support, and child-rearing goals in planned lesbian mother families. *Journal of Child Psychology and Psychiatry, and Allied Disciplines*, 45(4), 755–764. doi:10.1111/j.1469-7610.2004.00269.x

Bos, H., van Balen, F., and van den Boom, D. C. (2007). Child adjustment and parenting in planned lesbian-parent families. *American Journal of Orthopsychiatry*, 77(1), 38–48.

Bowen, J. R., Gibson, F. L., Leslie, G. I., and Saunders, D. M. (1998). Medical and developmental outcome at 1 year for children conceived by intracytoplasmic sperm injection. *The Lancet*, 351(9115), 1529–1534. doi:10.1016/S0140-6736(98)10168-X

Bowlby, J. (1951). Maternal care and mental health. *Bulletin of the World Health Organization*, 3, 355–534.

Bowlby, J. (1969). *Attachment and loss*. New York: Basic Books.

Bowlby, J. (1988). Developmental psychiatry comes of age. *Americal Journal of Psychiatry*, 145, 1–10.

Bradley, R. H., and Corwyn, R. F. (2002). Socioeconomic status and child development. *Annual Review of Psychology*, 53, 371–399. doi:10.1146/annurev.psych.53.100901.135233

Brazier, M., Campbell, A., and Golombok, S. (1998). *Surrogacy Review for health ministers of current arrangements for payments and regulation*. Report of the Review Team. Cm 4068. Department of Health, London.

Brewaeys, A., Ponjaert, I., van Hall, E. V, and Golombok, S. (1997). Donor insemination: Child development and family functioning in lesbian mother families. *Human Reproduction*, 12(6), 1349–1359.

Briggs-Gowan, M. J., Carter, A. S., Irwin, J. R., Wachtel, K., and Cicchetti, D. V. (2004). The brief infant–toddler social and emotional assessment: Screening for social-emotional problems and delays in competence. *Journal of Pediatric Psychology*, 29(2), 143–155.

Brodzinsky, D. M. (1987). Adjustment to adoption: A psychosocial perspective. *Clinical Psychological Review*, 7, 25–47.

Brodzinsky, D. M. (2006). Family structural openness and communication openness as predictors in the adjustment of adopted children. *Adoption Quarterly*, 9(4), 1–18.

Brodzinsky, D. M. (2011). Children's understanding of adoption: Developmental and clinical implications. *Professional Psychology: Research and Practice*, 42(2), 200–207. doi:10.1037/a0022415

Brodzinsky, D. M., and Evan B. Donaldson Adoption Institute (2011). *Expanding resources for children III: Research-based best practices in adoption by gays and lesbians*. New York: Evan B. Donaldson Adoption Institute.

Brodzinsky, D. M., and Pinderhughes, E. (2002). Parenting and child development in adoptive families. In M. H. Bornstein (ed.), *Handbook of parenting* (Vol. I, pp. 279–311). Hillsdale, NJ: Lawrence Erlbaum.

Brodzinsky, D. M., Schechter, D., and Brodzinsky, A. B. (1986). *Children's knowledge of adoption: Developmental changes and implications for adjustment*. Hillsdale, NJ: Lawrence Erlbaum.

Brodzinsky, D. M., Singer, L. M., and Braff, A. M. (1984). Children's understanding of adoption. *Child Development*, 55(3), 869–878.

Brodzinsky, D. M., Smith, D. W., and Brodzinsky, A. B. (1998). *Children's adjustment to adoption: Developmental and clinical issues*. Thousand Oaks, CA: Sage.

Brooks, D., and Goldberg, S. (2001). Gay and lesbian adoptive and foster care placements: Can they meet the needs of waiting children? *Social Work*, 46(2), 147–157. doi:10.1093/sw/46.2.147

Brooks-Gunn, J., Britto, P. R., and Brady, C. (1999). Struggling to make ends meet: Poverty and child development. In M. E. Lamb (ed.), *Parenting and child development in "nontraditional" families* (pp. 279–304). Mahwah, NJ: Lawrence Erlbaum.

Bryan, E. (1992). *Twins, triplets and more: Their nature, development and care*. London: Penguin.

Burns, L. H. (1990). An exploratory study of perceptions of parenting after infertility. *Family Systems Medicine*, 8(2), 177–189.

Bussey, K., and Bandura, A. (1999). Social cognitive theory of gender development and differentiation. *Psychological Review*, 106, 676–713.

Cahn, N. (2009). Necessary subjects: The need for a mandatory national donor gamete databank. *DePaul Journal of Health Care Law*, 12, 203.

Carson, C., Redshaw, M., Sacker, A., Kelly, Y., Kurinczuk, J. J., and Quigley, M. A. (2012). Effects of pregnancy planning, fertility, and assisted reproductive treatment on child behavioral problems at 5 and 7 years: Evidence from the Millennium Cohort Study. *Fertility and Sterility*, (5), 1–8. doi:10.1016/j.fertnstert.2012.10.029

Casey, P., Jadva, V., Blake, L., and Golombok, S. (2013). Families created by donor insemination: Father–child relationships at age 7. *Journal of Marriage and Family*, 75(4), 858–870. doi:10.1111/jomf.12043

Cassidy, J., and Shaver, P. R. (1999). *Handbook of attachment: Theory, research and clinical applications*. New York: Guilford Press.

Cederblad, M., Friberg, B., Ploman, F., Sjöberg, N. O., Stjernqvist, K., and Zackrisson, E. (1996). Intelligence and behaviour in children born after in-vitro fertilization treatment. *Human Reproduction*, 11(9), 2052–2057.

Chan, R. W., Raboy, B., and Patterson, C. J. (1998). Psychosocial adjustment among children conceived via donor insemination by lesbian and heterosexual mothers. *Child Development*, 69(2), 443–457.

Cherlin, A. J., Furstenberg, F. F., Chase-Lansdale, P. L., Kiernan, K. E., Robins, P. K., Morrison, D. R., and Teitler, J. O. (1991). Longitudinal studies of the effects of divorce on children in Great Britain and the United States. *Science*, 252, 1386–1389.

Chisholm, K. (1998). A three year follow-up of attachment and indiscriminate friendliness in children adopted from Romanian orphanages. *Child Development*, 69(4), 1092–1106. doi:10.1111/j.1467–8624.1998.tb06162.x

Clamar, A. (1989). *Psychological implications of the anonymous pregnancy*. New York and London: Plenum.

Coie, J. D., Coie, J. E., Lochman, R., Terry, R., and Hyman, C. (1992). Predicting early adolescent disorder from childhood aggression and peer rejection. *Journal of Consulting and Clinical Psychology*, 60(5), 783–792. doi:10.1037/0022-0 06X.60.5.783

Coleman, L., and Glenn, F. (2009). *When couples part: Understanding the consequences for adults and children*. London: One Plus One.

Collins, W. A., Maccoby, E. E., Steinberg, L., Hetherington, E. M., and Bornstein, M. H. (2000). Contemporary research on parenting: The case for nature and nurture. *American Psychologist*, 55(2), 218–232. doi:10.1037//0003-0 66X.55.2.218

Colpin, H., and Bossaert, G. (2008). Adolescents conceived by IVF: Parenting and psychosocial adjustment. *Human Reproduction*, 23(12), 2724–2730.

Colpin, H., Demyttenaere, K., and Vandemeulebroecke, L. (1995). New reproductive technology and the family: The parent–child relationship following in vitro fertilization. *Journal of Child Psychology and Psychiatry*, 36(8), 1429–1441.

Colpin, H., De Munter, A. D., Nys, K., and Vandemeulebroecke, L. (1999). Parenting stress and psychosocial well-being among parents with twins conceived naturally or by reproductive technology. *Human Reproduction*, 14(12), 3133–3137.

Colpin, H., and Soenen, S. (2002). Parenting and psychosocial development of IVF children: A follow-up study. *Human Reproduction*, 17(4), 1116–2223.

Conger, R., Conger, K., Elder, G., Lorenz, F., Simons, R., and Whitbeck, L. (1992). A family process model of economic hardship and adjustment of early adolescent boys. *Child Development*, 63, 526–541.

Conger, R., and Donnellan, M. (2007). An interactionist perspective on the socio-economic context of human development. *Annual Review of Psychology*, 58, 175–199.

Conger, R., Ge, X., Elder, G., Lorenz, F., and Simons, R. (1994). Economic stress, coercive family process, and developmental problems of adolescents. *Child Development*, 65, 541–561.

Cook, R., Bradley, S., and Golombok, S. (1998). A preliminary study of parental stress and child behaviour in families with twins conceived by in-vitro fertilization. *Human Reproduction*, 13(11), 3244–3246.

Cook, R., Golombok, S., Bish, A., and Murray, C. (1995). Disclosure of donor insemination: Parental attitudes. *American Journal of Orthopsychiatry*, 65(4), 549–559.

Covington, S. N., and Burns, L. H. (eds.). (2006). *Infertility counseling: A comprehensive handbook for clinicians.* Cambridge University Press.

Cox, M. J., Owen, M. T., Henderson, V. K., and Margand, N. A. (1992). Prediction of infant-father and infant-mother attachment. *Developmental Psychology*, 28(3), 474–483. doi:10.1037/0012-1649.28.3.474

Crawshaw, M. (2002). Lessons from a recent adoption study to identify some of the service needs of, and issues for, donor offspring wanting to know about their donors. *Human Fertility*, 5(16–12).

Crowl, A., Ahn, S., and Baker, J. (2008). A meta-analysis of developmental outcomes for children of same-sex and heterosexual parents. *Journal of GLBT Family Studies*, 4(3), 385–407. doi:10.1080/15504280802177615

Cummings, E. M., and Davies, P. (1994). *Children and marital conflict.* New York: Guilford Press.

Cummings, E. M., and Davies, P. T. (2010). *Marital conflict and children: An emotional security perspective.* New York and London: The Guildford Press.

D'Augelli, A. R., Rendina, H. J., and Sinclair, K. O. (2008). Gay and lesbian youth want long-term couple relationships and raising children. *Journal of LGBT Issues in Counseling*, 1(4), 77–98.

Daniels, K., Gillett, W., and Grace, V. (2009). Parental information sharing with donor insemination conceived offspring: A follow-up study. *Human Reproduction*, 24(5), 1099–1105. doi:10.1093/humrep/den495

Daniels, K. R., Grace, V. M., and Gillett, W. R. (2011). Factors associated with parents' decisions to tell their adult offspring about the offspring's donor conception. *Human Reproduction*, 26(10), 2783–2790. doi:10.1093/humrep/der247

Daniels, K. R., and Taylor, K. (1993). Secrecy and openness in donor insemination. *Politics and the Life Sciences*, 12(2), 155–170.

Daniels, K. R., and Thorn, P. (2001). Sharing information with donor insemination offspring: A child-conception versus a family building approach. *Human Reproduction*, 16(9), 1792–1796.

Darling, N., and Steinberg, L. (1993). Parenting style as context: an integrative model. *Psychological Bulletin*, 113, 486–496.

DasGupta, S., and Dasgupta, S. D. (2014). *Globalization and transnational surrogacy in India: Outsourcing life*. Lanham, MA: Lexington Books.

Davies, P. T., and Cummings, E. M. (1994). Marital conflict and child adjustment: An emotional security hypothesis. *Psychological Bulletin*, 116(3), 387–411. doi:10.1037/0033-2909.116.3.387

De Wolff, M. S., and van IJzendoorn, M. H. (1997). Sensitivity and attachment: A meta-analysis on parental antecedents of infant attachment. *Child Development*, 68(4), 571–591. doi:10.1111/j.1467-8624.1997.tb04218.x

Demo, D. H., and Acock, A. C. (1996). Family structure, family process, and adolescent well-being. *Journal of Research on Adolescence*, 6(4), 457–488.

Demuth, S., and Brown, S. L. (2004). Family structure, family processes, and adolescent delinquency: The significance of parental absence versus parental gender. *Journal of Research in Crime and Delinquency*, 41(1), 58–81. doi:10.1177/0022427803256236

DePaulo, B. M. (1992). Nonverbal behavior and self-presentation. *Psychological Bulletin*, 111(2), 203–243.

DeRosier, M. E., Kupersmidt, J. B., and Patterson, C. J. (1994). Children's academic and behavioral adjustment as a function of the chronicity and proximity of peer rejection. *Child Development*, 65(6), 1799–1813. doi:10.1111/j.1467-8624.1994.tb00850.x

Downey, G., and Coyne, J. C. (1990). Children of depressed parents: An integrative review. *Psychological Bulletin*, 108(1), 50–76.

Dozier, M., and Rutter, M. (2008). Challenges to the development of attachment relationships faced by young people in foster and adoptive care. In J. Cassidy and J. Shaver (eds.), *Handbook of attachment: Theory, research and clinical applications* (2nd edn., pp. 1083–1095). New York: Guilford Press.

Dozier, M., Zeanah, C. H., and Bernard, K. (2013). Infants and toddlers in foster care. *Child Development Perspectives*, 7(3). doi:10.1111/cdep.12033

Dunbar, N., and Grotevant, H. D. (2004). Adoption narratives: The construction of adoptive identity during adolescence. In M. W. Pratt and B. H. Fiese (eds.), *Family stories and the life course: Across time and generations* (pp. 135–161). Mahwah, NJ: Lawrence Erlbaum.

Dunn, J. (2004). Annotation: Children's relationships with their non-resident fathers. *Journal of Child Psychology and Psychiatry*, 45(4), 659–671. doi:10.1111/j.1469-7610.2004.00261.x

Dunn, J. (2008). *Family relationships, children's perspectives*. London: OnePlusOne.

Dunn, J., Cheng, H., O'Connor, T., and Bridges, L. (2004). Children's perspectives on their relationships with their non-resident fathers: Influences, outcomes and implications. *Journal of Child Psychology and Psychiatry*, 45(3), 553–566.

Dunn, J., Davies, L. C., O'Connor, T. G., and Sturgess, W. (2000). Parents' and partners' life course and family experiences: Links with parent–child relationships in different family settings. *Journal of Child Psychology and Psychiatry*, 41(8), 955–968.

Dunn, J., Davies, L. C., O'Connor, T. G., and Sturgess, W. (2001). Family lives and friendships: The perspectives of children in step-, single-parent and nonstep families. *Journal of Family Psychology*, 15, 272–287.

Dunn, J., Deater-Deckard, K., Pickering, K., O'Connor, T. G., and Golding, J. (1998). Children's adjustment and prosocial behavior in step-parent, single-parent, and non-stepfamily settings: Findings from a community study. *Journal of Child Psychology and Psychiatry*, 39(8), 1083–1095.

Dunn, J., O'Connor, T. G., and Cheng, H. (2005). Children's response to conflict between their different parents: Mothers, stepfathers, NR fathers, and NR stepmothers. *Journal of Clinical Child and Adolescent Psychology*, 34, 223–234.

Dunn, J., and Plomin, R. (1990). *Separate lives: Why siblings are so different.* New York: Basic Books.

Edwards, C. P., and Liu, W. (2002). Parenting toddlers. In M. H. Bornstein (ed.), *Handbook of parenting* (Vol. I, pp. 45–72). Hillsdale, NJ: Lawrence Erlbaum.

Ehlert, U. (2014, 7–9 May). Psychobiology of fatherhood: What we know and what we don't. In M. Lamb and L. Ahnhert (eds.), *Men as fathers: Interdisciplinary perspectives on fatherhood in the context of the family.* Zurich: The Jacobs Foundation.

Ehrensaft, D. (2008). When baby makes three, four or more: Attachment, individuation, and identity in assisted-conception families. *The Psychoanalytic Study of the Child*, 63, 3–23.

Elliot, J., and Vaitilingam, R. (2008). *Now we are 50: Key findings from the National Child Development Study.* London: The Centre for Longitudinal Studies.

Emery, R. E. (1988). *Marriage, divorce and children's adjustment.* Newbury Park, CA: Sage.

Erich, S., Hall, S. K., Kanenberg, H., and Case, K. (2009). Early and late stage adolescence: Adopted adolescents' attachment to their heterosexual and lesbian/gay parents. *Adoption Quarterly*, 12, 152–170.

Erich, S., Kanenberg, H., Case, K., Allen, T., and Bogdanos, T. (2008). An empirical analysis of factors affecting adolescent attachment in adoptive families with homosexual and straight parents. *Children and Youth Services Review*, 31(3), 398–404. doi:10.1016/j.childyouth.2008.09.004

Erich, S., Leung, P., and Kindle, P. (2005). A comparative analysis of adoptive family functioning with gay, lesbian, and heterosexual parents and their children. *Journal of GLBT Family Studies*, 1(4), 43–61. doi:10.1300/J461v01n04

Erich, S., Leung, P., Kindle, P., and Carter, S. (2005). Gay and lesbian adoptive families: An exploratory study of family functioning, adoptive child's behavior, and familial support networks. *Journal of Family Social Work*, 9(1), 17–32. doi:10.1300/J039v09n01

Erickson, M. F., Sroufe, L. A., and Egeland, B. (1985). The relationship between quality of attachment and behavior problems in preschool in a high-risk sample. *Monographs of the Society for Research in Child Development*, 50(1–2), 147–166. doi:10.2307/3333831

Ethics Committee of the American Society for Reproductive Medicine (2013a). Informing offspring of their conception by gamete or embryo donation: A committee opinion. *Fertility and Sterility*, 92, 1190–1193.

Ethics Committee of the American Society for Reproductive Medicine (2013b). Access to fertility treatment by gays, lesbians, and unmarried persons: A committee opinion. *Fertility and Sterility*, 100(6), 1524–1527.

Farr, R., Forssell, S. L., and Patterson, C. (2010a). Gay, lesbian, and heterosexual adoptive parents: Couple and relationship issues. *Journal of GLBT Family Studies*, 6(2), 199–213. doi:10.1080/15504281003705436

Farr, R., Forssell, S., and Patterson, C. (2010b). Parenting and child development in adoptive families: Does parental sexual orientation matter? *Applied Developmental Science*, 14(3), 164–178. doi:10.1080/10888691.2010.500958

Farr, R., and Patterson, C. (2013). Coparenting among lesbian, gay, and heterosexual couples: Associations with adopted children's outcomes. *Child Development*, 84(4), 1226–1240. doi:10.1111/cdev.12046

Fauber, R. L., and Long, N. (1991). Children in context: The role of the family in child psychotherapy. *Journal of Consulting and Clinical Psychology*, 59(6), 813–820. doi:10.1037/0022-006X.59.6.813

Fauser, B. C., Devroey, P., Diedrich, K., Balaban, B., Bonduelle, M., Delemarre-van de Waal, H. A., Estella, C., Ezcurra, D., Geraedts, J., Howles, C., Lerner-Geva, L., Serna, J., Wells, D., Evian Annual Reproduction (EVAR) Workshop Group 2011. (2014). Health outcomes of children born after IVF/ICSI: A review of current expert opinion and literature. *Reproductive BioMedicine Online*, 28, 162–182.

Feast, J. (2003). Using and not losing the messages from the adoption experience for donor-assisted conception. *Human Fertility*, 6(1), 41–45.

Fedewa, A. L., Black, W. W., and Ahn, S. (2014). Children and adolescents with same-gender parents: A meta-analytic approach in assessing outcomes. *Journal of GLBT Family Studies*, 11(1), 1–34. doi:10.1080/1550428X.2013.869486

Feldman, R., and Eidelman, A. I. (2005). Does a triplet birth pose a special risk for infant development? Assessing cognitive development in relation to intrauterine growth and mother–infant interaction across the first 2 years. *Pediatrics*, 115(2), 443–452. doi:10.1542/peds.2004-1137

Feldman, R., Eidelman, A. I., and Rotenberg, N. (2004). Parenting stress, infant emotion regulation, maternal sensitivity, and the cognitive development of triplets: A model for parent and child influences in a unique ecology. *Child Development*, 75(6), 1774–1791. doi:10.1111/j.1467-8624.2004.00816.x

Ferraretti, A. P., Goossens, V., Kupka, M., Bhattacharya, S., de Mouzon, J., Castilla, J. A., Erb, K., Korsak, V., and Nyboe Andersen, A. (2013). Assisted reproductive technology in Europe, 2009: Results generated from European registers by ESHRE. *Human Reproduction*, 28(9), 2318–2331. doi:10.1093/humrep/det278

Ferri, E. (1976). *Growing up in a one-parent family*. Slough: National Foundation for Educational Research.

Field, T. (1995). Psychologically depressed parents. In M. Bornstein (ed.), *Handbook of Parenting* (vol. IV, pp. 85–99). Hove: Lawrence Erlbaum.

Flaks, D. K., Ficher, I., Masterpasqua, F., and Joseph, G. (1995). Lesbians choosing motherhood: A comparative study of lesbian and heterosexual parents and their children. *British Journal of Developmental Psychology*, 31, 105–114.

Follain, J. (2014). Pope's 'shock' is setback for gays. *Sunday Times*, January 5, 2014.

Fonagy, P., Steele, H., and Steele, M. (1991). Maternal representations of attachment during pregnancy predict the organization of infant–mother attachment at one year of age. *Child Development*, 62(5), 891–905. doi:10.1111/j.1467–8624.1991. tb01578.x

Fox, N. A. (1995). Of the way we were: Adult memories about attachment experiences and their role in determining infant–parent relationships:

A commentary on van IJzendoorn (1995). *Psychological Bulletin*, 117(3), 404–410. doi:10.1037/0033-2909.117.3.404

Franz, S., and Allen, D. (2001). *Report to Health Canada: The offspring speak – an international conference of donor offspring.* Toronto, ON: Infertility Network.

Freeman, T., Bourne, K., Jadva, V., and Smith, V. (2014). Making connections: Contact between sperm donor relations. In T. Freeman, S. Graham, F. Ebethaj, and M. Richards (eds.), *Relatedness in assisted reproduction: Families, origins and identities.* Cambridge University Press.

Freeman, T., Jadva, V., Kramer, W., and Golombok, S. (2009). Gamete donation: Parents' experiences of searching for their child's donor siblings and donor. *Human Reproduction*, 24(3), 505–516.

Freud, S. (1933). *Psychology of women: New introductory lectures on psychoanalysis.* London: Hogarth Press.

Freud, S. (1953). Three essays on the theory of sexuality. In J. Strachey (ed.), *The standard edition of the complete works of Sigmund Freud* (Vol. VII, pp. 125–243). London: Hogarth Press. (Original work published 1905)

Freud, S. (1955). Beyond the pleasure principle. In J. Strachey (ed.), *The standard edition of the complete works of Sigmund Freud* (Vol. XVIII, pp. 3–68). London: Hogarth Press. (Original work published 1920.)

Fulcher, M., Sutfin, E. L., and Patterson, C. J. (2008). Individual differences in gender development: Associations with parental sexual orientation, attitudes, and division of labor. *Sex Roles*, 58, 330–341. doi:10.1007/s11199-007-9348-4

Garel, M., Salobir, C., and Blondel, B. (1997). Psychological consequences of having triplets: A 4-year follow-up study. *Fertility and Sterility*, 67(6), 1162–1165.

Garel, M., Salobir, C., Lelong, N., and Blondel, B. (2001). Development and behaviour of seven-year-old triplets. *Acta Paediatrica*, 90(5), 539–543.

Garmezy, N. (1991). Resilience and vulnerability to adverse developmental outcomes associated with poverty. *American Behavioral Scientist*, 34(4), 416–430. doi:10.1177/0002764291034004003

Gartrell, N., and Bos, H. (2010). US National Longitudinal Lesbian Family Study: Psychological adjustment of 17-year-old adolescents. *Pediatrics*, 126(1), 28–36. doi:10.1542/peds.2009-3153

Gartrell, N. K., Bos, H. M. W., and Goldberg, N. G. (2011). Adolescents of the U.S. National Longitudinal Lesbian Family Study: Sexual orientation, sexual behavior, and sexual risk exposure. *Archives of Sexual Behavior*, 40(6), 1199–1209. doi:10.1007/s10508-010-9692-2

Gartrell, N., Bos, H., Peyser, H., Deck, A., and Rodas, C. (2012). Adolescents with lesbian mothers describe their own lives. *Journal of Homosexuality*, 59(9), 1211–1229. doi:10.1080/00918369.2012.720499

Gartrell, N., Deck, A., Rodas, C., Peyser, H., and Banks, A. (2005). The National Lesbian Family Study: Interviews with the 10-year-old children. *American Journal of Orthopsychiatry*, 75(4), 518–524.

Gartrell, N., Peyser, H., and Bos, H. M. W. (2012). Planned lesbian families: A review of the U.S.A. National Longitudinal Lesbian Family Study. In D. M. Brodzinsky and A. Pertman (eds), *Adoption by Lesbians and Gay Men: A New Dimension in Family Diversity*. Oxford: Oxford University Press.

Gartrell, N., Rodas, C., Deck, A., Peyser, H., and Banks, A. (2006). The USA National Lesbian Family Study. Interviews with mothers of 10-year-olds. *Feminism and Psychology*, 16(2), 175–192.

Gates, G. J. (2013). *LGBT parenting in the United States*. Los Angeles, CA: The Williams Institute.

George, C., Kaplan, N., and Main, M. (1985). *Attachment interview for adults*. University of California, Berkeley.

Gershon, T. D., Tschann, J. M., and Jemerin, J. M. (1999). Stigmatization, self-esteem, and coping among the adolescent children of lesbian mothers. *The Journal of Adolescent Health*, 24(6), 437–445.

Ghevaert, L. (2010, February 9). What happens when surrogacy goes wrong: The recent Indiana surrogacy case in wider context. *BioNews* 545. Retrieved November 16, 2014 from www.bionews.org.uk/page_54415.asp

Gianino, M., Goldberg, A. E., and Lewis, T. (2009). Family outings: Disclosure practices among adopted youth with gay and lesbian parents. *Adoption Quarterly*, 12(3–4), 205–228. doi:10.1080/10926750903313344

Gibson, F., Ungerer, J. A., Leslie, G., Saunders, D., and Tennant, C. (1998). Development, behaviour, and temperament: A prospective, longitudinal study of infants conceived through in-vitro fertilization. *Human Reproduction*, 13, 1727–1732.

Gibson, F., Ungerer, J. A., McMahon, C., Leslie, G. I., and Saunders, D. M. (2000). The mother–child relationship following in vitro fertilisation (IVF): Infant attachment, responsivity, and maternal sensitivity. *Journal of Child Psychology and Psychiatry*, 41(8), 1015–1023.

Gibson, F. L., Ungerer, J. A., Tennant, C. C., and Saunders, D. M. (2000). Parental adjustment and attitudes to parenting after in vitro fertilization. *Fertility and Sterility*, 73(3), 565–574.

Glazebrook, C., Sheard, C., Cox, S., Oates, M., and Ndukwe, G. (2004). Parenting stress in first-time mothers of twins and triplets conceived after in vitro fertilization. *Fertility and Sterility*, 81(3), 505–511.

Gleicher, N., Campbell, D. P., Chan, C. L., Karande, V., Rao, R., Balin, M., and Pratt, D. (1995). Infertility: The desire for multiple births in couples with infertility problems contradicts present practice patterns. *Human Reproduction*, 10(5), 1079–1084.

Glennon, T. (2015). Legal regulation of family creation through gamete donation: Access, identity and parentage. In S. Golombok, J. Appleby, M. Richards, R. Scott and S. Wilkinson (eds.), *Regulating reproductive regulation*. Cambridge University Press.

Godman, K. M., Sanders, K., Rosenberg, M., and Burton, P. (2006). Potential sperm donors', recipients' and their partners' opinions towards the release of identifying information in Western Australia. *Human Reproduction*, 21(11), 3022–3026.

Goldberg, A. E. (2007). Talking about family: Disclosure practices of adults raised by lesbian, gay, and bisexual parents. *Journal of Family Issues*, 28(1), 100–131.

Goldberg, A. E. (2010). Studying complex families in context. *Journal of Marriage and Family*, 72(1), 29–34.

Goldberg, A. E. (2012). *Gay dads: Transitions to adoptive fatherhood*. New York University Press.

Goldberg, A. E., and Allen, K. R. (2013). Donor, dad, or …? Young adults with lesbian parents' experiences with known donors. *Family Process*, 52(2), 338–350.

Goldberg, J. S., and Carlson, M. J. (2014). Parents' relationship quality and children's behavior in stable married and cohabiting families. *Journal of Marriage and Family*, 76(4), 762–777.

Goldberg, A. E., Downing, J. B., and Moyer, A. M. (2012). Why parenthood, and why now? Gay men's motivations for pursuing parenthood. *Family Relations*, 61(1), 157–174.

Goldberg, A. E., Downing, J. B., and Sauck, C. C. (2008). Perceptions of children's parental preferences in lesbian two-mother households. *Journal of Marriage and Family*, 70(2), 419–434.

Goldberg, A. E., Kashy, D. A., and Smith, J. Z. (2012). Gender-typed play behavior in early childhood: Adopted children with lesbian, gay, and heterosexual parents. *Sex Roles*, 67(9–10), 503–515.

Goldberg, A. E., and Kuvalanka, K. A. (2012). Marriage (in)equality: The perspectives of adolescents and emerging adults with lesbian, gay, and bisexual parents. *Journal of Marriage and Family*, 74(1), 34–52.

Goldfarb, J., Kinzer, D. J., Boyle, M., and Kurit, D. (1996). Attitudes of in vitro fertilization and intrauterine insemination couples toward multiple gestation pregnancy and multifetal pregnancy reduction. *Fertility and Sterility*, 65(4), 815–820.

Goldsmith, H. H., Buss, A. H., Plomin, R., Rothbart, M. K., Thomas, A., Chess, S., Hinde, R. A., and McCall, R. B. (1987). Roundtable: What is temperament? Four approaches. *Child Development*, 58(2), 505–529. doi:10.2307/1130527

Goldstein, J., Freud, A., and Solnit, J. A. (1973). *Beyond the best interests of the child* (Vol. I). New York: The Free Press.

Golombok, S., and Badger, S. (2010). Children raised in mother-headed families from infancy: A follow-up of children of lesbian and single heterosexual mothers at early adulthood. *Human Reproduction*, 25(1), 150–157. doi:10.1093/humrep/dep345

Golombok, S., Appleby, J., Richards, M., Scott, R., and Wilkinson, S. (2015). *Regulating reproductive donation*. Cambridge University Press.

Golombok, S., Blake, L., Casey, P., Roman, G., and Jadva, V. (2013). Children born through reproductive donation: A longitudinal study of child adjustment. *Journal of Child Psychology and Psychiatry*, 54, 653–660. doi:10.1111/jcpp.12015.

Golombok, S., Brewaeys, A., Cook, R., Giavazzi, M. T., Guerra, D., Mantovani, A., Van Hall, E., Crosignani, P. G., and Dexeus, S. (1996). The European Study of Assisted Reproduction Families. *Human Reproduction*, 11(10), 2324–2331.

Golombok, S., Brewaeys, A., Giavazzi, M. T., Guerra, D., MacCallum, F., and Rust, J. (2002). The European Study of Assisted Reproduction Families: The transition to adolescence. *Human Reproduction*, 17(3), 830–840.

Golombok, S., Cook, R., Bish, A., and Murray, C. (1995). Families created by the new reproductive technologies: Quality of parenting and social and emotional development of the children. *Child Development*, 64(2), 285–298.

Golombok, S., Jadva, V., Lycett, E., Murray, C., and MacCallum, F. (2005). Families created by gamete donation: Follow-up at age 2. *Human Reproduction*, 20(1), 286–293.

Golombok, S., Lycett, E., MacCallum, F., Jadva, V., Murray, C., and Rust, J., Abdallah, H., Jenkins, J., and Margara, R. (2004). Parenting infants conceived by gamete donation. *Journal of Family Psychology*, 18(3), 443–452.

Golombok, S., MacCallum, F., and Goodman, E. (2001). The "test-tube" generation: Parent–child relationships and the psychological well-being of in vitro fertilization children at adolescence. *Child Development*, 72(2), 599–608.

Golombok, S., MacCallum, F., Goodman, E., and Rutter, M. (2002). Families with children conceived by donor insemination: A follow-up at age twelve. *Child Development*, 73(3), 952–968.

Golombok, S., MacCallum, F., Murray, C., Lycett, E., and Jadva, V. (2006). Surrogacy families: Parental functioning, parent–child relationships and children's psychological development at age 2. *Journal of Child Psychology and Psychiatry*, 47(2), 213–222.

Golombok, S., Mellish, L., Jennings, S., Casey, P., Tasker, F., and Lamb, M. E. (2014). Adoptive gay father families: Parent–child relationships and children's psychological adjustment. *Child Development*, 85(2), 456–468.

Golombok, S., Murray, C., Brinsden, P., and Abdalla, H. (1999). Social versus biological parenting: Family functioning and the socioemotional development of children conceived by egg or sperm donation. *Journal of Child Psychology and Psychiatry*, 40(4), 519–527.

Golombok, S., Murray, C., Jadva, V., Lycett, E., MacCallum, F., and Rust, J. (2006). Non-genetic and non-gestational parenthood: Consequences for parent–child relationships and the psychological well-being of mothers, fathers and children at age 3. *Human Reproduction*, 21(7), 1918–1924.

Golombok, S., Murray, C., Jadva, V., MacCallum, F., and Lycett, E. (2004). Families created through surrogacy arrangements: Parent–child relationships in the 1st year of life. *Developmental Psychology*, 40(3), 400–411.

Golombok, S., Olivennes, F., Ramogida, C., Rust, J., and Freeman, T. (2007). Parenting and the psychological development of a representative sample of triplets conceived by assisted reproduction. *Human Reproduction*, 22(11), 2896–2902. doi:10.1093/humrep/dem260

Golombok, S., Owen, L., Blake, L., Murray, C., and Jadva, V. (2009). Parent–child relationships and the psychological well-being of 18-year-old adolescents conceived by in vitro fertilisation. *Human Fertility*, 12(2), 63–72.

Golombok, S., Perry, B., Burston, A., Murray, C., Mooney-Somers, J., Stevens, M., and Golding, J., et al. (2003). Children with lesbian parents: A community study. *British Journal of Developmental Psychology*, 39(1), 20–33. doi:10.1037/0012-1649.39.1.20

Golombok, S., Readings, J., Blake, L., Casey, P., Marks, A., and Jadva, V. (2011). Families created through surrogacy: Mother–child relationships and children's psychological adjustment at age 7. *Developmental Psychology*, 47(6), 1579–1588. doi:10.1037/a0025292

Golombok, S., Readings, J., Blake, L., Casey, P., Mellish, L., Marks, A., and Jadva, V. (2011). Children conceived by gamete donation: The impact of openness about donor conception on psychological adjustment and parent–child relationships at age 7. *Journal of Family Psychology*, 25(2), 230–239.

Golombok, S., and Rust, J. (1993a). The measurement of gender role behaviour in pre-school children: A research note. *Journal of Child Psychology and Psychiatry*, 34(5), 805–811.

Golombok, S., and Rust, J. (1993b). The Pre-School Activities Inventory: A standardized assessment of gender role in children. *Psychological Assessment*, 5(2), 131–136. doi:10.1037//1040-3590.5.2.131

Golombok, S., Rust, J., Zervoulis, K., Croudace, T., Golding, J., and Hines, M. (2008). Developmental trajectories of sex-typed behaviour in boys and girls: A longitudinal general population study of children aged 2.5–8 years. *Child Development*, 79(5), 1583–1593.

Golombok, S., Scott, R., Wilkinson, S., Richards, M., and Appleby, J. (2015). *Regulating reproductive donation*. Cambridge University Press.

Golombok, S., Spencer, A., and Rutter, M. (1983). Children in lesbian and single-parent households: Psychosexual and psychiatric appraisal. *Journal of Child Psychology and Psychiatry*, 24(4), 551–572.

Golombok, S., and Tasker, F. (1996). Do parents influence the sexual orientation of their children? Findings from a longitudinal study of lesbian families. *British Journal of Developmental Psychology*, 32, 3–11.

Golombok, S., and Tasker, F. (2010). Gay fathers. In M. Lamb (ed.), *The role of the father in child development*. Hoboken, NJ: Wiley.

Golombok, S., and Tasker, F. (2015). Socio-emotional development in changing family contexts. In R. M. Lerner (series ed.) and M. E. Lamb (vol. ed.), *Handbook of child psychology and developmental science*, vol. III: *Social, emotional and personality development* (7th edn.). Hoboken, NJ: Wiley.

Golombok, S., Tasker, F., and Murray, C. (1997). Children raised in fatherless families from infancy: Family relationships and the socioemotional development of children of lesbian and single heterosexual mothers. *Journal of Child Psychology and Psychiatry*, 38(7), 783–791. doi:10.1111/j.1469–7610.1997. tb01596.x

Goodman, R. (1994). A modified version of the Rutter Parent Questionnaire including extra items on children's strengths: A research note. *Journal of Child Psychology and Psychiatry*, 35(8), 1483–1494.

Goodman, R. (1997). The Strengths and Difficulties Questionnaire: A research note. *Journal of Child Psychology and Psychiatry*, 38(5), 581–586.

Goodman, R. (2001). Psychometric properties of the Strengths and Difficulties Questionnaire. *Journal of the American Academy of Child Psychiatry*, 40(11), 1337–1345.

Goodman, S. H., and Brand, S. R. (2008). Parental psychopathology and its relation to child psychopathology. In M. Hersen and A. M. Gross (eds.), *Handbook of clinical psychology*, vol. II: *Children and adolescents* (pp. 935–965). Hoboken, NJ: Wiley.

Gosden, R. (2000). *Designing babies: The brave new world of reproductive technology*. New York: Freeman.

Gottlieb, C., Lalos, O., and Lindblad, F. (2000). Disclosure of donor insemination to the child: The impact of Swedish legislation on couples' attitudes. *Human Reproduction*, 15, 2052–2056.

Gottman, J. (1990). Children of gay and lesbian parents. In F. W. Bozett and M. B. Sussman (eds.), *Homosexuality and family relations* (pp. 177–196). New York: Harrington Park.

Graham, S. (2012). Choosing single motherhood? Single women negotiating the nuclear family ideal. In D. Cutas and S. Chan (eds.), *Families: Beyond the nuclear ideal.* London: Bloomsbury.

Graham, S. (2014). Stories of an absent "father": Single women negotiating relatedness from donor profiles. In T. Freeman, S. Graham, F. Ebethaj, and M. Richards (eds.), *Relatedness in assisted reproduction: Families, origins and identities* (pp. 212–231). Cambridge University Press.

Graham, S., and Braverman, A. (2012). ARTs and the single parent. In M. Richards, G. Pennings, and J. B. Appleby (eds.), *Reproductive donation: Practice, policy and bioethics.* Cambridge University Press.

Green, R., Mandel, J. B., Hotvedt, M. E., Gray, J., and Smith, L. (1986). Lesbian mothers and their children: A comparison with solo parent heterosexual mothers and their children. *Archives of Sexual Behavior*, 15(2), 167–184.

Greenfeld, D. A., and Seli, E. (2011). Gay men choosing parenthood through assisted reproduction: Medical and psychosocial considerations. *Fertility and Sterility*, 95(1), 225–229. doi:10.1016/j.fertnstert.2010.05.053

Gregg, E., Solomon, A., Johnson, S. C., Zaitchik, D., and Carey, S. (1996). Like father, like son: Young children's understanding of how and why offspring resemble their parents. *Child Development*, 67, 151–171.

Grossmann, K. E., and Grossmann, K. (1991). Attachment quality as an organizer of emotional and behavioral responses in a longitudinal perspective. In C. M. Parkes, J. Stevenson-Hinde, and P. Marris (eds.), *Attachment across the life cycle* (pp. 93–114). London: Routledge.

Grossman, K. E., Grossman, K., and Waters, E. (2005). *Attachment from infancy to adulthood.* New York: Guilford.

Grotevant, H. D. (1997). Family processes, identity development, and behavioral outcomes for adopted adolescents. *Journal of Adolescent Research*, 12, 139–161.

Grotevant, H. D. (1999). Adoptive identity development: New kinship patterns, new issues. In A. L. Rygvold, M. M. Dalen, and B. Saetersdal (eds.), *Mine–yours–oursand theirs: Adoption, changing kinship, and family patterns* (pp. 101–116). University of Oslo Press.

Grotevant, H. D. (2009). Emotional distance regulation over the life course in adoptive kinship networks. In G. Wrobel and E. Neil (eds.), *International advances in adoption research for practice* (pp. 295–316). Chichester: Wiley.

Grotevant, H. D., Dunbar, N., Kohler, J. K., and Esau, A. M. L. (2000). Adoptive identity: How contexts within and beyond the family shape developmental pathways. *Family Relations*, 49(4), 379–387. doi:10.1111/j.1741-3729.2000.00379.x

Grotevant, H. D., and Kohler, J. K. (1999). Adoptive families. In M. E. Lamb (ed.), *Parenting and child development in "nontraditional" families* (pp. 161–190). Mahwah, NJ: Lawrence Erlbaum.

Grotevant, H. D., McRoy, R. G., Wrobel, G. M., and Ayers-Lopez, S. (2013). Contact between adoptive and birth families: Perspectives from the Minnesota Texas Adoption Research Project. *Child Development Perspectives*, 7(3), 193–198. doi:10.1111/cdep.12039

Grotevant, H. D., Perry, Y. V, and McRoy, R. G. (2005). Openness in adoption: Outcomes for adolescents within their adoptive kinship networks. In D. M. Brodzinsky and J. Palacios (eds.), *Psychological issues in adoption. Research and practice* (pp. 167–185). Westport, CT: Praeger.

Grotevant, H. D., Rueter, M., Von Korff, L., and Gonzalez, C. (2011). Post-adoption contact, adoption communicative openness, and satisfaction with contact as predictors of externalizing behavior in adolescence and emerging adulthood. *Journal of Child Psychology and Psychiatry*, 52(5), 529–536. doi:10.1111/j.1469-7610.2010.02330.x

Grotevant, H. D., and Von Korff, L. (2011). *Adoptive identity*. In S. J. Schwartz, K. Luycks, and V. L. Vignoles (eds.), *Handbook of Identity Theory and Research*. New York: Springer.

Grover, S. A., Shmorgun, Z., Moskovtsev, S. I., Baratz, A., and Librach, C. L. (2013). Assisted reproduction in a cohort of same-sex male couples and single men. *Reproductive BioMedicine Online*, 27(2), 217–221. doi:10.1016/j.rbmo.2013.05.003

Grych, J. H., and Fincham, F. D. (1990). Marital conflict and children's adjustment: A cognitive-contextual framework. *Psychological Bulletin*, 108(2), 267–290. doi:10.1037/0033-2909.108.2.267

Grych, J. H., and Fincham, F. D. (1993). Children's appraisals of marital conflict: Initial investigations of the cognitive-contextual framework. *Child Development*, 64(1), 215–230. doi:10.1111/j.1467-8624.1993.tb02905.x

Grych, J. H., and Fincham, F. F. (eds.) (2001). *Child development and interparental conflict*. New York: Cambridge University Press.

Guasp, A., Statham, H., and Jennings, S. (2010). *Different families: The experiences of children with lesbian and gay parents*. London: Stonewall.

Gurdon, J. B. G. (2012). Human cloning could start within 50 years. *The Life Scientific*, BBC Radio 4.

Haberman, C. (2014, March 23). Baby M and the Question of Surrogate Motherhood. *New York Times*. Retrieved November 16, 2014 from www.nytime .com/2014/03/24/us/baby-m-and-the-question-of-surrogate-motherhood .html?_r=0

Hahn, C. S., and DiPietro, J. A. (2001). In vitro fertilization and the family: Quality of parenting, family functioning, and child psychosocial adjustment. *British Journal of Developmental Psychology*, 37, 37–48.

Hahn, S. J., and Craft-Rosenberg, M. (2002). The disclosure decisions of parents who conceive children using donor eggs. *Journal of Obstetrics and Gynecologic and Neonatal Nursing*, 31(3), 283–293.

Hansen, K., Johnson, J., Joshi, H., Calderwood, L., Jones, E., MacDonald, J., Platt, L., Rosenberg, R. M. Shepherd, P., Smith, K., and the Millennium Cohort Team. (2008). *Millennium Cohort Study first, second and third surveys: A guide to the datasets*. London: Institute of Education.

Hargreaves, K., and Daniels, K. R. (2007). Parents dilemmas in sharing donor insemination conception stories with their children. *Children and Society*, 21(21), 420–431.

Harold, G. T., and Conger, R. D. (1997). Marital conflict and adolescent distress: The role of adolescent awareness. *Child Development*, 68(2), 333–350.

Hay, D. A., Prior, M., Collett, S., and Williams, M. (1987). Speech and language development in preschool twins. *Acta Geneticae Medicae et Gemellologiae: Twin Research*, 33, 191–204.

Hayashi, K., Ohta, H., Kurimoto, K., Aramaki, S., and Saitou, M. (2011). Reconstitution of the mouse germ cell specification pathway in culture by pluripotent stem cells. *Cell*, 146(4), 519–532. doi:10.1016/j.cell.2011.06.052

Hayatbakhsh, M. R., Najman, J. M., Khatun, M., Mamun, A. A., Bor, W., and Clavarino, A. (2011). A longitudinal study of child mental health and problem behaviours at 14 years of age following unplanned pregnancy. *Psychiatry Research*, 185, 200–204.

Henderson, S. H., Hetherington, E. H., Mekos, D., and Reiss, D. (1996). Stress, parenting, and adolescent psychopathology in nondivorced and stepfamilies: A within-family perspective. In E. H. Hetherington and E. A. Blechman (eds.), *Stress, coping, and resiliency in children and families* (pp. 39–66). Mahwah, NJ: Lawrence Erlbaum.

Herbrand, C. (2008). Les normes familiales à l'épreuve du droit et des pratiques: Analyse de la parenté sociale et de la pluriparentalité homosexuelles (Ph.D. thesis, Université Libre de Bruxelles).

Hertz, R. (2002). The father as an idea: A challenge to kinship boundaries by single mothers. *Symbolic Interaction*, 25, 1–31.

Hertz, R. (2006). *Single by chance, mothers by choice. How women are choosing parenthood without marriage and creating the new American family*. New York: Oxford University Press.

Hetherington, E. M. (1988). *Parents, children, and siblings six years after divorce*. Cambridge University Press.

Hetherington, E. M. (1989). Coping with family transitions: Winners, losers and survivors. *Child Development*, 60, 1–14.

Hetherington, E. M., and Clingempeel, W. G. (1992). Coping with marital transitions: A family systems perspective. *Monographs of the Society for Child Development*, 57(2–3)

Hetherington, M., Cox, M., and Cox, R. (1982). Effects of Divorce on Parents and Children. In M. E. Lamb (ed.), *Nontraditional families: Parenting and child development* (pp. 233–288). Hillsdale, NJ: Lawrence Erlbaum.

Hetherington, E. M., and Stanley-Hagan, M. M. (1999). The adjustment of children with divorced parents: A risk and resiliency perspective. *Journal of Child Psychology and Psychiatry*, 40(1), 129–140.

Hetherington, E. M., and Stanley-Hagan, M. M. (2002). Parenting in divorced and remarried families. In M. Bornstein (ed.), *Handbook of parenting: Being and becoming a parent* (pp. 287–316). Mahwah, NJ: Lawrence Erlbaum.

Hicks, S. (2006). Maternal men – perverts and deviants? Making sense of gay men as foster carers and adopters. *Journal of LGBT Family Studies*, 2, 93–114.

Hines, M. (2004) *Brain gender*. Oxford University Press.

Hines, M. (2010). Gendered behavior across the life span. In M. E. Lamb and A. M. Freund (eds.) *The handbook of life-span development*. Vol. 2. *Social and Economic Development*. Hoboken, NJ: Wiley.

Hines, M. (2011). Prenatal endocrine influences on sexual orientation and on sexually differentiated childhood behavior. *Frontiers in Neuroendocrinology*, 32, 170–182.

Hoeffer, B. (1981). Children's acquisition of sex-role behavior in lesbian-mother families. *Americal Journal of Orthopsychiatry*, 51(3), 536–544.

Howe, D., and Feast, J. (2000). *Adoption, search and reunion*. London: British Association for Adoption and Fostering (BAAF).

Howes, P., and Markman, H. J. (1989). Marital quality and child functioning: A longitudinal investigation. *Child Development*, 60(5), 1044–1051.

Huggins, S. L. (1989). A comparative study of self-esteem of adolescent children of divorced lesbian mothers and divorced heterosexual mothers. *Journal of Homosexuality*, 18(1–2), 123–135. doi:10.1300/J082v18n01_06

Humphrey, H., and Humphrey, M. (1989). Damaged identity and the search for kinship in adult adoptees. *British Journal of Medical Psychology*, 62(4), 301–309.

Imber-Black, E. (1998). *The secret life of families*. New York: Bantam Dell.

Imrie, S., and Jadva, V. (2014). The long-term experiences of surrogates: Relationships and contact with surrogacy families in genetic and gestational surrogacy arrangements. *Reproductive BioMedicine Online*, 29, 424–435.

Isaksson, S., Skoog Svanberg, A., Sydsjö, G., Thurin-Kjellberg, A., Karlström, P.-O., Solensten, N.-G., and Lampic, C. (2011). Two decades after legislation on identifiable donors in Sweden: Are recipient couples ready to be open about using gamete donation? *Human Reproduction*, 26(4), 853–860.

Isaksson, S., Sydsjö, G., Skoog Svanberg, A., and Lampic, C. (2012). Disclosure behaviour and intentions among 111 couples following treatment with oocytes or sperm from identity-release donors: Follow-up at offspring age 1–4 years. *Human Reproduction*, 27(10), 2998–3007. doi:10.1093/humrep/des285

Jadva, V., Badger, S., Morrissette, M., and Golombok, S. (2009). "Mom by choice, single by life's circumstance..." Findings from a large scale survey of the experiences of single mothers by choice. *Human Fertility*, 12(4), 175–184. doi:10.3109/14647270903373867

Jadva, V., Blake, L., Casey, P., and Golombok, S. (2012). Surrogacy families 10 years on: Relationship with the surrogate, decisions over disclosure and children's understanding of their surrogacy origins. *Human Reproduction*, 27(10), 3008–3014. doi:10.1093/humrep/des273

Jadva, V., Casey, P., Readings, L., Blake, L., and Golombok, S. (2011). A longitudinal study of recipients' views and experiences of intra-family egg donation. *Human Reproduction*, 26(10), 2777–2782.

Jadva, V., Freeman, T., Kramer, W., and Golombok, S. (2009). The experiences of adolescents and adults conceived by sperm donation: Comparisons by age of disclosure and family type. *Human Reproduction*, 24(8), 1909–1919.

Jadva, V., Freeman, T., Kramer, W., and Golombok, S. (2010). Experiences of offspring searching for and contacting their donor siblings and donor. *Reproductive BioMedicine Online*, 20(4), 523–532.

Jadva, V., Freeman, T., Tranfield, E., and Golombok, S. (unpublished data). "Friendly allies in raising a child": A survey of men and women seeking elective co-parenting arrangements via a connection website.

Jadva, V., Imrie, S., and Golombok, S. (2014). Surrogate mothers 10 years on: A longitudinal study of psychological well-being and relationships with the parents and child. *Human Reproduction*. doi:10.1093/humrep/deu339

Jadva, V., and Imrie, S. (2014a). Children of surrogate mothers: Psychological well-being, family relationships and experiences of surrogacy. *Human Reproduction*, 29(1), 90–96. doi:10.1093/humrep/det410

Jadva, V., and Imrie, S. (2014b). The significance of relatedness for surrogates and their families. In F. Ebtehaj, S. Graham, M. Richards, and T. Freeman (eds.), *Relatedness in assisted reproduction: Families, origins, identities*. Cambridge University Press.

Jadva, V., Murray, C., Lycett, E., MacCallum, F., and Golombok, S. (2003). Surrogacy: The experiences of surrogate mothers. *Human Reproduction*, 18(10), 2196–2204.

Jaffari-Bimmel, N., Juffer, F., van IJzendoorn, M. H., Bakermans-Kranenburg, M. J., and Mooijaart, A. (2006). Social development from infancy to adolescence: Longitudinal and concurrent factors in an adoption sample. *Developmental Psychology*, 42(6), 1143–1153. doi:10.1037/0012-1649.42.6.1143

Jaffee, S. R., Moffitt, T. E., Caspi, A., and Taylor, A. (2003). Life with (or without) father: The benefits of living with two biological parents depend on the father's antisocial behavior. *Child Development*, 74(1), 109–126.

Jameson, P. B., Gelfand, D. M., Kulcsar, E., and Teti, D. M. (1997). Mother–toddler interaction patterns associated with maternal depression. *Development and Psychopathology*, 9(3), 537–550.

Jennings, S., Mellish, L., Casey, P., Tasker, F., Lamb, M., and Golombok, S. (2014). Why adoption? Gay, lesbian and heterosexual adoptive parents' reasons for adoptive parenthood. *Adoption Quarterly*, 205–226. doi: 10.1080/10926755.2014.891549

Johnson, M. H. (2010). Nobel Lecture/Nobel Prize Symposium in Honour of Robert G. Edwards, December 7, 2010. Retrieved January 5, 2015 from www.nobelprize.org/nobel-prizes/medicine/laureates/2010/edwards-lecture-pdf

Johnson, M. H. (2011). Robert Edwards: The path to IVF. *Reproductive BioMedicine Online*, 23(2), 245–262. doi:10.1016/j.rbmo.2011.04.010

Juffer, F., and van IJzendoorn, M. H. (2005). Behavior problems and mental health referrals of international adoptees: A meta-analysis. *JAMA: The Journal of the American Medical Association*, 293(20), 2501–2515. doi:10.1001/jama.293.20.2501

Juffer, F., and van IJzendoorn, M. H. (2007). Adoptees do not lack self-esteem: A meta-analysis of studies on self-esteem of transracial, international, and domestic adoptees. *Psychological Bulletin*, 133(6), 1067–1083.

Juffer, F., and van IJzendoorn, M. H. (2009). International adoption comes of age: Development of international adoptees from a longitudinal and meta-analytic perspective. In G. M. Wrobel and E. N. Neil (eds.), *International advances in adoption research for practice* (pp. 169–192). Chichester: Wiley-Blackwell.

Karpel, M. A. (1980). Family secrets: I. Conceptual and ethical issues in the relational context. II. Ethical and practical considerations in therapeutic management. *Family Process*, 19(3), 295–306.

Kazdin, A. E. (2000). Encyclopedia of Psychology. Washington, DC: American Psychological Association.

Kiernan, K. (2006). Non-residential fatherhood and child involvement: Evidence from the Millennium Cohort Study. *Journal of Social Policy*, 35(4), 651–669.

Kiernan, K., and Mensah, F. K. (2010). *Unmarried parenthood, family trajectories, parent and child well-being.* Bristol: The Policy Press.

Kirk, H. D. (1964). *Shared fate: A theory and method of adoptive relationships.* New York: Free Press.

Kirkpatrick, M., Smith, C., and Roy, R. (1981). Lesbian mothers and their children: A comparative survey. *American Journal of Orthopsychiatry*, 51(3), 545–551.

Klitzman, R., and Sauer, M. V. (2014). Creating and selling embryos for "donation": ethical challenges. *American Journal of Obstetrics and Gynecology.* http://dx.doi.org/10.1016/j.ajog.2014.10.1094

Klock, S. C., and Greenfeld, D. A. (2004). Parents' knowledge about the donors and their attitudes toward disclosure in oocyte donation. *Human Reproduction*, 19(7), 1575–1579.

Klock, S., and Maier, D. (1991). Psychological factors related to donor insemination. *Fertility and Sterility*, 56, 489–495.

Knoester, M., Helmerhorst, F. M., van der Westerlaken, L., Walther, F. J., and Veen, S. (2007). Matched follow-up study of five 8-year-old ICSI singletons: Child behaviour, parenting stress and child (health-related) quality of life. *Human Reproduction*, 22(12), 3098–3107.

Knoester, M., Helmerhorst, F. M., Vandenbroucke, J. P., van der Westerlaken, L. A. J., Walther, F. J., and Veen, S. (2008). Cognitive development of singletons born after intracytoplasmic sperm injection compared with in vitro fertilization and natural conception. *Fertility and Sterility*, 90(2), 289–296.

Kochanska, G., Kuczynski, L., Radke-Yarrow, M., and Welsh, J. (1987). Resolutions of control episodes between well and affectively ill mothers and their young children. *Journal of Abnormal Child Psychology*, 15(3), 441–456.

Kohlberg, L. (1966). A cognitive-development analysis of children's sex-role concepts and attitudes. In E. E. Maccoby (ed.), *The development of sex differences* (pp. 82–173). Stanford University Press.

Kohler, J. K., Grotevant, H. D., and McRoy, R. G. (2002). Adopted adolescents' preoccupation with adoption: The impact on adoptive family relationships. *Journal of Marriage and the Family*, 64(1), 93–104.

Kohnstamm, G. A., Bates, J. E., and Rothbart, M. K. (eds.) (1989). *Temperament in childhood.* Chichester: Wiley.

Kovacs, G. T., Wise, S., and Finch, S. (2013). Functioning of families with primary school-age children conceived using anonymous donor sperm. *Human Reproduction*, 28(2), 375–384.

Kreider, R. M., and Ellis, R. (2011). *Number, timing, and duration of marriages and divorces, 2009.* US Department of Commerce, Economics and Statistics Administration, US Census Bureau.

Ladd, G. W. (1990). Having friends, keeping friends, making friends, and being liked by peers in the classroom: Predictors of children's early school adjustment? *Child Development*, 61(4), 1081–1100. doi:10.1111/j.1467–8624.1990.tb02843.x

Lalos, A., Gottlieb, C., and Lalos, O. (2007). Legislated right for donor-insemination children to know their genetic origin: A study of parental thinking. *Human Reproduction*, 22(6), 1759–1768.

Lamb, M. (2010). *The role of the father in child development* (5th edn.). Hoboken, NJ: Jessop Hospital for Women.

Lamb, M. E. (2012). Mothers, fathers, families, and circumstances: Factors affecting children's adjustment. *Applied Developmental Science*, 16(2), 98–111.

Lamb, M. E. (2013). The changing faces of fatherhood and father–child relationships: From fatherhood as status to father as dad. In M. Fine and F. D. Fincham (eds.), *Handbook of family theories* (pp. 87–102). New York: Routledge.

Lamb, M. E., and Lewis, C. (2011). The role of parent–child relationships in child development. In M. H. Bornstein and M. E. Lamb (eds.), *Developmental science* (6th edn., pp. 469–518). New York: Psychology Press.

Lane, J. D., and Wegner, D. M. (1995). The cognitive consequences of secrecy. *Journal of Personality and Social Psychology*, 69(2), 237–253.

Lansford, J. E., Cebello, R., Abbey, A., and Stewart, A. J. (2001). Does family structure matter? A comparison of stepfather, and stepmother households. *Journal of Marriage and the Family*, 63, 840–851.

Leeb-Lundberg, S., Kjellberg, S., and Sydsjö, G. (2006). Helping parents to tell their children about the use of donor insemination (DI) and determining their opinions about open-identity sperm donors. *Acta Obstetricia et Gynecologica Scandinavica*, 85(1), 78–81.

Leiblum, S. R., and Aviv, A. L. (1997). Disclosure issues and decisions of couples who conceived via donor insemination. *Journal of Psychosomatic Obstetrics and Gynaecology*, 18(4): 292–300.

Leslie, G. I., Gibson, F. L., McMahon, C., Cohen, J., Saunders, D. M., and Tennant, C. (2003). Children conceived using ICSI do not have an increased risk of delayed mental development at 5 years of age. *Human Reproduction*, 18(10), 2067–2072. doi:10.1093/humrep/deg408

Leunens, L., Celestin-Westreich, S., Bonduelle, M., Liebaers, I., and Ponjaert-Kristoffersen, I. (2006). Cognitive and motor development of 8-year-old children born after ICSI compared to spontaneously conceived children. *Human Reproduction*, 21(11), 2922–2929. doi:10.1093/humrep/del266

Leunens, L., Celestin-Westreich, S., Bonduelle, M., Liebaers, I., and Ponjaert-Kristoffersen, I. (2008). Follow-up of cognitive and motor development of 10-year-old singleton children born after ICSI compared with spontaneously conceived children. *Human Reproduction*, 23(1), 105–111. doi:10.1093/humrep/dem257

Leung, P., Erich, S., and Kanenberg, H. (2005). A comparison of family functioning in gay/lesbian, heterosexual and special needs adoptions. *Children and Youth Services Review*, 27(9), 1031–1044. doi:10.1016/j.childyouth.2004.12.030

Levy-Shiff, R., Vakil, E., Dimitrovsky, L., Abramovitz, M., Shahar, N., Har-Even, D., et al. (1998). Medical, cognitive, and behavioural outcomes in school-age children conceived by in-vitro fertilization. *Journal of Clinical Child Psychology*, 27(3), 320–329.

Lindblad, F., Gottlieb, C., and Lalos, O. (2000). To tell or not to tell – what parents think about telling their children that they were born following donor insemination. *Journal of Psychosomatic Obstetrics and Gynecology*, 21, 193–203.

Lloyd, G., and Lacey, R. (2012a). *Understanding 21st century relationships: A compendium of key data* (Chapter 1: Partnership formation and dissolution). London: OnePlusOne.

Lloyd, G., and Lacey, R. (2012b). *Understanding 21st century relationships: A compendium of key data* (Chapter 2: Household composition and families). London: OnePlusOne.

Lutjen, P., Trounson, A., Leeton, J., Findlay, J., Wood, C., and Renou, P. (1984). The establishment and maintenance of pregnancy using in vitro fertilization and embryo donation in patient with primary ovary failure. *Nature*, 307, 174–175.

Luthar, S. S. (2006). Resilience in development: A synthesis of research across five decades. *Development and Psychopathology*, 3, 739–795.

Luthar, S. S., Crossman, E. J. and Small, P. J. (2015). Resilience in the face of adversities. In M. E. Lamb (vol. ed.) and R. M. Lerner (series ed.), *Handbook of child psychology and developmental science, vol. III: Social, emotional and personality development* (7th edn.). Hoboken, NJ.

Lytton, H., and Gallagher, L. (2002). Parenting twins and the genetics of parenting. In M. H. Bornstein (ed.), *Handbook of parenting* (Vol. I, pp. 227–253). Mahwah, NJ: Lawrence Erlbaum.

Mac Dougall, K., Becker, G., Scheib, J. E., and Nachtigall, R. D. (2007). Strategies for disclosure: How parents approach telling their children that they were conceived with donor gametes. *Fertility and Sterility*, 87(3), 524–533.

MacCallum, F., and Golombok, S. (2004). Children raised in fatherless families from infancy: A follow-up of children of lesbian and single heterosexual mothers at early adolescence. *Journal of Child Psychology and Psychiatry*, 45(8), 1407–1419.

MacCallum, F., and Golombok, S. (2007). Embryo donation families: Mothers' decisions regarding disclosure of donor conception. *Human Reproduction*, 22(11), 2888–2895.

MacCallum, F., Golombok, S., and Brinsden, P. (2007). Parenting and child development in families with a child conceived through embryo donation. *Journal of Family Psychology*, 21(2), 278–287. doi:10.1037/0893-3200.21.2.278

MacCallum, F., and Keeley, S. (2008). Embryo donation families: A follow-up in middle childhood. *Journal of Family Psychology*, 22(6), 799–808.

MacCallum, F., and Keeley, S. (2012). Disclosure patterns of embryo donation mothers compared with adoption and IVF. *Reproductive BioMedicine Online*, 24(7), 745–748. doi:10.1016/j.rbmo.2012.01.018

MacCallum, F., Lycett, E., Murray, C., Jadva, V., and Golombok, S. (2003). Surrogacy: The experience of commissioning couples. *Human Reproduction*, 18, 1334–1342.

Maccoby, E. E. (1998). *The two sexes: Growing up apart, coming together.* Cambridge, MA: Harvard University Press.

Maccoby, E. E. (2000). Parenting and its effects on children: On reading and misreading behaviour genetics. *Annual Review of Psychology*, 51, 1–27.

Maccoby, E. E. (2007). Historical overview of socialization research and theory. In J. E. Grusec and P. D. Hastings (eds.), *Handbook of socialization theory and research.* New York: Guilford Press.

Maccoby, E. E., and Martin, J. A. (1983). Socialization in the context of the family: Parent–child interaction. In P. H. Mussen (ed.), *Handbook of child psychology.* New York: Wiley.

Mahlstedt, P. P., LaBounty, K., and Kennedy, W. T. (2010). The views of adult offspring of sperm donation: Essential feedback for the development of ethical guidelines within the practice of assisted reproductive technology in the United States. *Fertility and Sterility*, 93(7), 2236–2246.

Main, M., and Cassidy, J. (1988). Categories of response to reunion with the parent at age 6: Predictable from infant attachment classifications and stable over a 1-month period. *Developmental Psychology*, 24(3), 415–426. doi:10.1037/0012-1649.24.3.415

Main, M., Goldwyn, R., and Hesse, E. (2003). *The adult attachment interview: Scoring and classification system* (Version 7.2). University of California, Berkeley.

Main, M., Kaplan, N., and Cassidy, J. (1985). Security in infancy, childhood, and adulthood: A move to the level of representation. *Monographs of the Society for Research in Child Development*, 50(1–2), 66–104. doi:10.2307/3333827

Main, M., and Solomon, J. (1990). Procedures for identifying infants as disorganized/disoriented during the Ainsworth Strange Situation. In M. T. Greenberg, D. Ciccetti, and E. M. Cummings (eds.), *Attachment in the preschool years: Theory, research, and intervention.* The University of Chicago Press.

Martin, C. L. (1993). New directions for assessing children's gender knowledge. *Developmental Review*, 13, 184–204.

Martin, C. L., Ruble, D. N., and Szkrybalo, J. (2002). Cognitive theories of early gender development. *Psychological Bulletin*, 128, 903–933.

Masten, A. S., and Coatsworth, J. D. (1998). The development of competence in favorable and unfavorable environments: Lessons from research on successful children. *American Psychologist*, 53(2), 205–220. doi:10.1037/0003-066X.53.2.205

Masten, A. S. Cutuli, J. J., Herbers, J. E., and Reed, J. M.-G. (2007). Resilience in development. In S. J. Lopez and C. R. Snyder (eds.), *The Oxford handbook of positive psychology* (pp. 117–131). Oxford University Press.

Mattes, J. (1997). *Single mothers by choice. A guidebook for single women who are considering or have chosen motherhood*. New York: Three Rivers Press.

Matthews, J. D., and Cramer, E. P. (2006). Envisaging the adoption process to strengthen gay- and lesbian-headed families: Recommendations for adoption professionals. *Child Welfare*, 85(2), 317–340.

Mayes, L. C, and Truman, S. D. (2002). Substance abuse and parenting. In M. H. Bornstein (ed.), *Handbook of parenting*, vol. IV: *Social conditions and applied parenting* (pp. 329–361). Mahwah, NJ: Lawrence Erlbaum.

McCall, R. B. (2011). Research, practice, and policy perspectives on issues of children without permanent parental care. *Monographs of the Society for Research in Child Development*, 76(4), 223–272. doi:10.1111/j.1540-5834.2011.00634.x

McGee, G., Brakman, S., and Gurmankin, A. (2001). Gamete donation and anonymity: Disclosure to children conceived with donor gametes should not be optional. *Human Reproduction*, 16(10), 2033–2036.

McLanahan, S. (2012). *Fragile families and children's opportunities*. Princeton University Press.

McLanahan, S., and Beck, A. N. (2010). Parental relationships in fragile families. *The Future of Children*, 20(2), 17–37.

McLanahan, S., and Sandefur, G. (1994). *Growing up with a single parent: What hurts, what helps*. Cambridge, MA: Harvard University Press.

McLoyd, V. C. (1998). Socioeconomic disadvantage and child development. *American Psychologist*, 53(3), 185–204. doi:10.1037/0003-066X.53.2.185

McMahon, C., and Gibson, F. L. (2002). A special path to parenthood: Parent–child relationships in families giving birth to singleton infants through IVF. *Reproductive BioMedicine Online*, 5(2), 179–186.

McMahon, C. A., Ungerer, J. A., Beaurepaire, J., Tennant, C., and Saunders, D. (1995). Psychological outcomes of parents and children after in vitro fertilization: A review. *Journal of Reproductive and Infant Psychology*, 13(1), 1–16. doi:10.1080/02646839508403227

McMahon, C., Ungerer, J. A., Tennant, C., and Saunders, D. (1997). Psychosocial adjustment and the quality of the mother–child relationship at four months postpartum after conception by in vitro fertilization. *Fertility and Sterility*, 68(3), 492–500.

Mellish, L., Jennings, S., Tasker, F., Lamb, M., and Golombok, S. (2013). *Gay, lesbian and heterosexual adoptive families: Family relationships, child adjustment and adopters' experiences*. London: British Association for Adoption and Fostering.

Mischel, W. (1966). A social learning view of sex differences in behavior. In E. E. Maccoby (ed.), *The development of sex differences* (pp. 56–81). Stanford University Press.

Mischel, W. (1970). Sex-typing and socialization. In P. Mussen (ed.), *Carmichael's manual of child psychology* (Vol. II, pp. 3–72). New York: Wiley.

Money, J. and Ehrhardt, A. (1972). *Man and woman, boy and girl*. Baltimore, MD: Johns Hopkins University Press.

Montgomery, T. R., Aiello, R. D., and Adelman, R. D. (1999). The psychological status at school age of children conceived by in vitro fertilization. *Human Reproduction*, 14, 2162–2165.

Morison, S. J., Ames, E. W., and Chisholm, K. (1995). The development of children adopted from Romanian orphanages. *Merrill-Palmer Quarterly*, 41(4), 411–430.

Murdoch, A. (1997). Triplets and embryo transfer policy. *Human Reproduction*, 12, 88–92.

Murray, C., and Golombok, S. (2005a). Going it alone: Solo mothers and their infants conceived by donor insemination. *The American Journal of Orthopsychiatry*, 75(2), 242–253. doi:10.1037/0002-9432.75.2.242

Murray, C., and Golombok, S. (2005b). Solo mothers and their donor insemination infants: Follow-up at age 2 years. *Human Reproduction*, 6, 1655–1660.

Murray, C., MacCallum, F., and Golombok, S. (2006). Egg donation parents and their children: Follow-up at age 12 years. *Fertility and Sterility*, 85(3), 610–618.

Murray, L. (1992). The impact of post-natal depression on mother–infant relations and infant development. *Journal of Child Psychology and Psychiatry*, 33, 543–561.

Mushin, D., Spensley, J., and Barreda-Hanson, M. (1985). Children of IVF. *Clinics in Obstetrics and Gynaecology*, 12(4), 865–876.

Nachtigall, R. D., Tschann, J. M., Szkupinski Quiroga, S., Pitcher, L., and Becker, G. (1997). Stigma, disclosure, and family functioning among parents of children conceived through donor insemination. *Fertility and Sterility*, 68(1), 83–89.

Nelson, J. A., and O'Brien, M. (2012). Does an unplanned pregnancy have long-term implications for mother–child relationships? *Journal of Family Issues*, 33(4), 506–526. doi:10.1177/0192513X11420820

Nixon, E., Greene, S., and Hogan, D. M. (2012). Negotiating relationships in single-mother households: Perspectives of children and mothers. *Family Relations*, 61(1), 142–156. doi:10.1111/j.1741-3729.2011.00678.x

Nuffield Council on Bioethics. (2012). *Novel techniques for the prevention of mitochondrial DNA disorders: An ethical review.* London.

Nuffield Council on Bioethics. (2013). *Donor conception: Ethical aspects of information sharing.* London.

Nygren, K. G., and Andersen, A. N. (2002). Assisted reproductive technology in Europe, 1999. Results generated from European registers by ESHRE. *Human Reproduction*, 17(12), 3260–3274. doi:10.1093/humrep/17.12.3260

O'Connor, T., Deater-Deckard, K., Fulker, D., Rutter, M., and Plomin, R. (1998). Genotype–environment correlations in late childhood and early adolescence: Antisocial behaviour problems and coercive parenting. *Developmental Psychology*, 34, 970–981.

O'Connor, T. G., Dunn, J., Jenkins, J. M., Pickering, K., and Rasbash, J. (2001). Family settings and children's adjustment: Differential adjustment within and across families. *British Journal of Psychiatry*, 179, 110–115.

Olivennes, F., Golombok, S., Ramogida, C., and Rust, J. (2005). Behavioral and cognitive development as well as family functioning of twins conceived by assisted reproduction: Findings from a large population study. *Fertility and Sterility*, 84(3), 725–733. doi:10.1016/j.fertnstert.2005.03.039

Orvaschel, H., Walsh-Altis, G., and Ye, W. (1988). Psychopathology in children of parents with recurrent depression. *Journal of Abnormal Child Psychology*, 16, 17–28.

Owen, L., and Golombok, S. (2009). Families created by assisted reproduction: Parent–child relationships in late adolescence. *Journal of Adolescence*, 32(4), 835–848. doi:10.1016/j.adolescence.2008.10.008

Palacios, J., and Brodzinsky, D. M. (2010). Adoption research. Trends, topics, outcomes. *International Journal of Behavioral Development*, 34(3), 270–284.

Palermo, G. (1992). Pregnancies after intracytoplasmic injection of single spermatozoon into an oocyte. *The Lancet*, 340(8810), 17–18.

Palermo, G., Joris, H., Devroey, P., and Van Steirteghem, A. C. (1992). Pregnancies after intracytoplasmic injection of a single spermatozoa into an oocyte. *Lancet*, 340, 17–18.

Pande, A. (2009). Not an "Angel", not a "Whore": Surrogates as "Dirty" workers in India. *Indian Journal of Gender Studies*, 16, 141–173.

Papaligoura, Z., and Trevarthen, C. (2001). Mother–infant communication can be enhanced after conception by in-vitro fertilisation. *Infant Mental Health Journal*, 22(6), 591–610.

Papp, P. (1993). The worm in the bud: Secrets between parents and children. In E. Imber-Black (ed.), *Secrets in families and family therapy* (pp. 66–85). London: W.W. Norton.

Papp, L. M., Cummings, E. M., and Goeke-Morey, M. C. (2005). Parental psychological distress, parent–child relationship qualities, and child adjustment: Direct, mediating, and reciprocal pathways. *Parenting: Science and Practice*, 5, 259–283.

Parker, J. G., and Asher, S. R. (1987). Peer relations and later personal adjustment: Are low-accepted children at risk? *Psychological Bulletin*, 102(3), 357–389. doi:10.1037/0033-2909.102.3.357

Parkhurst, J. T., and Asher, S. R. (1992). Peer rejection in middle school: Subgroup differences in behavior, loneliness, and interpersonal concerns. *Developmental Psychology*, 28(2), 231–241. doi:10.1037/0012-1649.28.2.231

Passmore, N., Foulstone , J. A., and Feeney, A. R. (2007). Secrecy within adoptive families and its impact on adult adoptees. *Family Relationships Quarterly*, 5, 3–5.

Patterson, C. J. (1995). Families of the Lesbian baby boom: Parents' division of labor and children's adjustment, *Developmental Psychology*, 31(1), 115–123.

Patterson, C. J. (2006). Children of lesbian and gay parents. *Current Directions in Psychological Science*, 15(5), 241–244. doi:10.1111/j.1467-8721.2006.00444.x

Patterson, C. J. (2009). Children of lesbian and gay parents: Psychology, law, and policy. *The American Psychologist*, 64(8), 727–736. doi:10.1037/0003-0 66X.64.8.727

Patterson, G. R. (1982). *Coercive family process.* Eugene, OR: Castalia.

Patterson, G. R., DeBaryshe, B. D., and Ramsey, E. (1989). A developmental perspective on antisocial behavior. *American Psychologist*, 44(2), 329–335. doi:10 .1037/0003-066X.44.2.329

Patterson, G. R., and Fisher, P. A. (2002). Recent developments in our understanding of parenting: Bidirectional effects, causal models, and the search for parsimony. In M. H. Bornstein (ed.), *Handbook of parenting*, vol. V: *Practical issues in parenting* (pp. 59–88). Mahwah, NJ: Lawrence Erlbaum.

Patterson, G. R., Reid, J. B., and Dishion, T. J. (1992). *Antisocial boys.* Eugene, OR: Castalia.

Paul, M. S., and Berger, R. (2007). Topic avoidance and family functioning in families conceived with donor insemination. *Human Reproduction*, 22(9), 2566–2571.

Perry, B., Burston, A., Stevens, M., Steele, H., Golding, J., and Golombok, S. (2004). Children's play narratives: What they tell us about lesbian-mother families. *American Journal of Orthopsychiatry*, 74(4), 467–479.

Pew Research Center. (2013). *Pew Social and Demographic Trends: The rise of single fathers*. Washington, DC: Pew Research Center. Retrieved November 16, 2014 from http://Pewsocialtrends.org/2013/07/02/the-rise-of-single-fathers/

Pinborg, A., Loft, A., Schmidt, L., Greisen, G., Rasmussen, S., and Andersen, A. N. (2004). Neurological sequelae in twins born after assisted conception: Controlled national cohort study. *British Medical Journal*, 329(7461), 311–317.

Pinborg, A., Henningsen, A.-K., and Malchau, S. S. (2013). Congenital anomalies after assisted reproductive technology. *Fertility and Sterility*, 99(2), 327–332.

Pleck, J. H. (2010). Fatherhood and masculinity. In M. E. Lamb (ed.), *The role of the father in child development* (5th edn., pp. 58–93). Hoboken, NJ: Wiley.

Plomin, R. (1990). *Nature and nurture: An introduction to human behavioral genetics*. Pacific Grove, CA: Brooks/Cole.

Plomin, R. (1994). Genetics and experience. *Current Opinion in Psychiatry*, 7(4), 297–299.

Plomin, R., and Daniels, D. (1987). Why are children in the same family so different from one another? *Behavioral and Brain Sciences*, 10(1), 1–16. doi:10.1017/S0140525X00055941

Ponjaert-Kristoffersen, I., Bonduelle, M., Barnes, J., Nekkebroeck, J., Loft, A., Wennerholm, U.-B., Tarlatzis, B. Peters, C., Hagberg, B., Berner, A., and Sutcliffe, A. G., (2005). International collaborative study of intracytoplasmic sperm injection-conceived, in vitro fertilization-conceived, and naturally conceived 5-year-old child outcomes: Cognitive and motor assessments. *Pediatrics*, 115(3), 283–289. doi:10.1542/peds.2004-1445

Ponjaert-Kristoffersen, I., Tjus, T., Nekkebroeck, J., Squires, J., Verté, D., Heimann, M., Bonduelle, M., Palermo, G., Wennerholm, U.-B., on behalf of the Collaborative study of Brussels, Göteborg and New York (2004). Psychological follow-up study of 5-year-old ICSI children. *Human Reproduction*, 19(12), 2791–2797. doi:10.1093/humrep/deh511

Potter, D. (2012). Same-sex parent families and children's academic achievement. *Journal of Marriage and Family*, 74, 556–571. doi:10.1111/j.1741-3737.2012.00966.x

Pryor, J., and Rodgers, B. (2001). *Children in changing families*. Oxford: Blackwell.

Radke-Yarrow, M., Cummings, E. M., Kuczynski, L., and Chapman, M. (1985). Patterns of attachment in two- and three-year-olds in normal families and families with parental depression. *Child Development*, 56(4), 884–893.

Ragoné, H. (1994). *Surrogate motherhood: Conception in the heart*. San Francisco: Westview Press.

Ratcliffe, G. C., Norton, A. M., and Durtschi, J. A. (2014). Early romantic relationships linked with improved child behavior 8 years later. *Journal of Family Issues*. doi:10.1177/0192513X14525618

Readings, J., Blake, L., Casey, P., Jadva, V., and Golombok, S. (2011). Secrecy, disclosure and everything in-between: Decisions of parents of children conceived by donor insemination, egg donation and surrogacy. *Reproductive BioMedicine Online*, 22(5), 485–495. doi:10.1016/j.rbmo.2011.01.014

Reichman, N., Teitler, J., and McLanahan, S. (2001). Fragile families: Sample and design. *Children and Youth Services Review*, 303–326.

Reynolds, J., Houlston, C., Coleman, L., and Harold, G. (2014). *Parental conflict: Outcomes and interventions for children and families*. Bristol: Policy Press.

Richards, M. (2000). Children's understanding of inheritance and family. *Child Psychology and Psychiatry Review*, 5(1), 2–8.

Rivers, D. (2010). In the best interests of the child: Lesbian and gay parenting custody cases, 1967–1985. *Journal of Social History*, 43(4), 917–943. doi:10.1353/jsh.0.0355

Rivers, I., Poteat, V. P., and Noret, N. (2008). Victimization, social support, and psychosocial functioning among children of same-sex and opposite-sex couples in the United Kingdom, 44(1), 127–134. doi:10.1037/0012-1649.44.1.127

Roberts, W. L. (1986). Nonlinear models of development: An example from the socialization of competence. *Child Development*, 57(5), 1166–1178.

Roberts, W. L., and Strayer, J. (1987). Parents' responses to the emotional distress of their children: Relations with children's competence. *Developmental Psychology*, 23(3), 415–422. doi:10.1037/0012-1649.23.3.415

Rodgers, B., and Pryor, J. (1998). *Divorce and separation: The outcomes for children*. York: Joseph Rowntree Foundation.

Rosenfeld, M. J. (2010). Nontraditional families and childhood progress through school. *Demography*, 47(3), 755–775.

Ruble, D. N., Martin, C. L., and Berenbaum, S. A. (2006). Gender development. In N. Eisenberg (ed.), *Handbook of child psychology* (vol. III, pp. 858–932). New York: Wiley.

Rueter, M. A., Keyes, M. A., Iacono, W. G., and McGue, M. (2009). Family interactions in adoptive compared to nonadoptive families. *Journal of Family Psychology*, 23(1), 58–66.

Rueter, M. A., and Koerner, A. F. (2008). The effect of family communication patterns on adopted adolescent adjustment. *Journal of Marriage and the Family*, 70(3), 715–727.

Rumball, A., and Adair, V. (1999). Telling the story: Parents' scripts for donor offspring. *Human Reproduction*, 14(5), 1392–1399.

Rutter, M. (1987). Psychosocial resilience and protective mechanisms. *American Journal of Orthopsychiatry*, 57, 316–331.

Rutter, M. (2006). *Genes and behavior: Nature–nurture interplay explained.* Malden, MA: Blackwell.

Rutter, M. (2007). Proceeding from observed correlation to causal inference: The use of natural experiments. *Perspectives on Psychological Science*, 2(4), 377–395. doi:10.1111/j.1745-6916.2007.00050.x

Rutter, M. (2012). Resilience as a dynamic concept. *Development and Psychopathology*, 24, 335–344.

Rutter, M., Beckett, C., Castle, J., Colvert, E., Kreppner, J., and Mehta, M., Stevens, S., and Sonuga-Barke, E. (2007). Effects of profound early institutional deprivation: An overview of findings from a UK longitudinal study of Romanian adoptees. *European Journal of Developmental Psychology*, 4(3), 332–350. doi:10.1080/17405620701401846

Rutter, M., Pickles, A., Murray, R., and Eaves, L. (2001). Testing hypotheses on specific environmental causal effects on behavior. *Psychological Bulletin*, 127(3), 291–324. doi:10.1037//0033-2909.127.3.291

Rutter, M. and Redshaw, J. (1991). Annotation: Growing up as a twin: Twin-singleton differences in psychological development. *Journal of Child Psychology and Psychiatry*, 32(6), 885–895. doi:10.1111/j.1469-7610.1991.tb01916.x

Rutter, M., Silberg, J., O'Connor, T., and Simonoff, E. (1999a). Genetics and child psychiatry: I. Advances in quantitative and molecular genetics. *Journal of Child Psychology and Psychiatry*, 40(1), 3–18. doi:10.1111/1469-7610.00422

Rutter, M., Silberg, J., O'Connor, T., and Simonoff, E. (1999b). Genetics and child psychiatry: II. Empirical research findings. *Journal of Child Psychology and Psychiatry*, 40(1), 19–55. doi:10.1111/1469-7610.00423

Rutter, M., Thorpe, K., Greenwood, R., Northstone, K., and Golding, J. (2003). Twins as a natural experiment to study the causes of mild language delay: I. Design; twin-singleton differences in language, and obstetrics risks. *Journal of Child Psychology and Psychiatry*, 44(3), 326–341. doi:10.1111/1469-7610.00125

Ryan, S. (2007). Parent–child interaction styles between gay and lesbian parents and their adopted children. *Journal of GLBT Family Studies*, 3, 105–132. doi:10.1300/J461v03n02

Ryan, S., and Cash, S. (2004). Adoptive families headed by gay or lesbian parents: A threat … or hidden resource? *University of Florida Journal of Law and Public Policy*, 15(3), 443–465.

Sampson, R. J., and Laub, J. H. (1994). Urban poverty and the family context of delinquency: A new look at structure and process in a classic study. *Child Development*, 65(2), 523–540. doi:10.1111/j.1467-8624.1994.tb00767.x

Scheib, J. E. (2003). Choosing identity-release sperm donors: The parents' perspective 13–18 years later. *Human Reproduction*, 18(5), 1115–1127.

Scheib, J. E., Riordan, M., and Rubin, S. (2005). Adolescents with open-identity sperm donors: Reports from 12–17 year olds. *Human Reproduction*, 20(1), 239–252. doi:10.1093/humrep/deh581

Scarr, S. (1992). Developmental theories for the 1990s: Development and individual differences. *Child Development*, 63(1), 1–19.

Scheib, J. E., and Ruby, A. (2008). Contact among families who share the same sperm donor. *Fertility and Sterility*, 90(1), 33–43.

Schoenmaker, C., Juffer, F., van IJzendoorn, M. H., and Bakermans-Kranenburg, M. J. (2014). Does family matter? The well-being of children growing up in institutions, foster care and adoption. In A. Ben-Arieh, F. Casas, I. Frønes, and E. Korbin (eds.), *Handbook of child well-being. Theories, methods and policies in global perspective* (pp. 2197–2228). Dordrecht, NL: Springer.

Schoppe, S. J., Mangelsdorf, S. C., and Frosch, C. A. (2001). Coparenting, family process, and family structure: Implications for preschoolers' externalizing behavior problems. *Journal of Family Psychology*, 15, 526–545.

Schover, L. R., Collins, R. L, and Richards, S. (1992). Psychological aspects of donor insemination: Evaluation and follow up of recipient couples. *Fertility and Sterility*, 57(3), 583–590.

Schuckit, M. A., and Smith, T. L. (1996). An 8-year follow-up of 450 sons of alcoholic and control subjects. *Archives of General Psychiatry*, 53(3), 202–210. doi:10.1001/archpsyc.1996.01830030020005

Serbin, L. A., Powlishta, K. K., and Gulko, J. (1993). Sex roles, status, and the need for social change. *Monographs of the Society for Research in Child Development*, 58(2), 93–95. doi:10.1111/j.1540-5834.1993.tb00391.x

Shehab, D., Duff, J., Pasch, L. A., Mac Dougall, K., Scheib, J. E., and Nachtigall, R. D. (2008). How parents whose children have been conceived with donor gametes make their disclosure decision: Contexts, influences, and couple dynamics. *Fertility and Sterility*, 89(1), 179–187. doi:10.1016/j.fertnstert.2007.02.046

Shelton, K. H., Boivin, J., Hay, D., van den Bree, M. B. M., Rice, F. J., Harold, G. T., and Thapar, A. (2009). Examining differences in psychological adjustment problems among children conceived by assisted reproductive technologies. *International Journal of Behavioral Development*, 33(5), 385–392. doi:10.1177/0165025409338444

Shiner, R. L., Buss, K. A., McClowry, S. G., Putnam, S. P., Saudino, K. J., and Zentner, M. (2012). What is temperament now? Assessing progress in temperament research on the twenty-fifth anniversary of Goldsmith et al.

(1987). *Child Development Perspectives*, 6(4), 436–444. doi:10.1111/j.1750-8606.2012.00254.x

Silverstein, L. B., and Auerbach, C. F. (1999). Deconstructing the essential father. *American Psychologist*, 54(6), 397–407. doi:10.1037/0003-066X.54.6.397

Singer, L., Arendt, R., Farkas, K., Minnes, S., Huang, J., and Yamashita, T. (1997). Relationship of prenatal cocaine exposure and maternal postpartum psychological distress to child developmental outcome. *Development and Psychopathology*, 9(3), 473–489.

Slade, A., Belsky, J., Aber, J., Lawrence, J., and Phelps, J. L. (1999). Mothers' representations of their relationships with their toddlers: Links to adult attachment and observed mothering. *Developmental Psychology*, 35(3), 611–619.

Smietana, M. (2011). Family-based affirmative action? Subversion and resilience strategies of gay father families (Ph.D. thesis, Universidad de Barcelona).

Smietana, M., Jennings, S., Herbrand, C., and Golombok, S. (2014). Family relationships in gay father families with young children in Belgium, Spain and the United Kingdom. In T. Freeman, S. Graham, F. Ebtehaj, and M. Richards (eds.), *Relatedness in assisted reproduction: Families, origins and identities*. Cambridge University Press.

Society for Assisted Reproductive Technology (2012). IVF success rates. *Society for Assisted Reproductive Technology*. Retrieved November 16, 2014 from www.sartcoronline.com

Söderström-Anttila, V., Sajaniemi, N., Tiitinen, A., and Hovatta, O. (1998). Health and development of children born after oocyte donation compared with that of those born after in-vitro fertilization, and parents' attitudes regarding secrecy. *Human Reproduction*, 13(7), 2009–2015.

Solomon, G. E. A., Johnson, S. C., Zaitchik, D., and Carey, S. (1996). Like father, like son: Young children's understanding of how and why offspring resemble their parents. *Child Development*, 67(1), 151–171. doi:10.1111/j.1467–8624.1996.tb01726.x

Sroufe, L. A. (1986). Bowlby's contribution to psychoanalytic theory and developmental psychology; Attachment: Separation: Loss. *Journal of Child Psychology and Psychiatry*, 27(6), 841–849. doi:10.1111/j.1469–7610.1986.tb00203.x

Stacey, J., and Biblarz, T. J. (2001). (How) does the sexual orientation of parents matter? *American Sociological Review*, 66(2), 159. doi:10.2307/2657413

Stams, G. J., Juffer, F., Rispens, J., and Hoksbergen, R. A. (2000). The development and adjustment of 7-year-old children adopted in infancy. *Journal of Child Psychology and Psychiatry*, 41(8), 1025–1037.

Stams, G.-J., Juffer, F., and van IJzendoorn, M. H. (2002). Maternal sensitivity, infant attachment, and temperament in early childhood predict adjustment in middle childhood: The case of adopted children and their biologically unrelated parents. *Developmental Psychology*, 38(5), 806–821. doi:10.1037//0012-1649.38.5.806

Steele, H., and Steele, M. (1994). Intergenerational patterns of attachment. In D. Perlman and K. Bartholomew (eds.), *Attachment processes during adulthood* (pp. 93–120). London: Jessica Kingsley.

Steele, H., and Steele, M. (2013). Parenting matters: An attachment perspective. In L. McClain and D. Cere (eds.), *What is parenthood? Contemporary Debates about the Family* (pp. 214–236). New York University Press.

Steele, M., Hodges, J., Kaniuk, J., Hillman, S., and Henderson, K. (2003). Attachment representations and adoption: Associations between maternal states of mind and emotion narratives in previously maltreated children. *Journal of Child Psychotherapy*, 29(2), 187–205. doi:10.1080/0075417031000138442

Steinberg, L. (2001). We know some things: Parent–adolescent relationships in retrospect and prospect. *Journal of Research on Adolescence*, 11(1), 1–19.

Steinberg, L. and Morris, A. S. (2001). Adolescent development. *Annual Review of Psychology*, 52, 83–110.

Steinberg, L. and Silk, J. S. (2002). Parenting adolescents. In M. H. Bornstein (ed.) *Handbook of parenting vol. I: Parenting children and older people*, pp. 103–133. Mahwah, NJ: Lawrence Erlbaum.

Steptoe, P. C., and Edwards, R. G. (1978). Birth after the reimplantation of a human embryo. *The Lancet*, 2(8085), 366.

Stevens, M., Golombok, S., Golding, J., and the ALSPAC Study Team (2002). Does father absence influence children's gender development? Findings from a general population study of preschool children. *Parenting: Science and Practice*, 2(1), 47–60. doi:10.1207/S15327922PAR0201

Stevenson, M., and Black, K. (1988). Paternal absence and sex-role development: A meta-analysis. *Child Development*, 59(3), 793–814. Retrieved November 16, 2014 from www.jstor.org/stable/10.2307/1130577

Stonewall (2010). *Including different families.* London: Stonewall Education Guides.

Strohschein, L. (2010). Generating heat or light? The challenge of social address variables. *Journal of Marriage and Family*, 72(1), 23–28. doi:10.1111/j.1741-3737.2009.00679.x

Suess, G., Grossman, K., and Sroufe, L. A. (1992). Effects of infant attachment to mother and father on quality of adaptation to preschool: from dynamic to individual organization of self. *International Journal of Behavioural Development*, 15, 43–65.

Sutcliffe, A. G., Taylor, B., Saunders, K., Thornton, S., Lieberman, B. A., and Grudzinskas, J. G. (2001). Outcome in the second year of life after in-vitro fertilisation by intracytoplasmic sperm injection: A UK case-control study. *The Lancet,* 357(9274), 2080–2084.

Sydsjö, G., Wadsby, M., Kjellberg, S., and Sydsjö, A. (2002). Relationships and parenthood in couples after assisted reproduction and in spontaneous primiparous couples: A prospective long-term follow-up study. *Human Reproduction,* 17(12), 3242–3250.

Tasker, F., and Golombok, S. (1995). Adults raised as children in lesbian families. *American Journal of Orthopsychiatry,* 65(2), 203–215.

Tasker, F., and Golombok, S. (1997). *Growing up in a lesbian family.* New York: Guilford Press.

Tasker, F. and Granville, J. (2011). Children's views of family relationships in lesbian-led families. *Journal of GLBT Family Studies,* 7, 182–199.

te Velde, E. R., van Baar, A. L., and van Kooij, R. (1998). Concerns about assisted reproduction. *The Lancet,* 1524–1525.

Thomas, A., Chess, S., Birch, H. G., Hertzig, M. E., and Korn, S. (1963). *Behavioral individuality in early childhood.* New York University Press.

Thompson, R. A. (2006). The development of the person: Social understanding, relationships, self, conscience. In W. Damon and R. M. Lerner (series eds.) and N. Eisenberg (vol. ed.), *Handbook of child psychology, vol. III: Social, emotional, and personalilty development* (6th edn., pp. 24–98). Hoboken, NJ: Wiley.

Thompson, R. A. (2008). Early attachment and later development: Familiar questions, new answers. In J. Cassidy and P. R. Shaver (eds.), *Handbook of attachment: Theory, research and clinical applications* (pp. 348–365). Guildford Publications.

Tornello, S. L., Farr, R. H., and Patterson, C. J. (2011). Predictors of parenting stress among gay adoptive fathers in the United States. *Journal of Family Psychology,* 25(4), 591–600. doi:10.1037/a0024480

Triseliotis, J. (1973). *In search of origins: The experience of adopted people.* London: Routledge.

Triseliotis, J. (1984). *Obtaining birth certificates.* London: Tavistock.

Triseliotis, J. (2000). *Identity formation and the adopted person revisited.* London: Jessica Kingsley.

Tronick, E. Z. (1989). Emotions and emotional communication in infants. *American Psychologist,* 44(2), 112–119. doi:10.1037/0003-066X.44.2.112

Trounson, A., Leeton, J., Besanka, M., Wood, C., and Conti, A. (1983). Pregnancy established in an infertile patient after transfer of a donated embryo fertilised in vitro. *British Medical Journal,* 286, 835–838.

Tully, L. A., Moffitt, T. B., and Caspi, A. (2003). Maternal adjustment, parenting and child behaviour in families of school-aged twins conceived after IVF and ovulation induction. *Journal of Child Psychology and Psychiatry*, 44(3), 316–325.

Turner, A. J., and Coyle, A. (2000). What does it mean to be a donor offspring? The identity experiences of adults conceived by donor insemination and the implications for counselling and therapy. *Human Reproduction*, 15, 2041–2051.

US Census Bureau (2012a). Single-parent households: 1980–2009. *Statistical Abstract of the United States*, 840.

US Census Bureau (2012b). Marriage and divorce rates by country: 1980–2008. *Statistical Abstract of the United States*, 840.

van Balen, F. (1998). Development of IVF children. *Developmental Review*, 18, 30–46.

van den Dries, L., Juffer, F., van IJzendoorn, M. H., and Bakermans-Kranenburg, M. J. (2009). Fostering security? A meta-analysis of attachment in adopted children. *Children and Youth Services Review*, 31(3), 410–421. doi:10.1016/j.childyouth.2008.09.008

van Gelderen, L., Bos, H. M. W., Gartrell, N., Hermanns, J., and Perrin, E. C. (2012). Quality of life of adolescents raised from birth by lesbian mothers: The US National Longitudinal Family Study. *Journal of Developmental and Behavioral Pediatrics*, 33(1), 17–23. doi:10.1097/DBP.0b013e31823b62af

van Gelderen, L., Gartrell, N. N., Bos, H. M. W., and Hermanns, J. M. A. (2012). Stigmatization and promotive factors in relation to psychological health and life satisfaction of adolescents in planned lesbian families. *Journal of Family Issues*, 34(6), 809–827.

van Gelderen, L., Gartrell, N., Bos, H., van Rooij, F. B., and Hermanns, J. M. A. (2012). Stigmatization associated with growing up in a lesbian-parented family: What do adolescents experience and how do they deal with it? *Children and Youth Services Review*, 34(5), 999–1006. doi:10.1016/j.childyouth.2012.01.048

van IJzendoorn, M. (1995). Adult attachment representations, parental responsiveness, and infant attachment: A meta-analysis on the predictive validity of the Adult Attachment Interview. *Psychological Bulletin*, 117(3), 387–403. doi:10.1037/0033-2909.117.3.387

van IJzendoorn, M. H., and De Wolff, M. S. (1997). In search of the absent father – meta-analyses of infant–father attachment: A rejoinder to our discussants. *Child Development*, 68(4), 604–609. doi:10.1111/j.1467-8624.1997.tb04223.x

van IJzendoorn, M. H., Schuengel, C., and Bakermans-Kranenburg, M. J. (1999). Disorganized attachment in early childhood: Meta-analysis of precursors, concomitants, and sequelae. *Development and Psychopathology*, 11(2), 225–249.

Vanfraussen, K. (2001). An attempt to reconstruct children's donor concept: A comparison between children's and lesbian parents' attitudes towards donor anonymity. *Human Reproduction*, 16(9), 2019–2025.

Vanfraussen, K., Ponjaert-Kristoffersen, I., and Brewaeys, A. (2003). Family functioning in lesbian families created by donor insemination. *American Journal of Orthopsychiatry*, 73(1), 78–90.

Vayena, E., and Golombok, S. (2012). Challenges in intra-family donation. In M. Richards, G. Pennings, and J. B. Appleby (eds.), *Reproductive donation: Practice, policy and bioethics*. Cambridge University Press.

Vangelisti, A. L., and Caughlin, J. P. (1997). Revealing family secrets: The influence of topic, function, and relationships. *Journal of Social and Personal Relationships*, 14(5), 679–705.

Von Korff, L., and Grotevant, H. D. (2011). Contact in adoption and adoptive identity formation: The mediating role of family conversation. *Journal of Family Psychology*, 25(3), 393–401.

Vukets, C. (2011, September 9). Surrogate mother's nightmare. *Toronto Star*. Retrieved November 16, 2014 from www.thestar.com/news/canada/2011/09/09/surrogate_mothers_nightmare.html

Wagenaar, K., Ceelen, M., van Weissenbruch, M. M., Knol, D. L., Delemarre-van de Wall, H. A., and Huisman, J. (2008). School functioning in 8- to 18-year-old children born after in vitro fertilization. *European Journal of Pediatrics*, 167, 1289–1295.

Wagenaar, K., van Weissenbruch, M. M., Knol, D. L., Cohen-Kettenis, P. T., Delemarre-van de Waal, H. A., and Huisman, J. (2009a). Behavior and socioemotional functioning in 9–18-year-old children born after in vitro fertilization. *Fertility and Sterility*, 92(6), 1907–1914. doi:10.1016/j.fertnstert.2008.09.026

Wagenaar, K., van Weissenbruch, M. M., Knol, D. L., Cohen-Kettenis, P. T., Delamarre-van de Wall, H. A., and Huisman, J. (2009b). Information processing, attention, and visual-motor function of adolescents born after *in vitro* fertilization compared with spontaneous conception. *Human Reproduction*, 24(4), 913–921.

Waagenaar, K., van Weissenbruch, M. M., van Leeuwen, F. E., Cohen-Kettenis, P. T., Delemarre-van de Waal, H. A., Schats, R., and Huisman, J. (2011). Self-reported behavioral and socio-emotional functioning of 11- to 18-year-old adolescents conceived by in vitro fertilization. *Fertility and Sterility*, 95(2), 611–616.

Wainright, J. L., and Patterson, C. J. (2006). Delinqency, victimization, and substance use among adolescents with female same-sex parents. *Journal of Family Psychology*, 20(3), 526–530. doi:10.1037/0893-3200.20.3.526

Wainright, J. L., and Patterson, C. J. (2008). Peer relations among adolescents with female same-sex parents. *Developmental Psychology*, 44(1), 117–126. doi:10.1037/0012-1649.44.1.117

Wainright, J. L., Russell, S. T., and Patterson, C. J. (2004). Psychosocial adjustment, school outcomes, and romantic relationships of adolescents with same-sex parents. *Child Development*, 75(6), 1886–1898. doi:10.1111/j.1467-8624.2004.00823.x

Waldfogel, J., Craigie, T.-A., and Brooks-Gunn, J. (2010). Fragile families and child wellbeing. *Future Child*, 20(2), 87–112.

Wegner, D. M., and Erber, R. (1992). The hyperaccessibility of suppressed thoughts. *Journal of Personality and Social Psychology*, 63(6), 903.

Wegner, D. M., and Lane, J. D. (2002). From secrecy to psychopathy. In J. Pennebaker (ed.), *Emotion, disclosure, and health*. Washington, DC: American Psychological Association.

Weinraub, M., Horvath, D. L., and Gringlas, M. B. (2002). Single parenthood. In M. H. Bornstein (ed.), *Handbook of parenting*, vol. III: *Being and becoming a parent* (pp. 109–140). Mahwah, NJ: Lawrence Erlbaum.

Weissman, M. M., Gammon, G., John, K., Merikangas, K. R., Warner, V., Prusoff, B. A., and Sholomskas, D. (1987). Children of depressed parents: Increased psychopathology and early onset of major depression. *Archives of General Psychiatry*, 44(10), 847–853. doi:10.1001/archpsyc.1987.01800220009002

Weissman, M. M., Warner, V., Wickramaratne, P., Moreau, D., and Olfson, M. (1997). Offspring of depressed parents 10 years later. *Archives of General Psychiatry*, 54(10), 932–940. doi:10.1001/archpsyc.1997.01830220054009

Werner, E. E., and Smith, S. (1982). *Vulnerable but invincible: A study of resilient children*. New York: McGraw-Hill.

Werner, E. E., and Smith, R. S. (1992). *Overcoming the odds: High risk children from birth to adulthood*. Cornell University Press.

Whiting, B., and Edwards, C. (1988). *Children of different worlds: The formation of social behaviour*. Cambridge, MA: Harvard University Press.

Wik, K. A., Keizer, R., and Lappegard, T. (2012). Relationship quality in marital and cohabiting unions across Europe. *Journal of Marriage and Family*, 74, 389–398. doi: 10.1111/j.1741-3737.2012.00967.x

Williams, J. M., and Smith, L. A. (2010). Concepts of kinship relations and inheritance in childhood and adolescence. *British Journal of Developmental Psychology*, 28(3), 523–546. doi:10.1348/026151009X449568

Wilson, G. S. (1989). Clinical studies of infants and children exposed prenatally to heroin. *Annals of the New York Academy of Sciences*, 562, 183–194. doi:10.1111/j.1749-6632.1989.tb21017.x

Winnicott, D. W. (1973). *The child, the family, and the outside world.* London: Penguin.

Wright, V., Schieve, L., Reynolds, M., Jeng, G., and Kissen, D. (2001). Assisted reproductive technology surveillance – United States. *Morbidity and Mortality Weekly Report,* 53(SS01), 1–20.

Wrobel, M., Grotevant, H. D., Berge, J., and Mendenhall, T. (2003). Contact in adoption: The experience of adoptive families in the USA. *Adoption and Fostering,* 27(1), 57–67.

Wrobel, G. M., Grotevant, H. D., Samek, D. R., and Von Korff, L. (2013). Adoptees' curiosity and information-seeking about birth parents in emerging adulthood: Context, motivation and behaviour. *International Journal of Behavioral Development,* 37(5), 441–450.

Wrobel, G. M., and Dillon, K. (2009). *Adopted adolescents: Who and what are they curious about?* Chichester: Wiley-Blackwell.

Youngblade, L. M., and Belsky, J. (1992). Parent–child antecedents of 5-year-olds' close friendships: A longitudinal analysis. *Developmental Psychology,* 28(4), 700–713. doi:10.1037/0012-1649.28.4.700

Zadeh, S., Freeman, T., and Golombok, S. (2013). Ambivalent identities of single women using sperm donation. *Revue Internationale de Psychologie Sociale,* 3, 97–123.

Zahn-Waxler, C., Duggal, S., and Gruber, R. (2002). Parental psychopathology. In M. H. Bornstein (ed.), *Handbook of parenting, vol. IV: Social conditions and applied parenting* (pp. 295–327). Mahwah, NJ: Lawrence Erlbaum.

Zegers-Hochschild, F. (2002). The Latin American Registry of Assisted Reproduction. In E. Vayena, P. Rowe, and P. Griffin (eds.), *Current practices and controversies in assisted reproduction.* Report of a WHO meeting. Geneva: World Health Organization.

Zegers-Hochschild, F., Mansour, R., Ishihara, O., Adamson, G. D., de Mouzon, J., Nygren, K. G., and Sullivan, E. A. (2013). International Committee for Monitoring Assisted Reproductive Technology: World report on assisted reproductive technology, 2005. *Fertility and Sterility,* 101(2), 366–378.

Zentner, M., and Shiner, R. L. (2012). *Handbook of temperament.* New York: The Guildford Press.

Zimmerman, M. A., Stoddard, S. A., Eisman, A. B., Caldwell, C. H., Aiyer, S. M., and Miller, A. (2013). Adolescent resilience: Promotive factors that inform prevention. *Child Development Perspectives,* 7(4), 215–220. doi:10.1111/cdep.12042

Index